IT'S ALL ABOUT THE MUSIC MARKETING STUPID

A PRACTICAL GUIDE TO MUSIC MARKETING

Kent Anderson and Jerry Brindisi

innovativeink
PUBLISHING

Cover image courtesy of Harrison Dilts and the Pabst Theater Group.
Cover design created by Sydni Dorsey.

innovativeink
PUBLISHING

www.innovativeinkpublishing.com
Send all inquiries to:
4050 Westmark Drive
Dubuque, IA 52004-1840

Published in the United States of America

CONTENTS

CHAPTER 1 BUSINESS OF MUSIC OVERVIEW   1

A BRIEF HISTORY OF THE BUSINESS OF MUSIC   2
CURRENT STATE OF THE MUSIC INDUSTRY   8
IDENTIFYING REVENUE STREAMS FOR ARTISTS   11
RESOURCES   12

CHAPTER 2 MUSIC PUBLISHING   13

COPYRIGHT   13
MECHANICAL LICENSE   16
PUBLIC PERFORMANCE   16
PERFORMING RIGHTS ORGANIZATIONS (PROS)   17
ASCAP   19
BMI   19
THE MECHANICAL LICENSING COLLECTIVE (THE MLC)   20
SOUNDEXCHANGE   20
SYNCHRONIZATION (OR SYNCH) LICENSE   22
SAMPLE LICENSE   23

MUSIC PUBLISHING 25
A MUSIC PUBLISHING DEAL 25
SELF-ADMINISTERED PUBLISHING 27
PUBLISHING ADMINISTRATION 27
SONGTRUST 28
RESOURCES 29

CHAPTER 3 MUSIC CONSUMPTION & THE TEAM 31

THE STATE OF THE MUSIC BUSINESS 34
THE TEAM 36
- A MANAGER 36
- A BOOKING AGENT 37
- A TOUR ACCOUNTANT / TOUR MANAGER 37
- A BUSINESS MANAGER 38
- A MERCHANDISING MAVEN 38

RESOURCES 40

CHAPTER 4 ESTABLISHING A BUSINESS ENTITY, INTELLECTUAL PROPERTY & RAISING CAPITAL 41

A BUSINESS MODEL 41
BUSINESS ENTITIES 43
- SOLE PROPRIETORSHIP / PARTNERSHIPS 44
- LIMITED LIABILITY COMPANY (L.L.C.) 44
- CORPORATIONS 45

COPYRIGHT (REVISITED) 45
TRADEMARK 46
PATENTS 47
RAISING CAPITAL 49
KICKSTARTER 51
INDIEGOGO 51
PATREON 52
RESOURCES 52

CHAPTER 5 DEFINING YOUR AUDIENCE 53

DETERMINING YOUR AUDIENCE 53
MUSIC GENRES 55
THE FOUR P's OF MARKETING 55
GEOTARGETING 57
DEMOGRAPHICS 59
PSYCHOGRAPHICS 59
OUTBOUND V.S. INBOUND MARKETING 61
RESOURCES 64

CHAPTER 6 PUBLICITY 65

UNDERSTANDING PUBLICITY 65
HOW TO BE YOUR OWN PUBLICIST 66
THE BIO 67
WHEN AND HOW TO CREATE A PRESS RELEASE 68
CREATING A BOILERPLATE 71
EMAIL MARKETING 71
THE MONTHLY NEWSLETTER 73
THE DATABASE (CRM) 74
RESOURCES 76

CHAPTER 7 YOUR DIGITAL HUB 77

ASSET PACKAGE 78
3 TYPES OF TRAFFIC 80
3 TYPES OF MEDIA 81
CONTENT MANAGEMENT SYSTEMS – (CMS) 81
RESOURCES 82

CHAPTER 8 BLOGGING & BRANDING 83

THE IMPORTANCE OF BLOGGING 83
THE IMPORTANCE OF BRANDING 87

ENDORSEMENT DEALS 89

SPONSORSHIP DEALS 90

CO-BRANDING 90

CAUSE MARKETING 91

THE ARTIST BRAND PROFILE (OR DECK) 92

RESOURCES 92

CHAPTER 9 SEO, CMS, GOOGLE SEARCH CONSOLE & CPC 93

WHAT THE F#*% IS SEO AND WHY IS IT IMPORTANT TO ME? 94

GOOGLE SEARCH CONSOLE 96

GOOGLE ANALYTICS 4 96

GOOGLE ADWORDS 97

GOOGLE ADSENSE 99

OPTIMIZING WEBSITE CONTENT & DESIGN 99

RESOURCES 100

CHAPTER 10 BOOKING, MARKETING SHOWS & TOURS & *THE PANDEMIC DID NOT KILL THE LIVE ENTERTAINMENT BUSINESS* (Contributor - Gary Witt) 101

A BRIEF HISTORY OF LIVE MUSIC VENUES 102

THE HISTORY OF CONCERT PROMOTION 103

THE KEY PLAYERS 105

THE PROMOTER & THE BOOKING AGENT 106

LIVE EVENT BOOKING 107

TOUR BOOKING 108

LIVE EVENT MARKETING 109

LIVE STREAMS 111

RESOURCES 112

CHAPTER 11 MAKING MONEY WITH MERCH 113

THE VALUE & OPPORTUNITY MERCH PRESENTS 113

PRINT ON DEMAND 116

THE MERCH TABLE   120
BUNDLING MERCH   121
MEET & GREETS   121
YOUR ONLINE MERCH STORE   122
RESOURCES   123

CHAPTER 12 SINGLES / SPOTIFY & DISTRIBUTION
(Contributor - Tony Klaczynski)   125

IT'S A SINGLES WORLD   129
DISTRIBUTION   131
SPOTIFY AND THE OTHERS DIGITAL SERVICE PROVIDERS (DSPS)   132
- LISTENER PLAYLISTS   133
- SPOTIFY EDITORIAL PLAYLISTS   134
- ALGORITHMIC PLAYLISTS   134
- COLLABORATIVE PLAYLISTS   134
PROMOTING YOUR SINGLE   135
ARTWORK   136
SPOTIFY FOR ARTISTS   137
SHOPIFY FOR SPOTIFY   139
TICKET SALES VIA SPOTIFY   140
CANVAS FOR SPOTIFY   140
A STRATEGY FOR SPOTIFY   140
RESOURCES   141

CHAPTER 13 VISUAL & MIXED MEDIA
(Contributor - Tony Klaczynski)   143

YOUTUBE   144
TIKTOK   146
INSTAGRAM REELS   150
WEB 3 AND NFTs   151
RESOURCES   152

CHAPTER 14 THE MARKETING PLAN   153

PROJECT OVERVIEW   156
TRACK LISTING   156
CREDITS, METADATA & DISTRIBUTION   156
MARKETING GOALS AND OBJECTIVES   157
THE TARGET AUDIENCE / ANALYTICS   157
SOCIAL MEDIA MARKETING   158
THE VIDEO   158
PUBLICITY   158
ADVERTISING   159
THE TEAM   159
THE TIMELINE   159
THE BUDGET   160
A PRACTICAL APPROACH   161
SINGLE RELEASES   161
ASSESSMENT   162
FOR CONSIDERATION   162
ADVANCE YOUR CAREER   163
RESOURCES   163

CHAPTER 15 SOCIAL MEDIA MARKETING *WELCOME TO THE JUNGLE* (Contributors - Chip Schutzman & Tony Klaczynski)   165

ONCE UPON A TIME   167
THE SOCIAL MEDIA PLATFORMS   170
LIKE A VIRGIN   172
IMAGING   172
STYLING   173
ARTWORK   173
CONTENT DEFINITION   173
RE-POSTS vs. REAL TIME POSTING   174
STRATEGY   175
FREQUENCY   176
REACH & ENGAGEMENT   176
ADVERTISING   177

THE SOCIAL MEDIA TIMELINE   178
THE DASHBOARD   179
CONCLUSION   179
RESOURCES   180

CHAPTER 16 TAXES FOR SELF-EMPLOYED ARTISTS, MUSICIANS & CREATIVES   181

TAXABLE INCOME   184
ALLOWABLE DEDUCTIONS   184
EMPLOYEE VS. INDEPENDENT CONTRACTOR   186
INDEPENDENT CONTRACTOR   187
WORK FOR HIRE AGREEMENT   187
W-2 – GETTING PAID AS AN EMPLOYEE   189
W9 – GETTING PAID AS A FREELANCER OR INDEPENDENT
   CONTRACTOR   189
FILING TAXES   190
CONCLUSION   191
DISCLAIMER   191

CHAPTER 17 MUSIC INDUSTRY DATA ANALYTICS (by Robert DiFazio)   193

ACKNOWLEDGEMENT   194
INTRO   194
HISTORY OF MUSIC INDUSTRY ANALYTICS   196
UNDERSTANDING DATA AND OPERATIONS   204
ANALYTIC DASHBOARDS   209
CONCLUSION   218

CHAPTER 18 NETWORKING   219

RESOURCES   222

PREFACE

"I wish there had been a music business 101 course I could have taken." -- Kurt Cobain

Although there exist many publications, online articles, YouTube instructional videos, online and in-person courses, many of these published by knowledgeable industry experts, there seems to be a void in putting all of these components into one comprehensive document. The purpose of this book is to provide insight and focus on key strategies in crafting, establishing, and building a brand encompassing various established entertainment marketing techniques.

The title for the book – IT'S ALL ABOUT THE ~~MUSIC~~ MARKETING STUPID is a nod to a former boss – the legendary Producer, Phil Ramone, (Aretha Franklin, Elton John, Bob Dylan, Paul McCartney, Ray Charles, Frank Sinatra, Paul Simon, David Sanborn, James Taylor, Billy Joel, and Stevie Wonder). It was 1996, and the internet had yet to insert itself into the public consciousness, yet our start-up was keenly aware of the potential of the dissemination of music over such a platform. Record labels were constantly searching for the next big thing. A&R people were still checking out bands, artists and DJs in clubs, and screening demo tapes. Data and analytics were largely absent and void from the music industry. It truly was ALL ABOUT THE MUSIC STUPID.

The office was located at 55 Broad Street, directly across the street from the New York Stock Exchange. The building the start-up company leased was previously that of the stock exchange tycoon Michael Milken, who famously pled guilty on felony charges for violating US Securities laws and sentenced to ten years in prison. The building itself provided two essential requirements.

a. The proximity to the NYSE & NASDAQ, and more importantly;
b. A T-1 line (the equivalent of what we all know today as high-speed internet access or ISDN, DSL or 5G today). Note: T-carrier systems offered entirely digital, full-duplex exchange of data that were rare, problematic to install and very expensive, yet vital to the company's success.

The company was one of the first to understand and embrace the potential of the distribution of music via the internet. The start-up leased numerous floors of the building and construction and build-out was continuous. A business plan was written and presented, and the company raised in excess of $70 million dollars in 1997.

There were entire floors devoted to developers and coders from all over the world (outside of the US) – as that was the only resource. The record label was located on the 12th floor. Upon stepping off the elevator, one was greeted with an antique movie theater ticket booth and a Queen Ann desk in Phil's office; indicating the disruption and convergence of what a few, early pioneers believed was the future of music delivery – the internet. The company explored and developed new technology in both audio, video transfer, and website design. With our various backgrounds in the music business, notable executives from radio, retail, press, distribution, and labels were all invited to the office for lunches and demonstrations of the future trans-fer of music / files over the internet. With Phil often holding court in the Conference Room with the T-1 line in place, the transfer of music over a high-speed infrastructure had a very short download / lag time. Over time, we came to realize that not one of the major industry executives we demonstrated this transfer of files to believed us. Rather, they looked at us puzzled, found no relevance to the music industry, and unanimously exclaimed, 'not in my lifetime,' and walked out of the room. Were they ever wrong. The disruption the music indus-try experienced as we moved from physical to digital consumption resulted in the recorded music business losing more than half its annual revenue. Fortunately, today, the trends have dramatically shifted, and the recorded music industry has an optimistic outlook. However, this has taken over twenty years to reverse. The preferred consumer format of entertainment no longer requires ownership, but rather access which today equates to our preferred methodol-ogy of entertainment consumption – streaming and on demand.

Phil had a reputation of embracing technology. A musical prodigy violinist, (trained at Julliard) his attraction to signing-up with the company was exploring the convergence of technology and music. To put it in perspective, one day while in a limo, his cell phone rang, he answered Pav, it was Pavarotti calling Phil on his mobile phone from Italy which, at the time, was remarkable. Another day, while working together, wrapped up in all this internet sensation, he had this idea, that technology does not make an artist — "It's all about the music stupid," which was then deemed the official record label screen saver of all computer monitors on our floor. Why this is ironic, at one point, essentially prior to the advent of the internet, it was, ALL about the music. Social media, streaming services, monthly listeners,' # of plays, views, and streams which are now the primary considerations in signing an artist to a major label didn't even exist.

Which begs the question, is it all about the music or is it all about the marketing? Obviously, this is a rhetorical question, with no right or wrong answer, however, one thing is certain, with few exceptions, marketing may be your optimal vehicle and pathway to making it in the music business. If one is to explore and understand that with few exceptions, your favorite artists all have assembled a team, large or small, who are working incessantly in building their career.

The recorded music business has been up double digits in revenue the past ten years thanks in large part to streaming services. There has never been a better time to be an artist and creator with countless ways of building your brand and being discovered. The challenge is how to get noticed despite all of the clutter and competition. The objective of this book is to provide you with ideas, concepts, and tools to do so — you just have to do the work.

It's our intent that this book, if nothing else; provides you a roadmap to a life as a full-time musician, artist, producer, aspiring tour manager, industry executive, or a creator, enabling you to quit your part-time job with the potential of realizing significant increased earnings from your craft.

I've had the good fortune of working with some of the most successful producers, artists, and talented, smart colleagues in the music industry. A select few of them have generously shared their knowledge regarding their respective area of expertise within the music industry. This book is an attempt to distill this information for you to understand, grasp and to digest strategies you can actually utilize in forging your career. It is our hope that we're successful in providing this pathway for you.

The authors and contributors of this book are colleagues and friends; one with a master's in information management. Another is the CEO of a multi-faceted entertainment organization that includes the booking, marketing, and hosting of over 700 events per year. My co-writer, Jerry Brindisi, has led music business programs in higher education for over 15 years and is the chair of the Business and Entrepreneurship department of one of the most well-known liberal art schools in America. And then there's me; I've had a truly multifaceted career; first as professional bassist, a record store manager, a Regional and National Sales Manager for major labels, a consultant, and as an adjunct professor. Cumulatively, it is our hope that you might find some of the ideas and marketing initiatives which we present, might equate in making a positive impact on your career. Read on if you dare (ha). Understand that if you are to implement some, most of, or all of the suggested methodologies in this playbook, you're in for a lot of work. Marketing, like creating music takes thought, planning, time, dedication, and commitment.

We wanted to add that by implementing the techniques and strategies outlined in this book in no way does it guarantee that you'll become a TikTok sensation or a viral Spotify artist achieving millions of streams. If that is your goal, we deem this limited marketing scope to be a very risky strategy in terms of career development. So, if you were hoping that somewhere in the book, we reveal the secret sauce to becoming a TikTok star or Spotify breakout artist – you'll be disappointed. The good news is, should you implement a few or all of the suggestions we offer, there's a strong likelihood that you will be better positioned in your career (assuming you of course have a talent). You'll be able to derive revenue from several different sources while not being reliant on just one or two.

I was fortunate to attend two universities, both with exceptional music programs. I was a member of the #1 jazz band at a Division 1 and a Big 10 school, an award-winning acoustic jazz septet, and studied with a world-class cellist and a celebrated principal bassist and instructor. My music lessons included sight reading, intonation, music theory, and improvisation - all of which are so vital and relevant to music. But what I learned many years later after landing my first gig in the music business, was that my instruction did not include anything about the *business of music*, let alone, the *marketing of music*. So, all of my experience has been on the job training for the past 30+ years. It is our hope that our introspective might provide for you an advantage many of us attending conservatories (then and now) were not exposed to.

This book will be obsolete the day it's published - as that is how quickly the digital music landscape is transforming. NFTs are being explored, TikTok artists are being signed, yet they too seem to be an unknown commodity. Authenticity and talent is an awesome recipe. But there's one more component - music marketing.

IT'S ALL ABOUT THE MUSIC MARKETING STUPID

DISCLAIMER: by no means does the constitution of this document ensure success. Success is predicated on a number of things; talent, marketing, the people one surrounds themselves with, etc. However, we can guarantee this – that if you were to adapt one, two, three or all of the ideas and recommendations presented in the following pages, you will be far better positioned in your career than should you decide not to.

TO CLARIFY: I'm a musician, a musicologist of sorts. I have a deep understanding of all forms of jazz, a deep appreciation for classical music, and possess a knowledge of popular music, rock, and R&B, as well as record labels, sidemen, and producers who were responsible for investing in and believing in making great music. The point being - in the end, I do truly feel it's about the music. There was a time when great music alone would prevail; today this is not necessarily the case. As a musician or artist, it's now essential that you allocate a portion of your time to music marketing. Even if you are an artist signed to a major record label, it is an expectation, and obligation to be involved in the marketing of your career. It is our aspiration that this book will offer you a practical sense of applying marketing strategies to enhance your talents. One thing we can say for certain; all of us, in the music business can cite more than one favorite record we worked, were told it was a 'priority' and would be a smash hit. And with all the major label monies beyond it - and for what-ever reason, it didn't find an audience. The missing element may have been ineffective or a lack of marketing to connect the project with the fans.

AUTHORS

KENT ANDERSON & JERRY BRINDISI

CONTRIBUTORS

ROBERT DIFAZIO
GARY WITT
CHIP SCHUTZMAN &
ANTONIO SALVADOR KLACZYNSKI

Please support live music and visit your local music or record store, invest in concert tickets, and attend shows and buy your favorite artist's merch!

ACKNOWLEDGEMENTS

KENT ANDERSON: This book is dedicated to my mom & dad. I thank them both for providing me with the confidence to offer my succinct honest and direct perspective, respectfully and with a hint of sarcasm and humor. Also, a special thanks to John Gehron for his initial insight and words of encouragement, and to Karen for your unwavering support and weekly toasts. A special thanks to my trusted and true friends who have provided their keen insight for select chapters. Specifically, I would like to thank my co-author, Jerry Brindisi for his tenacity, contributions, voice of reason, editing expertise, and acting as a moderator throughout the writing of this book. Gary Witt, a guy I once mentored who is now my idol. Another friend who's teaching acumen I tremendously respect and for graciously offering to take on the complex topic of analytics for us, Robert DiFazio. My dear friend Chip Schutzman for providing his expertise as it pertains to social media. And thanks to my *rockstar* Columbia College Chicago student, Tony Klaczynski for his expertise and candid insight into DSS and all things Spotify. And my pals; Freddie Breitberg, Carter Russell and #87 - Emery Moorehead.

JERRY BRINDISI: Thank you to Susan and my boys Luke and Gavin for giving me the inspiration and motivation for this project. To my siblings Geralyn, Angela, and Tony thank you for the guidance and continued support over the years. To my co-author Kent Anderson, thank you for involving me in this book. Your kind and gentle way is something we should all aspire to. I'd like to acknowledge those who have been influential and supportive throughout my "music business" career: Catherine Moore, Phil Galdston, Adam Anders, Nikki Anders, Philippe Ravanas, Mary Filice, Angelo Luciano, Dawn Larsen, Alex Endress, and Henric Lindstrom. I also want to thank my friends and colleagues at Columbia College Chicago.

A "special" thank you to my Mom and Dad for letting me be who I wanted to be and giving me everything I needed to do so. I love and miss you every day.

THANK YOU: Mick Stevanovitch, Loren Wells, Bill Giardini, Paul Natkin, Brian Rosenblatt, Bob Schnieders, Kelly D., Larry, Ryan Argast, Geoff Mayfield, Peter Mensch, Diane, Marcus Norris - Robert, Gary, Chip and Tony. With special thanks to the entire staff at *Kendall Hunt Publishing Company*, specifically our friends Greg J. Derosa, Stephanie Hyde and Angela Lampe for making this book a reality!

GRAPHIC DESIGN: Sydni Dorsey

COVER PHOTO COURTESY OF HARRISON DILTS AND THE PABST THEATER GROUP

EDITOR'S NOTE:

Music is a beautiful transformative way to express our individuality. Gun violence, bullying and hatred is not a characteristic of any true artist or musician. If you, or anyone in your circle, has a propensity with guns, has a prejudice, or is involved in questionable ethics, move away, this is not what music is about. As poets and creators, we have the ability to express and emit our emotions through our creative talents. Study the legends, and what you will discover is they moved away-from and lifted themselves out of harm's way by using their talents and their business acumen to utilize *music* as their platform. Historically the most successful of these artist's confronted discrimination, prejudice, violence, and war choosing the positive forum of popular music. As creative people, it's imperative to remain responsible. Be a role model while addressing controversy in a constructive way. Music in its finest form emits a message or emotion to provide insight, enlighten, and uplift.

ABOUT THE AUTHORS

KENT ANDERSON

Having an allure and love for music was evidenced first in his elementary school music class, his desire to take-up piano, trumpet and eventually bass lessons, Kent Anderson has parleyed that passion for the artform into a lifelong career in the music industry. A musician, producer, consultant, lecturer and as an adjunct professor, Kent Anderson draws from his vast background and experiences in the music business in his daily responsibilities. He has held key positions within the industry at *Virgin Records, GRP Records, N2K, Inc.* and as President of *A440 Music Group.* He is an Adjunct Faculty member of the *Columbia College Chicago Business & Entrepreneurship Department* where he instructs the *Business of Music, Entertainment Marketing, and Decision Making: Music Business.*

He first began his career in the music business managing record stores for the nation's largest music retailer – *Trans World Music Corp.* where he relocated to the Quad Cities, then Chicago then on to Short Hills, NJ and Greenwich, CT. Anderson was introduced to the founder of *GRP Records* and accepted a position in Chicago as the Mid-West Regional Sales Manager. After five-years in this position, Anderson was appointed to succeed his mentor, returning to New York to head-up the sales and marketing for the label alongside the esteemed Producer Tommy LiPuma. During his tenure at GRP the company was named the #1 Jazz Label in the world for five consecutive years, received more than 30 Grammy nominations and achieved annual domestic sales in excess of 25 million dollars.

Sharing in the vision of the integration of music and technology, Anderson served as Vice President under the tutelage of Phil Ramone at *N2K, Inc. (NASDAQ)*. The company demonstrated the future of the distribution of music via the internet through the creation of the first digital download in the history of recorded music with David Bowie, built communities around genre related websites, operated one of the first e-commerce stores, developed perhaps the first online music delivery mp3 player and produced the first 5.1 surround sound DVD. While at N2K, Mr. Anderson's sales and marketing efforts were recognized with *Billboard* magazine naming the label the *#1 Independent Jazz Label of the Year*, having the *#1 Best Selling Contemporary Jazz Recording*, and the *#1 Traditional Jazz Recording* (Dave Grusin Presents West Side Story).

While at *Virgin,* Anderson was responsible for all sales and marketing under the aegis of *Virgin Associated Labels* including: *Narada, Real World, Luaka Bop and Higher Octave.* In conjunction with the Music Business Association (formerly NARM), Anderson has produced four consecutive #1 *Billboard Jazz & Blues* chart compilation recordings.

As President and Executive Producer of more than twenty recordings, A440 was recognized with numerous accolades in the press, (Top 10 Jazz Album of the Year – *Chicago Tribune,* Best Female Jazz Vocalist of the Year – *L.A. Times*, Jazz Album of the Year – *Swing Journal*, Japan), a Grammy nomination and Best 5.1 Surround Sound Mix award. In 2005, Anderson has Managed and Produced recordings from artists as diverse as: Jackie Allen, Alice Peacock, Henry Johnson, New Soul Cowboys, Corey Wilkes, Steve Cole, and Carrie McDowell.

He grew up in Des Moines, Iowa, possesses a Bachelor of Arts degree from the University of Northern Iowa with a *Performance Degree on Double Bass,* (with additional studies at the University of Iowa). He played professionally for ten years performing and touring with big bands, jazz ensembles, orchestras, pit orchestras, R&B, and rock bands. Anderson is a voting member of The Recording Academy [the Grammys] and is an Eagle Boy Scout. He resides in Chicago, is the founder of *C Sharp Consulting*, and continues to enjoy practicing and playing gigs on both upright and electric bass.

JERRY BRINDISI

Jerry Brindisi's passion for the music industry evolved from his great love of popular music. His interest and experience has progressed from a desire to perform, write songs, record, and ultimately create music product. Mr. Brindisi is an Associate Professor and Interim Chair of the Business and Entrepreneurship Department at Columbia College Chicago. He is the Coordinator for the Music Business BA Program and oversees all music business courses and initiatives offered by the Department including International collaborations and study away programing. He enjoys serving as a faculty advisor and mentor to music business students. He is involved in department and program administration, curriculum development, teaching music business, coordinating interdisciplinary ventures, including AEMMP Practicum courses (student run record label, artist management, music publishing) and teaching music business.

Brindisi has an extensive background working in the music industry. He has been employed by Sony Music Entertainment Inc. as a Sales and Marketing Research Analyst in their Global Digital Business Group. He has also worked with the executive offices and the A&R departments of Warner Music Group's Asylum Records and Atlantic Records. As the studio manager for Ander's Music, he has had the opportunity to work closely with top industry leaders, attorneys, artists, managers, producers, and songwriters. Additionally, Mr. Brindisi has advised and counseled music artists and industry leadership on various industry issues including career advancement, publishing, marketing, promotion, and artist branding. His experience and research interests include record label operations, music publishing administration, marketing, audio production, and artist development. He previously served as a full-time faculty and program supervisor for the music business program at the State University of New York, Fredonia, where he taught courses such as Music Contracts, Music Copyright and Publishing, Music Marketing and Promotion and The Business of Music.

Brindisi earned a Master's degree in Music Business from New York University where he was honored for outstanding scholarship, leadership and service in the Graduate Music Business Program of the Steinhardt Department of Music and Performing Arts Professions. While attending NYU, he served as the assistant to the program director of Music Business. Mr. Brindisi holds a Bachelor's degree in Communication from SUNY at Buffalo with concentrations in public relations and advertising. He is a member of the Music and Entertainment Industry Educators Association (MEIEA), the Association of Arts Administration Educators, and is a recipient of the State University of New York Service to Students Award.

Once again, this is not the definitive book about the "music business," however, this book addresses numerous marketing ideas and strategies you need to capitalize on in maximizing the exposure and value of your music and your brand.

First of all, we've highlighted numerous revenue streams facilitated through organizations in which you should register – in an effort to not leave money on the table.

Additionally, we tackle a variety of topics including: demographic segmentation, being your own best publicist, Google Search Console, live performance, single release strategy, social media, data / analytics, and taxes.

To sign-up for our newsletter, blog, and podcast discussing relevant industry trends and perspectives, please do so by visiting www.musicmarketingstupid.com.

CONTRIBUTORS

ROBERT DIFAZIO

Robert serves as Clinical Assistant Professor and Coordinator of Music Business at the University of Illinois at Chicago (UIC) where he oversees the Bachelor of Arts in Music Business program. Robert is also Head of Research & Development at Song Sleuth where he oversees the development of analytic tools for the automatic recognition of user-generated music content on behalf of major labels, publishers, and rights societies. Robert holds a Bachelor of Science in Sound Recording Technology from DePaul University and a Master of Science in Management Information Systems from UIC.

GARY WITT

Arriving in Milwaukee via Chicago in 2002 following 19 years in the record business, Gary Witt is the CEO of the Pabst Theater Group, a multi-faceted entertainment organization whose activities include the booking, marketing and hosting of over 800 live events per year in and around the city of Milwaukee in iconic, creative places of public assembly that help to build community, loyalty and reinforce identity and heritage for Milwaukee.

CHIP SCHUTZMAN

Chip Schutzman is the president and founder of Miles High Productions, an online music marketing and promotion company founded in 2002. Chip has consulted and executed numerous online marketing campaigns for several platinum selling artists. Chip is a resident of Palm Springs and is a frequent guest lecturer at several universities including; Boston University, Berklee College of Music, Temple University, Columbia College Chicago and NYU.

ANTONIO SALVADOR KLACZYNSKI

Antonio Klaczynski aka Tony Klacz is a 21-year-old producer/songwriter, freelance writer, and media consultant as well as the co-founder and CEO of the entertainment accelerator True Groovy Media. Since founding True Groovy Media his freshman year of college, Klacz has worked with talent throughout the US and Brazil in music, as well as visual media and marketing, always with a dedicated passion for community building and reimagining industry norms.

1

BUSINESS OF MUSIC OVERVIEW

Let's discuss the purpose of this textbook. The drivers of success for a recording artist are predicated on a number of things, some of which may be talent, being at the right place at the right time, knowing someone, YouTube views, Spotify plays, or perhaps even dumb luck. There has always existed a small yet elite tier of superstar artists reaping huge financial rewards. This book is not about them, but rather about you and developing your career. What we intend to set-forth in this book is a strategic method of maximizing your fans and ultimately creating numerous revenue streams. Today there exists more opportunities than ever for an artist to be able to sustain a comfortable lifestyle while pursuing a full-time career as an "Artist." Although we will most commonly be referring to you as the artist or band, the content is also applicable for any aspiring instrumentalist, artist manger, journalist, photographer, videographer, or music business entrepreneur.

What will be presented, set forth and required of you will be a detailed and tedious investment in your time and energy. It will involve only a minimal financial investment to implement the plan. However, your initial challenge will be to conduct the research and to set up the select projects we will discuss in various chapters throughout the book. Once you have completed building out the platforms and created these various digital assets, the bigger challenge will be to continue to evolve, develop, and utilize these tools in an ongoing fashion.

Are you aware that it has recently been calculated that 'success' for an artist now relies approximately on 50% talent and recording, the other 50% is marketing? [Ref: Matt Leblanc]

By the end of the book, you will have established a marketing strategy that if pursued develop an audience and generate consistent revenue for yourself or your band, your artist, or your brand. This methodology will be particularly effective in sub-genre categories outside of Hip-Hop and Pop in finding and building your audience. Another possible outcome of implementing the recommendations' provided include developing a following and generating enough plays and views to put you on the radar of a major or indie record label.

A BRIEF HISTORY OF THE BUSINESS OF MUSIC

Before one can easily understand and maximize opportunities in what was described 25 years ago as the *new paradigm*, it's important to know where we came from to better understand how best to exploit them today. There are several credible textbooks on the business of music, and this book is not intended to compete with but rather compliment them. This first chapter is provided as a brief history and summary of the business of music, enabling us to focus on the marketing strategy we plan to implement in subsequent chapters.

It's fair to assume the earliest music business financial transactions revolved around Classical music and opera of the 18th century. The business of music was limited to a few select individuals; essentially one had to either be a composer, a musician, or a copyist. Live performances drew audiences. Demand brought patrons who created a demand for tickets and created a new phenomenon, the paying audience. Attending a classical music performance was generally an audience comprised of a rather elite group of affluent individuals. Composers became rock stars, commissioned to compose by royalty. The orchestras throughout European cities such as Vienna, London, Paris and in New York, Philadelphia and Boston evolved to legendary status.

The business remained largely unchained until Thomas Edison invented the phonograph player in the late 1800's. RCA Victor, Columbia and others-built factories to manufacture the phonograph players and subsequently recognized a need to create record labels. The technology allowed for the commercialization of recorded music as demand grew for recordings. The labels created structure, guidance and financial support and accounting for the artist, in much the same way as they operate today. This evolution of record labels fostered in a whole new cadre of jobs for record executives, A&R (artist and repertoire), to sales and marketing personnel, and distribution. Recording studios were built and technology evolved providing the opportunity to multi-track. The business began to expand and jobs in music such as recording studios, sound engineers, managers and agents, inventors and manufacturers of recording equipment and manufacturing plants for physical good (LPs, cassettes, CDs, posters) began to materialize. The 45 RPM, a small piece of vinyl having only one song on side A and one on side B quickly became a dominant configuration of the music business. This phenomenon created pop stars having hit singles experiencing sales never previously achieved. It became a singles business with record companies selling millions of singles. Coincidentally, we live in a singles driven world today.

The business evolved as the popular format transitioned to the LP. Demand provided opportunity and independent record labels and regional distributors were started by entrepreneurs throughout the country. LPs allowed consumers to own 12-14 songs of an artist on one record. This 12" piece of vinyl included cover art vividly depicting the artist's image or brand, complete with album credits and liner notes. The format had an intrinsic value to the consumer. Nearly every household in America housed at least one record player and a record collection.

A number of circumstances of the 1960s had a significant impact on the development of the recorded music business. In 1964, per FCC rule, AM radio stations could no longer simulcast on FM creating a need for additional content. The population explosion after World War 2 meant the "baby boomers" were now teenagers, the primary demographic for rock music. Again, demand provided opportunity and film and television also began to support music and musical artists. Additionally, 1960s saw the British Invasion with artists such as the Beatles and the Stones being elevated to superstar status. FM radio began to gain in popularity with the youth. Tracks were no longer limited to 3 minutes; the music could now expand to 5 – 7 or even 11 minutes per song. The counterculture of the 60s and 70's, the Viet-Nam war and Woodstock were all reflected in the songwriting. The FM radio DJs played these records which reflected the times. The entire youth culture was listening to the same music, from R&B to rock. Audiences grew allowing artists to fill bigger venues. It's relatively easy to argue the 70's was the greatest decade in the history of popular music. Many of these acts have achieved legendary status and the consumption of the artists' music has endured. This is clearly evidenced in the RIAA Gold & Platinum chart.

The 80s marked the introduction of the compact disc to the consumer. The advent of lossless digital audio made the compact disc instantly the preferred format of music for the consumer. Accompanying the improved digital audio, was a high price tag generating recorded music sales previously never realized. As a result of this technical revolution in audio, consumers flocked to record stores to re-purchase their favorite recordings. Not only were consumers purchasing new music, but they were also buying catalog recordings to own their favorite recordings on this new digital format. This marked another technological breakthrough and change in format which, throughout the 90s translated into the music business posting its greatest earnings in recorded music history. The compact disc remained the dominant format of choice for the consumer for almost 2 decades. That is, until the world wide web and con-nectivity reached critical mass. The *disruption* impacted a variety of businesses negatively, but perhaps none more than the recorded music industry. CD Rom drives were shipped with computers, blank CDs were a fraction of the price of a commercial CD, and the consumer now had the ability to rip that CD borrowed from a friend with no degradation in audio quality. Further negatively impacting the sales of recorded music was the proliferation of illegal file sharing services

The industry simply was not ready for change and remained in denial of the digital transfor-mation that they seemingly were unwilling to embrace. Consumers were frustrated in having to purchase a $15-18 CD to discover only one or two "good" songs. One year before the turn of the century in 1999 Napster, a little project by college student Shawn Fanning went online. By 2000, the online file-sharing service was being sued by record labels and musicians for allowing users to download digital files of songs illegally. By July of 2020 a federal judge in San Francisco shut down the popular music swapping web site — saying the online company encourages "wholesale infringement" against music industry copyrights. What the industry was not prepared for is what happened next – within days a number of other illegal file shar-ing services went online. Many were located in offshore locations or in territories outside the US jurisdiction. According to the RIAA the US Recording Industry realized an all-time high in 1999 of nearly 14 billion dollars. By 2010 the US recorded music revenue had been so dramat-ically impacted from the ripping of CDs and illegal file sharing that it reached a precipitous low of approximately half that amount in 2010.

In the late 90's the music business remained in a continual denial of the rapid evolution of music being transferred over the internet. It took a technology company, not a music company to revolutionize the business. On April 28, 2003, Apple opened the iTunes Store, a software based online digital media store and opened the legal digital marketplace. When it opened,

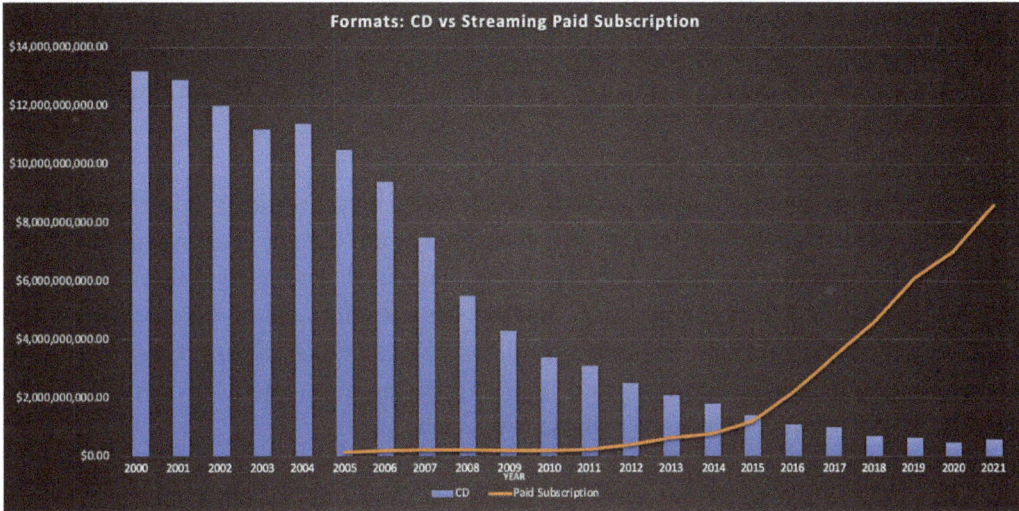

Formats: CD vs Streaming Paid Subscription

it was the only legal digital catalog of music to offer songs from all the major and most indie labels. (iTunes Store from Wikipedia)

Despite Apple now providing a legal download service for the consumer the proliferation of illegal file-sharing, downloading and the ripping of CDs continued at an alarming rate. At the height of this popular consumer trend the music industry experienced its weakest sales in 25 years. In 2006 a 23-year-old Swedish entrepreneur had an idea, since people are stealing music, why not offer it to them for free. Unlike the illegal file sharing services, this service would have a beautiful, searchable interface with no chance of the consumer downloading a virus or malware. The creators would ultimately be paid from advertising, plus the company would offer a paid ad free subscription tier as well. So as folklore has it, Daniel Ek met with the heads of the Majors in Sweden and pitched them the idea, that his software might eviscerate illegal file sharing altogether. With illegal file sharing hovering around 80% in the country, the record executives essentially realized they had nothing to lose. Within months of launching, the recorded music industry in Sweden noticed a dramatic decrease in illegal file sharing. Over the next few years this model was replicated in several other European countries proving numerous times over that Spotify was the savior technology company here to rescue the music business. Ek's position was that Spotify discouraged online music piracy by providing a low-cost alternative and that the service would over time generate substantial royalties for the music industry. Ultimately Ek was able to convince the heads of the Majors here in the

US that embracing his platform was in their best interest as well and terms of licensing deals were negotiated. In July of 2011, Spotify launched in the US. Apple countered with its own streaming service and today, streaming accounts for 85(+) % of all music consumption in the US. (RIAA – Mid Year 2020).

Back in the day, decisions to sign artists were largely based on gut instincts. If you were one of the fortunate few that sent in a demo or was discovered by an A&R guy checking your band out in a club, chances are you were signed to a multiple album deal. The initial release was guaranteed typically having 3-5 'option periods.' The label has the opt to opt on the options, not the artist. So, if the artist's sales are performing well, then you continue to make record 2, 3 and 4. However, during the course of any option period, it's up to the label to decide to carry on or drop the artist by sending your Manager a pink slip in the mail.

The label the artist was signed to then had a distribution deal in place, most often with one of The Majors. These distribution companies owned and operated pressing and manufacturing plants for LPs, cassettes, CDs, etc. The typical cost for distribution was 14-20% right off the top, which is deducted from the artist's royalties. The salesforce was strategically located in major markets and in the hometowns of the corporate offices of national and independent chains. Nearly every record store in America was paid a weekly visit from their salesperson who would present them with a new release book typically 6-8 weeks prior to street date, (now referred to as release date). Each store or chain had a designated 'buyer' with whom the salesperson would meet with to discuss the potential success and necessary initial quantity of product to order. However, there was certainly a process in place to influence the number of units the buyer might bring into their warehouse, chain or directly into a single store. Priority or superstar artists' size of the orders were greatly influenced by the amount of money the label was willing to pay for sale price and premium positioning of the physical music releases in the stores. This systematic process was universally known as *co-op advertising* where the label would fund advertising for the retailer. In return the title was offered to the consumer with sale pricing & positioning. Let's not forget, the label had already invested anywhere from $40,000 – 500,000 to record, mix and master the record and then spend another substantial sum of money ($30,000 – 100k) to make a music video. This price & positioning cost would vary wildly based on the sales history (if any), early and anticipated radio airplay, touring and opportunities offered by the retailers. For example, a single mom & pop shop might have a weekly ad in a city's free newspaper, a cut in there, plus sale pricing and prominent positioning out of the artist's bin might cost a hundred bucks. For this the salesperson in communication with the label's VP of Sales would approve these co-op dollars. In the event of a superstar release, there was an IOU (Initial Orders Upfront) of how many projected units needed to be shipped to provide adequate supply for the demand. At the time a mini advertisement in the Best Buy four-color national Sunday newspaper insert would cost upward of $30,000. These rates would increase during the 4th quarter holiday selling season. So, with order in hand, co-op ad dollars allocated the order was placed in the system. From there the distribution company assumed the responsibility and had the ability to pick, pack and ship via truck lines the heavy boxes of physical goods to fill an order placed by a chain of stores or a single record store.

Another intriguing observation about the music industry is that physical goods are 'returnable.' Product was brought into warehouses and stores essentially on consignment. So, if something doesn't sell, the store clerk can box it up and return it to the distributor for full price, minus a re-stocking fee. And about that 'price and positioning' for product we spoke of – remember sale pricing was also given to advertised product. So, for developing artist or superstars alike – their new release might have a list price of $16.99 – with a sale sticker of $12.99. This routine practice of having new releases be on sale seems somewhat unique and strange in comparison to most other business models. If Armani is releasing a brand-new fall line – when it is released and placed in a retail store it is introduced at full price and is largely non-returnable. In most other retail environments, product is not sale priced upon release but rather the sale price would be applied several months after the item failed to sell at full price. Unlike the fashion and consumer goods industries, today, for the most part, music product is nearly all digital – with little need to concern a label about obsolescent inventory and returns. Today, by understanding metrics and your audience, you have the ability to make limited runs of CDs and vinyl with little financial risk and exposure.

It's important to understand that prior to streaming services and paid downloads, records (which is a catch all phase for all formats such as LPs, CDs, cassettes, even a full album in digital form.) were sold in record stores and in big box mass merchandisers. At that time as an independent artist, it was very difficult and tedious to gain placement for your one sole release in a record store. Yes, you might have been able to strike a deal with one shop in your community but getting into the national chains of the day such as Tower Records, Musicland, Best Buy and numerous midsize regional chains and indie stores across the country was not possible. If, however, you, as an artist got signed to a record label, they had the infrastructure to solicit and announce the forthcoming release of your record, to promote, pick, pack and ship the physical goods into every store. Most importantly they had the ability and clout to invoice and collect the money due to the label who would then in turn calculate royalties due the artist, if any. Beginning around the turn of the century indie stores and regional chains began to close, culminating with Tower Records declaring bankruptcy in 2004. It also bears pointing out the #1 consumer driver in influencing a music purchase at the time was terrestrial radio. Then with the advent of music being delivered to the consumer via digital transmissions, terrestrial radio station listenership began to decline. Today when asked, 'when was the last time you actually listened to terrestrial radio'; often, a young person simply cannot recall. This illustration points out the importance of having a deal with a record label, who's #1 marketing objective was to get their artist's new single on the radio. Oftentimes today, radio is monitoring social media and is adding a record based on the number of organic streams. Making radio the last to the party rather than breaking the record by adding it early on. This is best illustrated in countless instances, with such artists as Glass Animal, Billie Eilish and BTS. Eilish for example self-released her song 'Ocean Eyes' when she was 13 years old by uploading it to streaming service Soundcloud. The song exploded driving interest in her from fans, record labels, etc. The song currently has close to 900 million streams on Spotify.

CURRENT STATE OF THE MUSIC INDUSTRY

Let's continue exploring the opportunities that exist today with the barriers of entry lessened or removed altogether. With the advent of Digital Audio Workstations (DAW) and software such as Pro Tools and Logic, it is now more affordable and completely possible to make a hit record on a home computer. Such was the case with H.E.R., as well as Billie Eilish and her brother, producer Finneas. Of course, a session in a professional recording studio has distinct advantages ranging from the prestige of a major studio to the caliber of mics, preamps, and outboard gear with the sonic quality of the recording being somewhat superior. The point however being that it is no longer 100% essential that you have a significant recording fund to make a record.

With video editing software and Go Pro type cameras, or even your mobile phone the same as above applies to video production. Do to the fact that one needed to create a storyboard, hire hair and make-up, wardrobe, a video production crew with state-of-the art video recording equipment – a modest budget for a music video at that time was around $30,000. Today, not only can you create a hi-def music video for one tenth of the price, if you were to utilize a friend or student majoring in film, that needs some content for their demo reel, you may be able to get this accomplished for little or nothing.

With streaming now accounting for 85% of recorded music revenue, it's easy to get fixated on the number of streams you might have as an artist. Unfortunately, as a developing / independent artist you should assume, (unless you hit the lottery and create a viral sensation), that your payments received from your digital distributor (DistroKid, CD Baby, Tunecore, Amuse or AWAL), alone will be insufficient to sustain your career. We are all aware the challenge today is the per stream rate being paid to owners of sound recording copyrights holders (The Masters) and songwriters (music publishing) remains remarkably low.

So, if one were to analyze the understand the number of streams it takes to earn **one dollar**, here's some numbers to cause one to pause.

When calculating the over-all payout per stream rate, when taking into consideration discounts for family sharing plans, student subscriptions, add supported freemium plans and

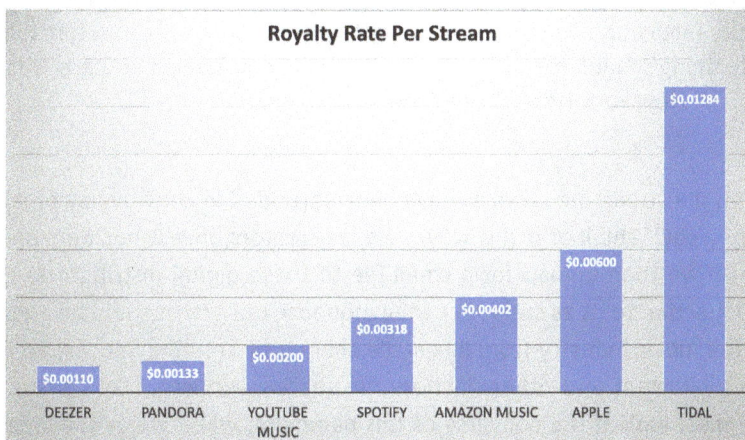

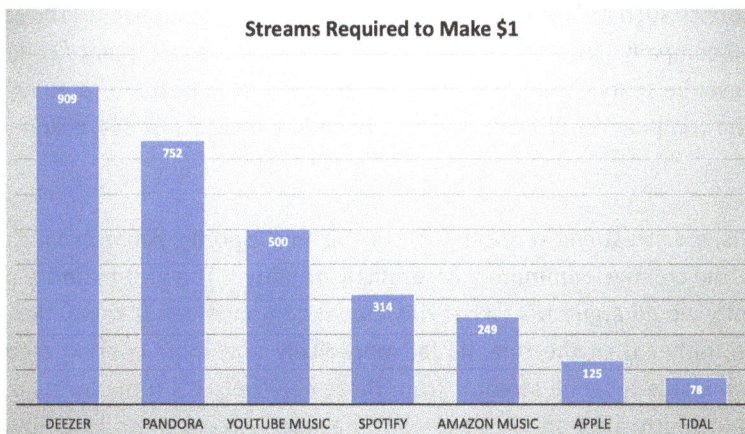

Royalty Rate Per Stream

Platform	Rate
DEEZER	$0.00110
PANDORA	$0.00133
YOUTUBE MUSIC	$0.00200
SPOTIFY	$0.00318
AMAZON MUSIC	$0.00402
APPLE	$0.00600
TIDAL	$0.01284

Streams Required to Make $1

Platform	Streams
DEEZER	909
PANDORA	752
YOUTUBE MUSIC	500
SPOTIFY	314
AMAZON MUSIC	249
APPLE	125
TIDAL	78

paid subscriptions - a rule of thumb, the per stream rate equates to $0.005 cents per stream as the average barometer. Utilizing this formula an artist having 300 million plus plays equates to $1.5 million in revenue. If we were to reduce this number by 50% to 150 million streams, that would represent revenue of $750,000. And if we were to reduce this again by half, to 75 million streams that would roughly equate to $375,000. Do the math again, reduce by two-thirds to 25 million streams and your payout would be around $12,500.

In Britain, more than 150 artists, including stars like Paul McCartney, Kate Bush and Sting, signed a letter asking Prime Minister Boris Johnson for reforms in the streaming economy. In the United States, a new advocacy group, the Union of Musicians and Allied Workers, has waged a guerrilla campaign against Spotify, demanding higher payouts. The terms of record companies' contracts with artists, like royalty rates and ownership of recordings, are under more scrutiny than ever. Even streaming's fundamental accounting rules have been getting a fresh look. [Source: The New York Times, May 7, 2021]

Since inception, the streaming services have been shrouded in controversy regarding the per stream rate they pay. Think of it this way – we, as creators, invest our time and expense to create art which we then upload for a small fee to these digital distributors. They in turn, provide a vital function to us as creators – they monetize our art. It could be argued that Daniel Ek 'saved' the music industry from illegal file sharing by creating Spotify; an ad supported alternative to Bit-Torrent and other offshore file sharing services. Let's assume this to be true: then we must look at the converse of this paradigm; when we as the creative community upload our WAV files to our distributor of choosing, recognize that we are providing free content to a service such as Spotify to build their brand and market value. They are after all a publicly traded company [NYSE: SPOT] and although they act as a tracing / collection agency of sorts, the revenue splits under a million plays are modest at best. In so doing, our content has enabled the company (Spotify) to realize a valuation in excess of $54 billion [Forbes: April 23, 2021].

The question is, are streaming services such as YouTube, Spotify, Amazon Music, and others compensating the creative community accordingly or fairly? The vast majority of, as the creative community would argue NO. What this model demonstrates is that unless you are the rare exception, rather than the rule, its far more likely that most content creators will not realize any formidable revenue streams from these services. It's futile for us to explore the revenue splits in depth, after-all, they are what they are. Accept them and move on. Should you care to learn more about how these low rates are being challenged, explore NMPA.org. The National Music Publishers' Association represents the interests of songwriters and music publishers. They are heavily vested in this fight.

Today, with music being so readily available, fans have the ability to dig deep into the genre of their choosing. Terrestrial radio, television performances, awards shows such as the Grammy's are experiencing precipitous decreases in viewership. The result of a performance having little or no effect on an artist's impact in music consumption. What this shows us, is that most of us don't care, have our own rabbit-hole of music we're in to, and simply aren't into the handful of artists' who are the pop artists de-jour.

IDENTIFYING REVENUE STREAMS FOR ARTISTS

With so much music being readily available and continually being created and released globally, its far more difficult than ever to achieve critical mass. It has been reported that 100,000 tracks are being uploaded to Spotify and other Digital Service Providers each day. The new vision may be, to find your community and maximize their loyalty and friendship. You may come to discover that 50,000 dedicated fans will be sufficient for you to create your small army. Don't misunderstand, the strategy to releasing a single is important, and focusing on maximizing Spotify and streaming plays is a good idea. But plays should not be your only focus. We will take a fairly in-depth look at building an identity / a brand, identifying and tapping into strategies, organizations and provide suggestions so that, streaming revenue is not the only focus of your energy and form of income.

Predicated either by necessity or one's steadfastness in retaining ownership of master sound recordings, today it is possible and becoming more prevalent to do so. The most obvious example and poster child for the DIY methodology would be *Chance The Rapper*. With this every growing desire and trend of artist owned masters, some labels are finding it necessary to be flexible and open to exploring licensing or distribution deals providing you with ownership of your masters. It should be noted: the book assumes you have no recording agreement of any kind, and therefore the assumption is you will be the sole owners of your master sound recordings, music publishing and other intellectual property created.

So, if we are to examine the current state of the music industry, there are numerous reasons to be optimistic. First, year-end sales for the past six years for the recorded music industry have experienced significant, steady growth. More than 60,000 artists hit the milestone of reaching 100,000+ monthly listeners on Spotify at some point during 2020 — up 42% from 2019. The barriers of entry have been essentially removed. No longer do you (the artist) need a record deal to have any chance of success. To the contrary, there has never been a more ideal time to be an artist than today. It's never been more affordable to record, mix and master, shoot a music video, and have the possibility of global distribution and reach. You can join one of the Performing Rights Organizations (PROs), obtain a mechanical license, submit your music for synch licensing opportunities, and secure a publishing administration agreement — all online! More details of this will be covered in book.

We will take a positive and optimistic viewpoint at the strategies and opportunities that exist today for you as an artist, a business, a band, or brand, (or any combination thereof). Specifically, we will explore numerous tools on how to grow a fan base, the benefits of database marketing, utilizing analytics to determine demographic and psychographic segmentation, a dedicated website having an ecommerce component, social media marketing, crowdsourcing and merch to name a few.

Start thinking – is the music business primarily about art or about business?

Resources

Historia de la Música / History of Music (subtitled / subtitulado)
From Phonographs to Spotify: A Brief History of the Music Industry
2021 Year-End Music Industry Revenue Report | RIAA

2

MUSIC PUBLISHING

If you are not familiar with, or could use a refresher course in; copyright, public performances, synch, and sample licenses' we will briefly explore them here so that you might better understand the importance of intellectual property. Additionally, we will explore the many facets of music publishing.

COPYRIGHT

What is copyright and why is it so important to music creators?

According to the U.S. Copyright Office, Copyright is: A form of protection provided by the laws of the United States for "original works of authorship", including literary, dramatic, musical, architectural, cartographic, choreographic, pantomimic, pictorial, graphic, sculptural, and audiovisual creations. "Copyright" literally means the right to copy but has come to mean that body of exclusive rights granted by law to copyright owners for protection of their work. Copyright protection does not extend to any idea, procedure, process, system, title, principle, or discovery. Similarly, names, titles, short phrases, slogans, familiar symbols, mere variations of typographic ornamentation, lettering, coloring, and listings of contents or ingredients are not subject to copyright.

Stated more simply: Copyright is the exclusive legal right, given to an originator to print, publish, perform, film, or record literary, artistic, or musical material, and to authorize others to do the same.

What exclusive rights do you gain with a copyright?

A copyright owner is provided with six exclusive rights in their created work. The owner, as well as authorized third parties, have the right to:
1. reproduce the work (replicate the work in any physical or digital format)
2. distribute the work (stream or otherwise make the music publicly available)
3. prepare derivatives of the work (remixes, edits and acappella versions)
4. publicly perform the work (in a small nightclub, a concert hall or on the radio) and,
5. publicly display the work. (i.e., in music - visual images of Getty images, album art-work, logos and trademarks
6. digital transmission or public performance or a sound recording via digital audio transmission. This applies only to the sound recording. The distinction between the composition and sound recording will be discussed below.

Without copyright, music compositions and recorded music would have little monetary value. In music, there exist two copyrights in a song:
1. one for the composition and the other
2. for the sound recording (the Master).

Compositions are usually owned by songwriters and/or music publishers. Sound recordings are typically owned by indie artists or record labels. Copyright in a composition is the most valuable asset of a songwriter and due to numerous variances, may be a formidable revenue stream on an annualized basis. Essentially every time a record is streamed, played on the radio, placed in a motion picture or TV commercial or even played in a restaurant or club; the songwriter is theoretically compensated. So, if you are a songwriter and your song is your own original expression, and it is fixed in tangible form (e.g., recorded) – and assuming that you are the sole songwriter / composer of this composition then you own the copyright to that song. You are considered the author of the work. Generating income from songwriting is the definition of *music publishing.*

In the US, the copyright of a song endures for 70 years beyond the death of the last surviving composer of a song. Copyrights may be inherited, transferred, or sold. Be aware however, if you feel as though someone has stolen your copyright you are only able to seek damages through the court system in cases of copyright infringement when your song has been previously registered with the US Copyright and trademark office. To protect their songs, the vast majority of professional songwriters register their songs with the US Copyright Office. Registering a copyright is as easy as preparing and submitting an application with the appropriate filing fee and a submission of the copyrighted material. Should you wish to file a copyright, you may do so by visiting the url below.

https://www.copyright.gov/

Copyright owners are able to grant permission for others to use their compositions for a particular purpose. This process is called licensing. The rights which can be licensed correspond with the 'exclusive rights' indicated above and there are a few ways in which some of these rights are "bundled" into a particular type of license. We'll discuss them. The administration of music copyrights and licensing is what music publishing is all about. Make sense?

Entire books have been written dedicated to copyright and music publishing, so if you are not too familiar with songwriting and licenses, it would be beneficial for you to take a closer in-depth look for yourself. For our purposes, it's essential that you have a basic understanding of revenue streams for songwriters. Some key takeaways include:

1. In order for you to record a song you did not perform; it will be necessary for you to file for a mechanical license. You can obtain a mechanical license from Songfile or Easy Song License.
2. If you play live music in a restaurant or club, know that there exists a strong likelihood that the establishment has purchased a public performance license. This license allows you to perform copywritten songs you did not write at music venues large or small.
3. Streaming services such as Apple Music and Spotify have negotiated rates with the publishers, so that you as a songwriter get paid when your song is streamed. The rate for streaming is at present approximately $0.06 per 100 streams, although this number seems minuscule at best, it becomes meaningful for songwriters having compositions that have achieved 10s if not 100s of millions of streams. The songwriter formula is approximately $1,000 earned for every 1.6 million streams.

Next, we need to address the 2nd copyright in music, specifically the master sound recordings, which like the songs themselves are considered intellectual property. Master sound recordings are typically owned by the record label, but in the case of an indie artist – you yourself (by default), own your master sound recordings. Like a songwriter, as the owner of a master sound recording, you are eligible for compensation in numerous ways for the exploitation of the masters. Also know that streaming services such as Apple Music and Spotify have negotiated rates with the majors and indie label representatives, so that you as a master sound recording owner also get paid when your song is streamed. The average per-stream royalty for both the composition and recording on Spotify is around half a penny. The sound recording average is about $0.0038 per stream. Again, although this number seems minuscule at best, it becomes meaningful for the owner of a master that has achieved 10s if not 100s of millions of streams.

MECHANICAL LICENSE

A mechanical license is a type of license issued by a copyright owner of a music composition or song to do a "cover" of that song or if a portion of it (sample) is used and reproduced. We're talking about the rights to a song/composition itself, not a recording. The statutory rate set by the Copyright Royalty Board is currently 9.1 cents and is expected to be raised to 12 cents in 2023. This rate is payable to songwriters as compensation per song in a physical format such as an CD, or a digital download. It is paid for each copy manufactured and distributed.

PUBLIC PERFORMANCE

A "public performance" of music is defined in the U.S. copyright law to include any music played outside a normal circle of friends and family. Songwriters, composers, and music publishers have the exclusive right to play their music publicly and to authorize others to do so under the copyright law. This is known as the "Performing Right". This right was designed to enable and encourage music creators to continue to create music.

Public performances" encompass a variety of things, such as:
    Radio and television stations playing music
    Live concerts
    Night clubs/bars and restaurants with live or recorded music including jukeboxes
    Retail stores playing music over a central sound system
    Music on hold on telephone systems
    Music in elevators, hotel lobbies and department stores

Whether it's a festival, a nightclub, a hotel lobby, a theater, or a stadium, it's the legal responsibility of the owner/operator of a performance space/venue to ensure that the necessary rights and licenses have been obtained with respect to all copyrighted music which is performed at that venue regardless of a non-profit or for-profit business. Venue owners/operators purchase blanket licenses on an annual basis. This license provides them with the legal authorization to perform (live or recorded music) of all works managed by the respective Performing Rights Organization (PRO).

Now that we have an understanding of what exactly defines a public performance, and as a songwriter and/or performer, you are now aware that you are entitled to compensation every time your song is deemed a public performance. The question is, *who* collects this money on your behalf and allocates your fair share to you. It seems like quite an arduous task collecting money from *public* performance revenue from venues, radio spins, streams, or synchs of your compositions and/or recorded music in the U.S., let alone throughout the world. The objective here is to walk you through what is admittedly a somewhat confusing and complicated network of collection societies one must register with in an effort to ensure you are amassing all the monies and royalties due you. The following is a breakdown of the organizations which you should be intimately familiar (registered) with that facilitate this task.

PERFORMING RIGHTS ORGANIZATIONS (PROS)

Perhaps you're familiar with the PROs here in the US. If not, here's a quick summary. At present there are four PROs in the US. They are ASCAP, BMI, SESAC and GMR. PROs represent songwriters *only* and are not responsible for the collection of monies associated with the master sound recording, that responsibility lies with other entities which we will introduce later. The role of a performing rights organization is to collect monies on behalf of you as a songwriter associated with *live performances* in locations such as retail stores, festivals, nightclubs – essentially all public spaces utilizing live, streamed or prerecorded music. The monies collected from live performances are calculated and divided up proportionally among PRO songwriters. These monies are called publishing royalties. The license or blanket license is granted by the copyright holders to parties who wish to use copyrighted works publicly.

Playing live music in an establishment comes with a price. You see, precedent exists when around the turn of the 20th century, composer Victor Herbert was dining in a restaurant where the in-house orchestra was playing one of his songs "Sweethearts." Herbert contended that he should be paid a royalty for the performance. The proprietor's position was that since no admission was being charged, the performance was "not for profit" and did not constitute infringement. ASCAP brought a suit against the restaurant in Herbert v. Shanley Co. ASCAP convinced the Supreme Court that public performances in restaurants, despite no fee being charged, was an unauthorized "public performance for profit." Justice Holmes wrote an opinion that stated "Restaurants are not charities, when they play music, it must be in the interest of profit even if they do not charge at the door. Saying in part, "if music didn't pay, it would be given up. The "Herbert Principal" has had a powerful impact on copyright theory and legislation to this day.

The US Copyright Office has done a remarkable job in legislating government regulations for copyright holders including songwriters to earn money from their music. One of the ways songwriters earn money from their composition copyrights is through public performances. This created a need for organizations to track the number of individual public performances, hence created the need for the Performing Rights Organizations or PROs. Essentially all public spaces playing live, or recorded music are required to purchase a public performance license. Each club, venue, hotel, restaurant or retail shop purchase blanket licenses on an annual basis. The cost of each license is approximately 2% of the gross annual revenue of each establishment. This translates into about 5% of gross revenue the owner/operators must purchase from the four PROs in order to have the privilege of playing music in their establishment. Two of these organizations are essentially by invitation only, so for our purposes, we will explore the two performing rights organizations, which you as a songwriter should consider joining. Again, understand, the PROs represent songwriters only and are not responsible for collecting revenue on behalf of the master sound recording owner (i.e., the record label). So, if you are a songwriter in the US, you should join either ASCAP or BMI to act as your agent. PROs are mandated for collections within their respective territories, so BMI & ASCAP only collect for performance rights in the US. Note: there exist reciprocal PROs in nearly all countries throughout the world which operate within the same guidelines within their designated territories. We will also explore how best to collect your publishing monies from these other territories throughout the world later in the chapter.

To reiterate, there are four collection societies in the US – ASCAP, BMI, SESAC and GMR. The last two are by invitation only, (for songwriters with a proven track record of hit singles), so for the time-being, move on. They'll contact you when you've written more than one hit single. Assuming, you have yet to write a hit single, become either an ASCAP or BMI songwriter. If you're a songwriter not yet affiliated with a PRO add it to the top of your to-do list.

ASCAP

The American Society of Composers, Authors and Publishers (ASCAP) is home to more than 800,000 music creator members across all genres – representing the greatest names in music, and thousands more in the early stages of their careers. ASCAP is the only PRO in the US owned and governed by their members. They license over 16 million songs to the businesses that play them publicly, and then send the money to its members as royalties. This is accomplished with the use of cutting-edge technology to process over one trillion performances every year - more than any PRO in the world. Registration requires a one-time fee of $50. [Source: ASCAP]

BMI

Broadcast Music, Inc. (BMI) is the bridge between songwriters and the businesses and organizations that play music publicly. As a global leader in music rights management, BMI serves as an advocate for the value of music, representing over 17 million musical works created and owned by more than 1.1 million songwriters, composers and publishers. BMI was founded in 1939 and operates as a non-profitmaking performing right organization. BMI is now the largest music rights organization in the US and continues to nurture new talent. Registration is free to join. [Source: BMI]

So, your question might be, which of these two organizations should I join. Essentially, they both do the same thing and both organizations are extremely adept at collecting and distributing monies on behalf of songwriters. Combined, the four organizations collect more than three billion dollars annually and distribute these monies to their members using a pro rata formula. In making a determination which PRO to join conduct research on the organizations to determine which of your favorite songwriters have joined which society. That may give you a good indication on which to join. At the same time, consider how much is the fee to join, what benefits do they offer, what digital content, workshops and showcases are offered. Do they offer discounts on instrument insurance and software? Do they provide career advice? Once you join one of these societies, be sure to take advantage of the various resources and benefits they provide. Then once initially established, do your best to develop a personal relationship, make yourself known (network) with one of the publishers or a staff member.

THE MECHANICAL LICENSING COLLECTIVE

The Mechanical Licensing Collective (The MLC) is a nonprofit organization designated by the U.S. Copyright Office which is a direct result of Congress passing the historic *Music Modernization Act* of 2018. As a result, in 2020, The MLC collected a historical amount of unmatched royalties in the amount of $424 million from the likes of Spotify, Apple, Amazon, Google, Soundcloud and others. In January 2021, The MLC began administering blanket mechanical licenses to streaming and download services (digital service providers or DSPs) in the United States. The MLC then collects these royalties due under those licenses from the DSPs (MSPs, *music streaming services*) and pays songwriters, composers, lyricists, and music publishers.

In the simplest of terms, The MLC changes the way songwriters are paid when their music is being played on interactive streaming services. This includes the major players like Spotify, Amazon and Apple. So essentially, it's their job to collect digital audio mechanical royalties (on behalf of songwriters), from eligible streaming services (MSPs) in the United States who elect to secure blanket licenses from The MLC. They have established a massive database in an effort to accomplish said task. The MLC is not a PRO and provides a separate function for songwriters. One way or the other, if you're a songwriter, here's another organization to place on your to do list. You can become a member by registering directly, or by utilizing a third party to do so on your behalf, (more on that later).

> Anyone who is entitled to receive digital audio mechanical royalties in the United States will need to become a "Member" of The MLC. This will include music publishers, administrators and self-administered songwriters, composers, and lyricists. Be sure to register your works with the MLC. To be clear, The MLC, like the PROs only represents and collects on behalf of songwriters and not the owners of the master sound recording. The MLC will however, pay self-administered songwriters or their designated music publishing entity. By law, The MLC's services are free for all of its Members. [Source: The MLC]

SOUNDEXCHANGE

SoundExchange collects royalties from non-interactive streaming services such as Pandora, Music Choice and 3,000+ digital radio stations including SiriusXM. SoundExchange collects monies on behalf of performers and sound recording master rights owners, (i.e., record labels) for 'non interactive' digital performances.

> SoundExchange provides royalty solutions for sound recordings and publishing, serving as a critical backbone to today's digital music industry. The organization collects and distributes digital performance royalties on behalf of more than 250,000 recording artists' and master rights owners,' (i.e., record labels) and administers direct agreements on behalf of rights owners and licensees. To date, SoundExchange has paid out more than $7 billion in royalties. [Source: SoundExchange]

If you are an artist and you own your master sound recordings or own a label, you should register with SoundExchange to administer collections for the sound recording copyright. SoundExchange has more than 32 million recordings in their repertoire database and now represents 14% of the entire U.S. recorded music industry's revenues.

So, once again, if you are a performer and/or master rights sound recording owner here's another organization which will be incumbent for you to register with. If you don't, you're simply leaving money on the table.

The PROs represent a different copyright than SoundExchange. ASCAP, BMI, SESAC and GMR collect performance revenue for the owners of the copyrighted musical work (the song, the composition, the songwriter), i.e., music publishers, songwriters, and composers. SoundExchange on the other hand, collects performance revenue for owners of the sound recording copyright (the master) and for featured and nonfeatured artists. SoundExchange, therefore, performs a different function and does not compete with ASCAP, BMI or The MLC.

In summary, both SoundExchange and the The MLC are relatively new nonprofit entities established by the U.S. Copyright office. So, if you are a songwriter and were not previously familiar with The MLC, you should now understand that it is incumbent for you to register with them. If you're an independent artist releasing your own master, and/or, you are a 'featured artist' you should most certainly register your performances and recordings with SoundExchange. If your serous, if this pertains to you or persons in your orbit, it would be smart to adhere to these recommendations. Why leave money on the table?

SYNCHRONIZATION (OR SYNCH) LICENSE

If someone intends to use music in combination with a video clip, or in a film, or television commercial then they must first obtain a synchronization license. Synch licenses are granted by two parties:
1. the songwriter and
2. the master sound recording owner.

A synch license is issued once both parties grant the approval. The licensing revenue is then typically split 50/50 between the songwriter and the master sound recording owner. There is no statutory rate for sync licensing. Rather, rates are determined and based on market conditions and project budgets, and nuanced considering the particular use of the song in the project. For example, a song featured as the title track for a feature film would likely cost more than if that same track was just embedded in a scene of the film. The prominence of the song, how it's used, the duration of time, and any number of other factors might be considered in determining the rate that will be paid to the copyright owners.

The first criteria the decision makers in sync licensing (music supervisors or a creative at an advertising agency) are initially seeking music that is wholly owned or controlled. In its simplest of forms, a cover song, or a performance of a song you did not write and do not have a relationship with the songwriter, would exclude them from sync licensing consideration. The reason being, they are seeking a turnkey solution whereby they can easily gain the approval of the songwriter(s) and the owner of the master sound recording. The fees for sync licensing varies wildly, from $0 to $500 for an independent artist in say a local television commercial to tens of, if not hundreds of thousands of dollars for major artist placement in a major motion picture or a commercial.

OK, so perhaps we're getting ahead of yourselves, if you're not already familiar with a music supervisor – they are the ones entrusted with finding the right song at the right price for a perfect placement in a film, a sit-com, or any other specific usage (digital or otherwise) in which music is synchronized to moving pictures (including stills).

You might be wondering about all of the content you consume or are exposed to that has music synced to it on online platforms such as TikTok and YouTube. Because of the very nature of how these platforms function, where users upload videos that often include music which technically, they do not own the rights to, they negotiate agreements with record labels and music publishers. This allows users of the platform to sync music to their content without having to secure a license. The platforms themselves pay a blanket license inclusive of the entire catalog of music from publishers and labels. Micro-sync royalties are royalties generated in this manner and generally are for short form videos that have the potential for significant views. Songwriters collect performance royalties for these uses through their affiliated PRO. Mechanical royalties are collected and distributed by mechanical rights organizations such as the MLC and the Harry Fox Agency.

There exist numerous 3rd parties that, for a fee of course, will assist you in finding placements. One bit of advice is to develop a personal relationship with your contact at your publishing company or with an agency. After all this is a relationship driven business.

SAMPLE LICENSE

If you intend to incorporate any portion of a song you did not write or own the master to into your new piece of music, you must obtain a sample license. Just like a sync licenses, sample licenses must be obtained from two (2) parties: the songwriter and the master sound recording owner. A sample license is issued once both parties grant the approval. In addition to an advance, a royalty may be involved as well. The licensing revenue is then typically split 50/50 between the songwriter and the master sound recording owner.

Because of the ease in which samples of sound recordings can be used in developing new works, it is tempting to do so without obtaining the proper license. For some genres of music, it is common practice to sample recordings and incorporate it into new works. Know that if you are doing so without the proper licensing in place, you are setting yourself up for failure. Imagine you do this and your track starts to take off. Now you have a real problem. If a label is interested in you because of this track, you are not in a position to work with the label as it pertains to this song. If you haven't cleared the rights for the sample, the track is useless to a label as they cannot risk the liability of releasing it. Frankly, neither can you. It's a real legal liability. Any use of a copyrighted work without permission of the copyright owner(s) is called copyright infringement.

TERMS OF A LICENSE

What follows are some initial, basic terms that need to be considered and included in any music licensing agreement. These also factor into the cost of the license for the sync:

Territory – Territory refers to places in which the "synced" content will be used or broadcasted. Does the licensee intend to use your music in a 30 second television commercial to be shown throughout the country, or is your music being used as a bed in a local spot with a car wash? What is the scope of the possibility? Does the language in the license include world-wide, to accommodate internet broadcasts

Term – Term refers to the length of time or duration in which the license will be valid. If for example your song were placed in a motion picture, it presumably would be licensed in perpetuity, as the film will endure in a digital format for years to come. Suppose you write a holiday song for a limited run local radio commercial. Presumably, this license would be for a period of only 30-60 days leading up to the holiday. The agreement may include an option to extend or renew annually.

Media – The type of media in which the synced audiovisual content will be exploited will need to be defined in the license. Most licensors will request your song be included for "all media," which encompasses the internet. Similar to a sample license, make certain that the duration and specific portion of the song for the usage is specified.

Fee – Typically the fee the licensee would be willing to pay would be offered as an "all-in" fee. Meaning the amount offered is to be split with the record label who likely owns the recording. It is customary for the fee to be split 50 / 50 with the record label. However, if you own the master recording you would be entitled to the entire amount.

ROYALTY FREE MUSIC

This is a term in music licensing in which it is understood the user pays a one-time fee to the songwriter and record label and is free to use it with no further financial obligation. The company you license the music from pays the royalty fees. There exist numerous royalty-free music distribution platforms, whereby you can upload a hi quality digital file of your track. You can then essentially determine your own price of free, $50 or what-ever you deem appropriate. Understand that the creator (let's assume a video director) once purchasing your "royalty-free" track will have the ability to re-use your music in other future projects – just be aware.

Although there is a great deal of money to be made in music licensing, some creators decide to charge nothing for the royalty free license, rather viewing it as marketing and exploitation. Understand that in the early stages of your career and music licensing, royalty-free will be the structure most often utilized by independent production companies, and advertising agencies.

MUSIC PUBLISHING

We've discussed music publishing and the importance of it, but what exactly is it? *Generating money from song writing is called music publishing.* Any person or company involved in this activity is a music publisher. Although you have successfully registered with SoundExchange and a PRO – guess what, that's not enough. You see, there exist omissions these organizations displace in collecting money for mechanical royalties for songwriters from the streaming services. Hence you next need to enter into some type of a music publishing deal. So, what are your options?

A MUSIC PUBLISHING DEAL

Music publishing is the business of acquiring, administering, marketing, and promoting musical compositions. The music publishing industry is dominated by 5 major publishers: Universal Music Publishing, Sony Music Publishing, Warner / Chappell, Kobalt, and BMG. There are, however, literally hundreds of smaller, independent music publishers, most of whom focus on a particular genre. A music publisher's' responsibility is to create and seek promotion and licensing placements of songs in film, television, and commercials for example. The benefits of entering into a music publishing deal will typically include:
- administering copyrights,
- collecting streaming revenue,
- negotiating licenses,
- setting up co-writes
- establishing demo budgets
- pitching your songs to artists, producers, and A&R teams

Music publishers seek out successful songwriters and entice them to sign a long-term agreement which typically includes an advance, or upfront payment. For a songwriter with a major label recording agreement and a successful track record of writing hit records, securing a music publishing deal is relatively easy. Music publishers will actively seek you out in an effort in securing a publishing deal. The terms of a music publishing deal typically include an advance of money, while you relinquish 50% of your publishing income and ownership of your songs for the term of the agreement.

The primary responsibility of a music publisher is the exploitation of your songwriting. Again, earning money from songwriting is called *music publishing*. Although one concedes 50% of the gross revenue in a music publishing deal, you can begin to appreciate that forfeiting half of one's earnings from songwriting is advantageous and in one's best financial interest. A typical publishing deal involves an advance, and the commitment of pitching your songs for placements with artists, labels, motion pictures, video games, etc. This is the preferred way to go for hit songwriters, as nearly all are offered and enter into a publishing agreement. If you have had the good fortune of entering into a publishing deal, congratulations. Just be wary of the fact that some individuals/companies may offer you a "deal" but not really be established or in the best position and with the appropriate contacts to secure licensing for your music. You will need to do your research and make sure you are dealing with a reputable and successful music publisher. Ask for references.

Now assuming you have not been offered, nor entered into a music publishing deal, it would be highly recommended that you, for the time being, register for a publishing administration deal. Most publishing admin deals have an opt out option, allowing you to end the term and relationship once you're offered a publishing deal. You may recall that they are adept at collecting music publishing royalties on a global basis. However, their services typically do NOT include the exploitation of your songwriting for placement in films and television. So, for the time being, seeking out synch licensing opportunities will be up to you and your team.

However, if you have only a modest catalog, with modest success at this point, then you are not necessarily enticing to music publishers. You may have to wait until you have established a track record, and achieved some KPIs (key performance indicators) such as a significant number of streams or views. So, then what are your options?

SELF-ADMINISTERED PUBLISHING

If you're not ready or uncertain about entering into a publishing deal, one option is to self-administer your publishing. You will need to set-up your own vanity publishing entity whereby you own all rights in your songs and you are eligible for 100% of all royalties collected and have full control of the compositional copyright. Although incurring no collection fees from a publisher may sound tempting and financially prudent, understand music publishing is a tedious task and without assistance, may distract from the creative songwriting process. Self-publishing may be a viable option should you have a team or even one dedicated individual to assist you in the marketing, promotion, and collections of your songs. Recognize, that self-publishing is an option, and if done properly can prove to be quite financially compelling. However, it may be a bit risky in that, once again it's quite possible you might be leaving money on the table.

PUBLISHING ADMINISTRATION

Should you be overwhelmed with the arduous task of self-administering, or not offered nor seeking a full publishing deal there is an efficient and turn-key alternative for songwriters. This would be to enter into a Publishing Administration deal. A Music Publishing Administrator acts as a music publishing company responsible for administering, registering and collecting publishing royalties from global societies on behalf of the songwriters they represent. The beauty of this arrangement is that you retain 100% of the ownership of the copyrights, the term of the agreement is relatively short (1-2 years), the registration fee is low, you do not need to create your own vanity music publishing company and the commission for the administration is typically a modest 10-15%. They maintain reciprocal arrangements with the PROs in the various foreign territories throughout the world. The key here is, in a publishing admin deal they collect *global* streaming services revenue on your behalf. Meaning, they collect for you as a songwriter throughout the world. One caveat, Publishing Admin deals typically do not offer an advance and they do not provide creative or marketing services. However, this should not preclude you from considering entering into such an agreement.

SONGTRUST

SongTrust provides access to the largest network of over 60 pay sources and collection societies in over 245 countries world-wide to collect all your publishing royalties. As the world's largest global royalty collection service, SongTrust streamlines the music publishing administration for over 3 million songs from over 350,000 songwriters. There is a one-time fee of a hundred dollars per writer to join and they retain a 15% commission of the monies they collect on your behalf. [Source: SongTrust]

So, if you have not yet figured it out, it's likely the ideal publishing arrangement for you to enter into would be a publishing admin deal. There are several service providers to choose from. If you use CD Baby for example as your distributor, they offer CD Baby Pro publishing admin. They take a commission of 15% of the publishing royalties and 9% of the mechanical royalties. The drawback here, is they only collect on music released through CD Baby and they will not collect money for songs you write or co-write that are distributed through another distributor. TuneCore is another option for distribution of your music, they too offer publishing administration. They retain a 10% commission; however, you don't have to release music through them in order to use their publishing admin services. The largest publishing administration company in the US is SongTrust. CD Baby Pro actually outsources their publishing admin to SongTrust.

It's worth noting that should you sign-up with SongTrust or CD Baby Pro Publishing or any other distributor which offers publishing administration, some will also register your copyrights on your behalf with The MLC. This in and of itself, is another very compelling reason to join SongTrust, or CD Baby Pro Publishing for example, to simplify and streamline your ability to manage your publishing rights. Both organizations are free to register. The one-time registration fee with SongTrust is currently $100. Pro Publishing with CD Baby currently costs $29 per single and $69 per album annually. A publishing admin deal as an independent songwriter may be an ideal arrangement for you until which time you might be offered and enter into a full publishing deal.

Please note that entering into any of the above referenced music publishing deals is an exclusive arrangement. Lastly, in addition to registration, and transparent accounting from all of the previously referenced organizations, their websites provide useful portals for FAQs, news, educational videos and tutorials. Take advantage of these free, educational resources.

RESOURCES

ASCAP

BMI

SongTrust

The MLC

SoundExchange

Pharrell and Rick Rubin Have an Epic Conversation

Jeff Tweedy's Songwriting Masterclass | Broken Record (Hosted by Malcolm Gladwell)

Kendrick Lamar Meets Rick Rubin and They Have an Epic Conversation | GQ

Paul McCartney Breaks Down His Most Iconic Songs | GQ

How to write one song (according to Jeff Tweedy)

Best Music Licensing Companies

3

MUSIC CONSUMPTION

Before we continue, it's important to understand what defines *music consumption* - and how its basic formulas translate into sales. It's easy to understand with physical sales, it's simple, you pay money at an indie record store for a CD or LP, that one transaction or sale is scanned and digitally uploaded to be included in the weekly accrual of the *Billboard* charts. Of course, this is a bit of oversimplification, but you get the point.

Calculating the sales of music pre-SoundScan (known today as the MRC) was a guesstimate at best. One of the entry level jobs at a label was calling stores on a weekly basis to obtain the past week's 'store report.' In an effort to 'influence' the reports; concert tickets, electronic equipment, merch, etc. would be offered to a store owner/manager in an effort to secure a #1 or top 10 chart position on the *Billboard Top 200*. Then in 1991 retail chains as well as mom & pop record stores were offered compensation for providing this sales information to Sound-Scan. Nearly every store in the nation at the time signed up. By scanning the bar codes of each CD, LP or cassette sold into a handheld computer, SoundScan was able to track and compile the first accurate sales data in March of 1991. One week later the first published *Billboard Top 200* chart incorporating the technology, turned the charts upside down. For the first time in history, the recorded music industry had accurate metrics to include in their decision making.

10 years later Apple introduced the iTunes Store offering paid digital downloads. What was immediately observed, was this a la carte format transformed the music business from a full album-oriented consumer offering into a singles business overnight. This in turn necessitated the creation of a formula for calculating the sales of digital downloaded singles. A determination was made that the sale of 10 paid downloads would equal the equivalent of 1 album sale.

What deems an artist's career as successful? Success may be predicated on a few things; the number of live shows per year you play, the value of your music publishing, or how much money you generate from your merch store. Today most however might answer, 'the number of Spotify streams.' So how are streams calculated and what is music consumption and how does it translate into sales?

The advent of streaming once again necessitated a calculation for a specific number of streams that would be the equivalent to one album sale. The short answer is 1,500 on demand streams equal the sale of one full album (in any format). Known as SEA (streaming equivalent album) - 1,500 song streams from an album are treated as the equivalent to one purchase of the album. To differentiate subscription users from those using the freemium version, two tiers of on-demand audio streams exist.

> *The Album Award counts album sales, song sales and on-demand audio and/or video song streams at the formula of 1,500 on-demand audio and/or video song streams = 10 track sales = 1 album sale. [RIAA]*

> Streams on the Billboard 200 album chart will also be weighted by tier. TIER 1 will be for paid subscription audio streams where 1,250 streams will now equal 1 album unit, and TIER 2 will be ad-supported audio streams where 3,750 streams will equal 1 album unit. [Hypebot]

Now, to put this all-in perspective with the streaming services paying roughly $0.006 per stream one needs 250,000 streams on Spotify in order to make a $1000. In other words, if everyone listened to you track five times on Spotify, you would need to sell out the equivalent of the combined occupancy of Madison Square Garden, the Hollywood Bowl, and Red Rocks Amphitheater. That's a lot of fans.

We all have a basic understanding of the tens if not hundreds of millions one track has the potential to rack-up on Spotify alone (excluding Apple, Amazon, Tidal, et al). However, just like in America where the top 1% possess nearly forty percent of the nation's wealth, the top tier Spotify achievers mirror the same discrepancy in stature and financial wealth. Yes, there are numerous artists we can all cite that most everyone has listened to or at least heard of, but in comparison to the sheer number of creators releasing music, they too represent a minuscule percent. Now if all of this sounds like a monumental challenge, that's because it just may be. Spotify created a website *Loud & Clear* to provide transparency and facts about the money the platform distributes. Essentially, the site quantifies the number of artists whose recording catalogs and publishing income have generated certain financial thresholds per year. In 2020 Spotify made the following information available.

- The $50k per-year club had 13,400 members
- The $100k-plus-per-year club had 7,800 artists
- The $500k-plus-per-year club had 1,820 artists
- And the $1 million-plus-per-year club counted 870 artists

The 2021 Lound & Clear statistics revealed the following Spotify updates;
- Paid out more than any other service – $7B
- For the first time, over 1,000 artists generated over $1 million on Spotify
- For the second year running, Spotify paid out more than a billion dollars to publishing rights holders
- Over 50,000 artists generated $10,000 from Spotify alone

Editor's note: Make no mistake about it, 7 billion in paid monies to rights holders is substantial, to say the least. However, the last bullet point brings only further credence to the fact that only the top approximate 1-4% are earning a living from Spotify. While an annual payment of ten thousand dollars, would be greatly appreciated by us all, (and although Spotify makes no claims to the contrary) illustrates the fact that revenue derived from streaming services, in and of itself, will not be sufficient in sustaining a career.

Not to pour fuel on the flames, but then take into account the number of artists / creators (podcasters, et al), who have content on Spotify. Just exactly how big is the competition? There are an estimated 60,000 tracks uploaded to Spotify every day. The service itself has in excess of 70 million tracks and according to Founder - Daniel Ek as of 2020 there are 8 million creators on Spotify.

So, the figure of $50,000 annually is representative of a middle-income standard of living salary in the US. But as you can also see from their own numbers, the members of this group number less than 15,000. The point being, if you are one of the talented and fortunate who can achieve anyone of these financial tiers, you have our adoration and respect. There's also a strong likelihood you are signed to a major label. If you have your doubts about achieving 1,250,000 plays per year on Spotify, then the additional content and ideas from here on out, should act as guidance in complimenting your streaming income with the addition of other ancillary revenue sources.

THE STATE OF THE MUSIC BUSINESS

United States recorded music revenues grew 9.2% in 2020 to $12.2 billion at estimated retail value. This is the fifth consecutive year of growth for the industry, as paid subscription services continued to be the primary driver of revenue increases and reached a record number of subscriptions. Streaming music's share of total revenues grew to 83%. [Source: RIAA 2020 Year-End Music Industry Revenue Report]

On an annualized basis the recorded music industry seems to be poised for continued growth. Recognize this is a very bold statement yet predicted by many. If you are an artist or an individual aspiring for a career in the music business, this trend should be both inspiring and motivating news for you. It's a great time to be getting into the music business.

Actually, there may never have been or be a better time to be an artist or to carve out a career in the music industry than that which exists today. The barriers to entry have been either reduced or essentially removed altogether. If you're an audio engineer and own a DAW or home studio, or you have a friend who does, the cost associated with recording no longer requires a budget. Distribution is no longer a problem; all one needs to do is upload your WAV files to the digital distributor of your choosing at minimal cost, if any. So, what's the problem? In a word – *marketing.* The most common mistake an indie artist, not signed to a label makes, is to put all of one's efforts *and* resources into the recording, giving little or no thought to the marketing of the release. Simply uploading a track and releasing it globally with little or no set-up will likely not produce the results you would like. Somehow thinking and believing that your one track is so undeniably brilliant that it will undoubtedly get discovered by tens if not hundreds of thousands of new fans is hubris. This is a very flawed formula and a recipe for disappointment if not disaster altogether. Unfortunately, the sheer number of creators versus the elite group earning six figures annually from Spotify is minuscule. It does however remain all too obvious that generating a significant number of plays on the streaming services is of vital importance. The point being, building a community of fans and followers will provide you with other revenue streams outside of the music streaming services (MSS), and in so doing will ultimately impact your streaming numbers.

So, the challenge today is how to be heard and how to distinguish yourself from all the clutter. The ease and ability of anyone to be able to release music is that there no longer exists a gatekeeper or filter for the music. The consequences of which, it's likely you're competing with clutter. Just because someone owns a DAW does not make them a brilliant artist. To the contrary perhaps they are one of the guilty ones contributing to all the clutter. For example, as we stated there are approximately 60,000 tracks per day uploaded by creators to Spotify, and that number is projected to be as much as a quarter million a day in the next 3-5 years. With no criteria, can all of this be quality music? Of course not. And even if it was, we all like different genres of music, after all that's the foundation of music. Not everyone likes everything. Sure, there are a handful of artists appealing to the masses, but even they are not known by everyone. So, what you need to do is find your niche and develop your own fan base.

First, determine who is you audience is. And once that's accomplished, work tirelessly to communicate to them and build this fan base. What you will ultimately discover is that marketing to your fans is highly cost effective, gratifying and most importantly they will make a significant impact in driving your revenue. This will all happen when you implement some of the ideas set forth as well as your own creative efforts you will discover in reaching your fans. Now if you're an artist reading this and are thinking, I'm a creative person, I want to make music, why do I need to do this stuff? The answer is you don't altogether if you build a team around you. Do keep in mind, that you WILL be involved and WILL need to contribute to your team's efforts. If you prefer to not be the only one out front in this crusade, this for example is where a good Manager, or your friend who is a social media maven can fill these roles. Either way, the work must get done. While we're on the subject, let's discuss options and the importance of you creating a team around your career.

THE TEAM

With few exceptions, to be successful in the music business you must be likable, humble, and always receptive to other people's ideas and opinions. If these traits and characteristics speak to you, then there's a good chance you have done a fair amount of networking already. If that's the case, some of your team members may already be in your orbit.

Roles and titles of persons you might consider adding to your team may include;
- A Manager
- A Booking Agent
- A Tour Accountant / Tour Manager
- An Entertainment Attorney
- A Business Manager
- A Digital Marketing Guru
- A Merchandising Maven

MANAGER

The manager is the liaison and point person for an artist. They should either have or develop a keen understanding of the music business. Aside from this book, there are numerous other publications as well as podcasts and video resources from which to learn. A manager can be an advocate for you, instrumental in making business decisions, orchestrating record releases and tours, assist in booking gigs, and implementing merchandising strategies. The value of a good manager is particularly useful in negotiations, conflict resolution and crisis intervention. The implementation of a manager in your career removes you the artist from being the point person in creative and financial negotiations. However, the most vital job a manager can provide is promoting the artist and finding and collecting all the monies due to them. No gig in the industry demands a closer 24/7 relationship with an artist or band than this position.

Do you put a relationship between your manger and yourself in writing? Do you hire an entertainment attorney to draft a *Management Agreement* between the two of you? The answer is, it's up to you. You can conduct business on a handshake or if both parties are more comfortable, you can put it in writing. Keep in mind however, that initially the stakes may be very low for all involved. If everyone is doing their job, that can change quickly and once there is money on the table, it may be better to have an agreement in place that outlines the responsibilities and expectations of each party. This could ease the complications that success may present. If you're an aspiring manager, one thing you may want to include in the agreement is what's referred to as a 'sunset clause.' If in the event your artist blows up and becomes huge, they will gain the attraction of notable, more seasoned mangers and management firms. A sunset clause will protect you should the two of you deiced to part ways. The clause typically provides you with a reduced management fee for three consecutive years following the dissolution of your services. An artist management agreement is exclusive to the artist, meaning you cannot sign with another individual wanting to also act as your manager. Management agreements are not exclusive to managers as their income is tied to you as well as their other artists' success.

A Manager can be instrumental in selecting and overseeing the various individual responsibilities of your entire team.

BOOKING AGENT

The primary function of a booking agent is to secure and facilitate live performance opportunities. A good agent works with two parties – the artist and the venue / promoter. Not wanting to burn bridges, the objective of an agent is to cut a fair deal between both parties making it a win/win situation. Agents have relationships with promoters and venue owners and pitch the artists they represent. Once a verbal offer has been reached, an 'option' is held on that date and time for that promoter. This signals the initiation of a *Live Performance Agreement* outlining the specific terms of the performance. The document includes details such as the date, time and duration of the performance, fee, deposit, cancellation and boilerplate, and standardized clauses. Accompanying the Live Performance Agreement is the *Technical Rider.* A tech rider includes details as they pertain to hospitality, ground transportation, stage plot, dressing room requirements, number of complimentary (comp) tickets, merch, parking, etc.

TOUR ACCOUNTANT / TOUR MANAGER

A Tour Accountant / Tour Manager is the point person in dealing with promoters, venues, ticketing agents, the band and crew. Day to day responsibilities include advancing the show (confirming all the details in advance), confirming reservations, logistics (moving the band and crew from point A to point B), while collecting and accounting for performance fees. An aspiring tour manager can make themselves even more indispensable if they have some accounting background and the ability to detail all income and expenses of a tour or show. On smaller shows and tours, a tour manager can also act as a front of house sound engineer.

A good tour manager is a very organized individual who is highly disciplined and performs well under pressure. Understand that being a tour manager is a very demanding job. Although you may be touring the world, don't have the misconception that, you will 'see the world'. In all likelihood, you will not be visiting tour markets as a 'tourist'. A tour manger is the last to bed, the first up, and on wi-fi constantly working out of the venue's Production Office advancing shows, load-in, coordinating ground transportation to the venue for sound-check, the show, then load-out and return to the hotel, initiating lobby calls in the morning, for the tour bus and a number of other responsibilities as issues arise. Compensation is typically based on a day or weekly rate.

BUSINESS MANAGER

You need a business manager once your career becomes a business. A business manager's primary function is to supervise an artist's business affairs. Although not essential, most business managers have an accounting background or are registered CPAs. The scope of services a business manager can provide include accrual accounting, the creation and maintaining of payroll, provide tax services and making investments on behalf of their client. In the music industry, this role is specialized due to the potential for revenue from multiple sources as well as the uniqueness of those sources such as recorded music, intellectual property ownership, publishing, and touring. Business management firms exist that focus solely on entertainment industry clients. Compensation is typically based on an hourly rate.

MERCHANDISING MAVEN

This individual's responsibilities might be to build and monitor your ecommerce store, oversee inventory management of physical merch while monitoring and providing accounting for merchandise purchased and sold. This responsibility could easily be appointed to a band member, a super fan, or an intern. Initially compensation may be in the form of free merch or a percentage of net revenue from merch sales.

FOR YOUR CONSIDERATION

It could be argued that the two most vital team members of all these positions would be a manager and a booking agent. However, recognize that both jobs are compensated in the form of a percentage of monies earned. Mangers for example typically charge between 15-20% while an agent typically works for 5-10% of gross. Understand, these percentages are based off gross revenue, (before expenses). So, if you get a gig for $1,000 – can you afford to give up 200 bucks to the manager and a hundred bucks to the agent? Now of course, if your guarantee from the promoter is six figures, paying these commissions is no problem. But in our $1,000 scenario, can you afford to give up 300 bucks right off the top? And what if you're playing a club date with a $500 guarantee - can you afford to give up $150 before expenses? If the answer is no – then possibly, you might consider putting a team together from within your existing network. Think of your friends, band members, and classmates. Who do you trust? Who has the aptitude for one of these gigs? The history of the music business provides numerous examples of where a band and a manager were both admitted novices but trusted and believed in each other and learned on the job. A perfect example would be Chance the Rapper and his (now former) Manager, Pat Corcoran. Admittedly, neither knew much about the biz but trusted in each other and made decisions together.

You can choose to go it alone or set up a team you can afford as you begin to build your career. Ideally, the people you assemble on your team share in your vision. If you believe and trust in each other, then immediate money in one's pocket will not be the motivating factor to get involved and do the work. But rather, all are on board for the long haul. The end-game dividend or payday will be worth the effort and investment in time.

So, for example, let's just say that your best friend assumes the role of Artist Manager. Same might possibly hold true for another friend, or band member for that matter, who is a maven at social media and the web. What about booking shows? Perhaps this is something you can take on yourself, or your Manger can take on in the early stages. Certainly, you can reach out to a licensed regional booking agency – however, keep in mind if your guarantee is low or for the door, the money simply isn't attractive to an agent. Recognize that 10, 15 or 20% of nothing equals nothing. Out of necessity this puts forth the alternate plan to enlist your friends, and your band members.

Trust is all well and fine, but what if success comes sooner than later, and now your act is attractive to professional managers and agents. You don't wanna leave the small team of friends who helped you along the way feeling they can get left behind. To avoid this scenario, you should consider having an attorney draft some sort of a document – creating a partnership with the team and/or band members. Remember, basically they are all working for free. When setting up your Team, this might prove to be an ideal time to conduct research on the entertainment attorneys in your vicinity or working with other acts having a similar statute as yourself.

Here's one last perspective on creating a team around you. Think about the fact that nearly all athletes participating in so called 'individual sports' such as tennis, golf, car racing, cycling, snowboarding, etc. all have a team in place around them. They have sports managers, they have "coaches", strength and fitness experts, caddies, dietitians, etc. So, if your undecided about establishing a team around you, perhaps recognizing this will influence your decision.

RESOURCES

Loud&Clear
How Chance The Rapper's Manager, Pat Corcoran, Reimagined the Music Business | Blueprint
TOUR MGMT 101
They played in a tiny café . . . there were four people in the audience
How Scooter Braun Went From Promoting Parties to Building An Entertainment Empire | Blueprint

4

ESTABLISHING A BUSINESS ENTITY & INTELLECTUAL PROPERTY

A BUSINESS MODEL

What's a Business Model? It's a roadmap of how the operation of a business becomes successful by identifying costs associated with production and marketing, identifying revenue streams, the customer base, potential products, and details of financing.

"All it really meant was how you planned to make money" (Harvard Business Review)

A business model addresses the fundamental question every Manager or Artist must ask themselves; how do we plan to make money? Can we create content for licensing, generate revenue from ticketing and merch sales, provide a service, build a subscription business, etc. Essentially, you... thinking of yourself as a company must determine the activities you can engage in and how you can generate revenue and make a profit.

Think about all the activities and costs associated with creating, manufacturing, and marketing your single, EP, or establishing your brand. Then think about all the activities you will explore and pursue in finding and reaching your target market, transacting a merch sale, or delivering consistently profitable shows. Develop a one sentence mission statement. Think of your objectives 6, 12 and 24 months from now. What is the value proposition that you believe exists for an audience of yours and how you will monetize those relationships and associations?

A great way to organize your thoughts and get your head around what your business model could be is to use the Business Modal Canvas. Created by Alexander Osterwalder, of Strategyzer, the Business Model Canvas provides a structure for you to think about important elements of a strong business model. The Business Model Canvas outlines 9 building blocks listed below with relevant examples for: artists, managers, and entrepreneurs.

1. Customer Segments – paying customers, fans, super-fans, and avid listeners
2. Value Proposition – products and services offered to your customer segments / your unique selling points, brand recognition
3. Channels – your website / blog, social media, database, and newsletter (Mailchimp), music distribution as well as live performance
4. Customer Relationships – your network and fans and the relationships you foster
5. Revenue Streams – merch store, live shows and merch sales, music publishing and collection societies, ASCAP or BMI, licensing, Patreon, etc
6. Key Resources – home studio (DAW), intellectual property, WAV files, website, merch, digital tools, social media, and your network
7. Key Activities – in all likelihood would include, but not limited to, music and digital content creation, networking, fan building, social media engagement, booking shows and rehearsing
8. Key Partners – your band members, musicians, your producer and manager and your team are your most valuable key partners. Outside of the obvious we have other key partner relationships one needs to have and develop including: talent buyers, sponsorship (cross promotional) relationships, brands, songwriters, music and production collaborators, performance rights organization, etc
9. Cost Structure – what you spend money on to run your business such as instruments, touring expenses, studio time, social media advertisements, etc

BUSINESS MODEL CANVAS EXAMPLE

KEY PARTNERS	KEY ACTIVITIES	VALUE PROPOSITION	CUSTOMER RELATIONSHIPS	CUSTOMER SEGMENTS
Tunecore	Songwriting	Creative Marketing	College Communities	New Fans
BMI	Recording	Geo-Targeting Marketing	Emails and Newsletters	Super Fans
SongTrust	Performances	Memorable Performances		Peer Musicians
Sound Exchange	Networking	The Brand		Bloggers / Reviewers
Manager	Marketing			
Booking Agent				

KEY RESOURCES
Customer Relationships
Industry Relationships
Home Studio

CHANNELS
Social Media
Press Releases ?PR
Database / Mailing Lists
Blog
Live Shows

COST STRUCTURE
Marketing
Website
Studio Equipment
Performance Gear
Management Fee
Agency Fee

REVENUE STREAMS
Music Publishing
Merch.
Live Shows
DSPs
Crowdsourcing
Synch Licensing

BUSINESS ENTITIES

Consider your band/group or yourself, as an independent artist, as a business that should be set-up accordingly. Declaring the assets and ownership in writing to avoid potential conflict in the future should be a priority. For example, who owns the name, who can continue to use the name should the band break up? Do you all have equal voting rights and if so, how do you fire one member of the band that's got an attitude problem that the rest of the other members are sick of, or simply not delivering on stage when performing? How do you replace this member? Who owns the publishing?   If there are four members in your band, do you agree to split all publishing equally at 25% each, or do only the 'songwriters' get paid?

Beyond considering your music career as a business venture you can legally establish it as a business entity. There are four legal entities in which to organize your business:
• Sole Proprietorship
• Partnership
• Limited Liability Company (LLC)
• Corporation

SOLE PROPRIETORSHIP / PARTNERSHIPS

If you have a 'wedding band' and you are the leader and are responsible for hiring other musicians, or a D.J. and oversee investing and transporting sound and lights, you can either choose to set your operation up as a sole proprietorship or, should you have a partner(s) it may be more appropriate to organize yourselves as a partnership. Although both entities are affordable to create there are some drawbacks in organizing your business as a sole proprietorship or a partnership. While these are the simplest forms of business to organize, realize a sole proprietorship is not a separate legal entity from the owner. It simply refers to the person who owns the business and ultimately that person is responsible for its debts. A partnership on the other hand is a legal entity which is typically put in writing amongst the partners. However, in both cases, the income earned from your business is declared on your own personal tax return. So, if for example you pay your band members in cash (as many musicians prefer), you will not have a record of your disbursements and could potentially be taxed on the gross (total amount of revenue brought in), not the net (revenue minus expenses) monies paid-out to your band.

LIMITED LIABILITY COMPANY (L.L.C.)

Perhaps the better choice, may be to organize as an L.L.C. (a Limited Liability Company). A Limited Liability Company encompasses the best of both worlds, combining the pass through of taxes through the business with the limited liability of a corporation. An L.L.C. is a legal corporate structure in the United States. Your attorney can help you file the proper documentation with the state when forming an L.L.C. Once filed with the state your L.L.C. will be issued a tax ID number enabling you to open a bank account and conduct business in the name of the company. The L.L.C. will file a separate tax return from that of your own, showing profits and losses shared by the members. As long as you have not personally guaranteed any loans, each of you, as members will be shielded from personal liability for business debts. You can see where this would be particularly beneficial if you were organizing a new band/group. You would now be able to obtain a credit card in the name of the business and make purchases on behalf of the business. Let's assume the four of you in a band, as members decide to invest $10,000 in sound and lights and then after six months of rehearsals breaks-up, in general the creditors will not be able to look to you as members or individuals for financial shortfall.

CORPORATIONS

A corporation is a legal entity which is separate and apart from those who created it and carry on as operators. Like an L.L.C. a corporation must file papers with the state government. A corporation enjoys all the benefits derived from an L.L.C. such as filing a separate tax return, shielding members from personal debt, etc. Additional benefits include the issuance of stock, the ability to raise capital, the creation of corporate bylaws, and unlimited life (meaning that the entity can continue when members quit, retire, or die). Stocks can be issued, transferred, or sold. Setting up a corporation is more time consuming and costly than an L.L.C. One thing to consider is initially setting up your business as an L.L.C., and as the business grows in its scope you may then find it advantageous or necessary to re-organize as a corporation.

Any attorney can assist you in creating a partnership, L.L.C. or corporation, however, this might be the ideal opportunity to seek out an Entertainment Attorney. They are more than capable of establishing your band or brand as a legal entity. The benefits in having a relationship with an entertainment attorney is that they are familiar with recording contracts and the typical clauses contained within, plus they are familiar with licensing deals and ideally have relationships with other artists and labels. A good entertainment attorney can be instrumental in securing and / or negotiating a recording agreement on your behalf, review a distribution agreement, negotiate a sync or merchandising license on your behalf. Do your research, ask around, and speak with potential entertainment lawyers. Select one and build a relationship – seek their opinion on which legal entity to organize your artistry, band or brand around. What criteria should you utilize in selecting an attorney? Determine if your prospective attorney specializes in music business law including intellectual property and digital media management. Have they been successful in dealing with music artists, record labels, and artist managers? What is their reputation? Do they expect to be paid hourly, on retainer, or will they work for a percentage of your gross income contingent on your ability to generate revenue. This will depend on a few factors including the stage you are at in your career.

COPYRIGHT (REVISITED)

By now, you should have a comprehensive idea of copyright and its value to the music business. Without copyright, the music business would not exist, as music would not be valued the same way.

As detailed in Chapter 2, Copyright is the exclusive legal right, given to an originator or an assignee to print, publish, perform, film, or record literary, artistic, or musical works. Unique in music, is that there exist two distinct and separate copyrights. One for the composition and the other for the master sound recording. The composition is typically owned by the song-writer(s) or publisher and the master sound recording is typically owned by the record label. Music is copywritten when fixed in a tangible form. Technically speaking a 'tangible form' would be your Pro-Tools session files, any means of recording a performance or handwritten or software generated sheet music for example. However, should you wish to protect your compositions from theft, copying, or infringement you must file your compositions with the US Copyright Office. A copyright endures for 70 years beyond the passing of the last surviving author, composer, or lyricist. This longevity of the term provides successful songwriters and music publishing companies with tremendous valuation and as attractive acquisitions for long term investment groups and major publishers.

Copyright has created a tremendous value in both music publishing and in the ownership of the master sound recordings. Today, many forward-thinking artists are weighing the advantages of retaining ownership of their own masters rather than signing with a label who will assume the ownership of the sound recordings in perpetuity. Never lose sight of the value of good song-writing and ownership of the Masters in the music business – it's where the money is.

TRADEMARK

Do you have a logo? As an artist, band, brand, or business, if you do not already, you would be well advised to create a logo. This logo can then in turn be registered with the US Trademark and Patent Office. You may file for a trademark for a name, an image, or a phrase. When filing for a trademark the Trademark and Patent Office will search their database for any conflicts or previous assignees. Filing for a trademark early in your career will ensure that you do not inadvertently build your career utilizing a name or moniker already trademarked, (i.e., Lady A) thus, avoiding a disaster. Can you imagine successfully building your fan base only to discover an attorney representing someone else sending you a cease-and-desist letter notifying you must stop using your name or image or else face a lawsuit. Once registered the trademark provides you with the exclusive ownership and the right to utilize the name, image, or phrase in all mediums in marketing, promotion, and branding. Once claimed and the trademark has been filed you may utilize the ™ symbol while the application is pending. Once the trademark is granted you will be able to utilize the federal registration symbol ® in conjunction with your name, your image, or a phrase. Once again, it is best advised to engage the assistance of your attorney in filing for a trademark on your behalf.

PATENTS

A patent is applied for and is issued by the US Patent and Trademark Office for an invention. For example, should you create a unique software plug-in, or effects pedal you would be eligible to apply for a patent. And once granted the patent, it protects you as the exclusive owner of that original 'invention' for a term of 20 years. Should a music manufacturing company learn of your invention or design and wish to utilize your patent in one of their products, you could then negotiate a license with them, granting them the ability to do so. This could be a source of significant revenue. Although there are three types of patents, the two applicable to music manufacturing would be a utility or design patent. Should you believe you have created an invention, machine, process or design it would be best advised to again engage the assistance of your attorney in filing for a patent on your behalf.

An example of an artist who was successful in applying for patents for his inventions is Edward Van Halen. Recognized as one of the greatest guitarists of all time, Edward Van Halen was granted multiple patents during his lifetime for inventions that were directly related to his craft and the use of his instrument. The example below is a patent for a supporting device that allows users to play string instruments in a manner similar to that of a keyboard. Known for his "tapping" technique this device allowed Edward Van Halen an alternate voice and unique approach to playing guitar. Another patent of Edward Van Halen is the *D-Tuna* which is a device that allows guitarists to drop the intonation of a low E string on a guitar utilizing a locking tremolo system to a D without having to unlock and manually retune the string. This device is still in production today and sold under the EVH brand.

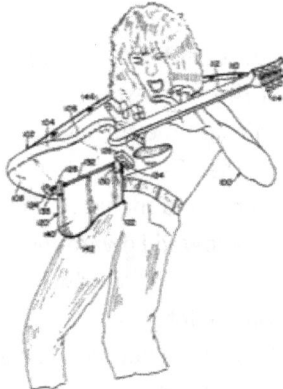

Edward L. Van Halen. United States Patent Number 4,656,917. April 14, 1987. United States Patent and Trademark Office.

IT'S ALL ABOUT THE MUSIC MARKETING STUPID

RAISING CAPITAL

We have explored numerous revenue streams you might pursue or employ in your career. But what are your options if you determine you need to raise some capital (or cash)?

Let's assume you and your band intend to raise some funds for a buildout of your band's studio (in the same way Wilco works – in your own space) or to fund the recording and marketing of your next EP. Start-ups (particularly in the tech world) find it necessary to raise substantial amount of funds for R & D (research and development). Writing a formal *business plan* with an accompanying 3-year *cash flow projection* is essential. Once completed, they would then hope to schedule meetings with VCs (venture capitalists), who specialize in investing (in this example) the tech sector. And if presented correctly, after much due diligence, the VC firm may agree to invest in the company and in return would take an equity position in the ownership of the company or a percentage of future revenues, or both. Either way this is a tedious process that requires a great deal of upfront work compiling a comprehensive business plan and cash flow projections. Or perhaps you can get lucky and discover someone in the band has a rich uncle you can approach, that might lend you the money as a favor. This type of investor is what is described as an 'angel investor.' Capital (money) is raised in these two ways every day for all types of business ventures. However, securing the money is no easy feat, and certainly is not guaranteed.

Another way of raising money is through the creation of a crowdfunding project. Let's assume you want to record a new EP, this time you would like to record it in a professional recording studio, hire a professional producer and engineer, and pay to have it properly mixed and mastered. After conducting some research, you estimate that in order to do so, you may need fifteen thousand dollars. Plus, it would be ideal to have 3 -5 thousand dollars for marketing and tour support. The problem is, you don't have an extra fifteen or twenty grand lying around. You might be able to solve this problem by employing a crowdfunding or fan funded campaign. If you have developed your database, this is where it can kick in to reach out to make your fans aware of your newest crowdfunding project. Anyone can participate and contribute for as little as ten dollars to several thousand dollars. Although there are others, the most popular platforms for setting-up and administering a crowdfunded campaign for an artist or band are Kickstarter, Indiegogo, and Patreon.

Fan funded or crowdfunding has been instrumental in the initial capital raise for tech start-ups, video game developers, motion picture film productions, sound recordings, design and tech projects, the arts, book publishing, and music. Essentially, the idea of crowdfunding is to raise large sums of money, from a large number of followers all contributing small amounts of money. In exchange for a 'fans' contribution (or pledge) they are provided with an incentive such as a gift, a t-shirt, a merch bundle, or an experience.

Fan funding only works if you have a database of fans that you can email and connect with. The platform you use will help you manage the campaign and continually engage and grow your audience.

Once you have selected the most appropriate platform for your project, you must set a financial 'goal' you hope to achieve with the campaign. Note: several of the platforms work in an *all or nothing model,* which means if you don't hit your financial goal, the project goes unfunded.

Next you must set-up your campaign. It's common practice that you record a talking-head video documenting the explanation, rationale, or usage in your seeking this specific amount of capital or money. What kind of special gifts can you dream-up and provide in exchange for contributions? Pledge amounts typically start at $10, increasing exponentially, topping out between five to ten thousand dollars. Chicago based pop / rock band Marina City recently held a successful Kickstarter project. They had a somewhat ambitious goal of $35,000 and exceeded this by a couple of thousand dollars. They were very creative in the gifts they developed and offered. For example, for a pledge of $200 the band would perform a 3-song acoustic set at your home (limited to the Chicagoland area), a one-on-one songwriting session for $300, record a cover of your choice for $1,000, or a full band private show (including sound and lights) for $5,000. It's interesting to note they had 335 backers pledged $37,331 in total, representing an average pledge of around $100.

The $50 tier dominates, bringing in almost 25% of all earnings. Surprisingly, $100 is a not too distant second at 16%. $25 brings in a healthy chunk too, but the overwhelming conclusion from this data is that people don't mind paying $50 or more for a project they love. It's also worth contemplating going well beyond $100 into the $250 and $500 tiers: they scored relatively high pledging rates compared to other expensive tiers. The lower tiers — less than $25 — are so statistically insignificant (barely bringing in a combined 5% of all pledges). [Source: Music Business Journal Berklee College of Music]

What the data illustrates is the fact that the lower price tiers are far less effective than those starting at $25.00. Keep it simple stupid. Giving too may low tiered options to contribute small sums of money, in a way, will provide less incentive instead of more. This could reduce the total overall goal of the campaign. By eliminating or having only one lower tier price-point of $10, pledgers are forced to think big in terms of their donations and the rewards offered. Think of it as a type of silent action.

KICKSTARTER

Kickstarter is one of the biggest names when it comes to crowdfunding, known for helping tech and creative entrepreneurs fund their projects before getting a loan or raising money for venture capital. The company has raised over $6.5 billion since its inception in 2009. Potential funders can browse a number of ventures from arts and film to publishing.

Kickstarter is an all-or-nothing platform, which means that you don't get your funds unless you complete your campaign and reach your goal. It also means that the funder's credit card won't be charged unless you meet your campaign goal. The fee is 5% on top of processing payment charges (3% to 5%) per transaction. There's a 14-day waiting period for funds if you raise enough money [Source: The Balance of Small Business]

INDIEGOGO

Indiegogo users are usually creating campaigns for tech innovations, creative works, and community projects. The crowdfunding platform works similarly to Kickstarter, except it doesn't have an exclusively all-or-nothing fundraising model.

Users choose between two options: fixed and flexible funding. Fixed is best for fundraisers where your project needs a certain amount of money, while flexible is good for campaigns where you'll benefit from any funding. With flexible funding, you will get your funds whether or not you meet your goal; with fixed funding, all funds are returned to your donors if you do not meet the campaign goal.

There are no fixed funding fees for campaigners who do not meet their goal, as opposed to 5% for flexible funds and fixed funds that do meet their goals. There's also a processing fee of 2.9% and $0.30 per transaction. The minimum goal for either type of fundraiser is $500. [Source: The Balance of Small Business]

PATREON

Patreon is popular among digital creatives, such as YouTubers, podcasters, and bloggers. As opposed to you collecting one-off campaign donations, you have a subscription model where patrons regularly contribute a set amount of money every month or per creation.

The site allows artists to form relationships with their fans, and creators can even deliver exclusive content to their Patreon subscribers as an incentive to continue funding them. Suffice to say, this service works best if you regularly share work on your personal platform. Otherwise, pledgers do have the option of canceling their subscription if creators don't produce content.

Patreon offers three plan tiers that take a percentage of the monthly income earned on the platform: Lite (5%), Pro (8%), and Premium (12%). The site boasts over 8 million active patrons and over 250,000 creators. However, one drawback with Patreon is that it doesn't market creators as much as sites such as Indiegogo or Kickstarter, which have entire verticals and pages on their projects for potential donors to browse. [Source: The Balance of Small Business]

RESOURCES

U.S. Copyright Basics
TED: The art of asking – Amanda Palmer
TED: How artists can (finally) get paid in the digital age – Jack Conte

5

DEFINING YOUR AUDIENCE

Ok so we've covered the important and necessary mechanics you or the artist you represent need to consider and act on to establish your business, your team and, the means to collect all the monies you're entitled to. As creative people, now think about being equally creative in your marketing efforts as you are in developing your music. What follows is an introduction to the largely adopted segmented marketing strategies you can employ in developing your career.

> Forget the notion that you can market to everybody – you simply can't! You don't have enough time, money, or resources.

DETERMINING YOUR AUDIENCE

What is marketing? The *American Marketing Association* defines marketing as "simply the performance of business activities that direct the flow of goods and services from the producer to the consumer." Creating business activities (and a buzz) that generates awareness and exploitation opportunities for your music and brand to consumers (your audience/fans) is all you need to do. This sounds pretty simple right? The luxury of a big budget is not necessarily the answer as evidenced by The Majors success rate of only 5%, (yes that's correct – it's largely rumored that one of twenty) releases actually turns a profit. Let's assume for argument's sake that 50% of all artists signed to the majors are successful, recoup and receive royalties, what about the other 50%. They didn't make money. The genius he was, Prince wasn't signed to Warner Brothers because of his talent, but rather his ability to sell out *First Avenue* in Minneapolis. He had found his audience. If your long-term goal is to get signed to a label, then the first objective is to find an audience and build a tribe.

> Data from the BLS shows that approximately 20% of new businesses fail during the first two years of being open, 45% during the first five years, and 65% during the first 10 years. Only 25% of new businesses make it to 15 years or more. Investopedia

So, what we can learn from this? A sizable marketing budget is no guarantee of success. Money alone doesn't break a record – a buzz does, or generating excitement and activity related to your music. Conversely, methodically, over a period of time with little or no budget it is possible to make inroads and build a fanbase. The mistake commonly made by a developing artist is to extend a great deal of effort, time, and resources (budget) into the recording yet having little or no strategy or knowledge of what to do next other than releasing the track through a digital service like CD Baby or Distrokid. That's not a marketing strategy. Setting up the release of a single or EP should be a thoughtful process of targeted marketing that may take several weeks to implement and execute successfully. Keep in mind that Digital Service Providers are uploading approximately 100,000 tracks per day. That's a lot of clutter to compete against no matter how good your music is. In a future chapter we will explore how to properly set up the release of a single or an EP. It's not possible to make informed decisions about where, what and when to advertise, and promote until which time you have done your own research in determining your target market.

Building you own dedicated fan base, is the most important aspect of building a career. A cover band that earns $3,000 – 5k a night and play most weekends, can equate to a modest lifestyle and that's a pretty smart bet. However, there's little to no upside. Should your goal be to create original content as a band or brand and become a household name in your community, city, state, country, or the world, it will be necessary for you to consciously build an audience. You see, it can truly happen – you can sustain a comfortable lifestyle as an artist, if you build your brand.

MUSIC GENRES

All genres of music have a market, specific to that genre and audience and fans. Out of necessity you must declare the genre of music you work within. It will be necessary for you to be specific in declaring your genre or the category which your music fits into. Pick your genre wisely – House, Indie, K-pop, Pop, Punk, Rock, Metal, R&B, Hip-Hop, Rap, Latin, Country, Garage, Blues, Techno, EDM – you decide. At some point, you will be asked, "who do you sound like?" – the most off-putting answer might be – "We/I don't; sound like anybody." That's a terrible answer – because a verbal description and comparison to a recognizable artist is paramount in gaining peoples curiosity. You need to speak intelligently about your music and have the ability to articulate what you sound like. This is necessary for a number of reasons. Know you will be asked to declare your genre and cite comparable artists on many of the digital services. It is imperative you declare your genre and similar styled artists for this reason. Focus on creating music that appeals to the audience of your genre. Generally speaking, you need to stay within some confines of a genre or genres, however being sufficiently different from others may be an advantage. Another way to look at genres is to consider the various radio formats. Whether it's a terrestrial radio station, streaming or satellite radio, stations identify with a particular "format" - catering and targeting to a specific audience. Radio is built on advertising revenue and in an effort to sell time on a station, they have conducted extensive market research into their audience. It might be easier for you to identify a radio station that you think might play your music and align your target market or audience with that of the station. Then do your best to tap into that research.

So, what's involved in marketing music? We will initially explore some basic marketing strategies that are universally employed by professional marketers and advertising agencies. We must first understand the basics of marketing and explore customer segmentation – identifying and marketing to the right audience. We'll start from the beginning with the basic *Marketing Mix* and expand on it.

THE FOUR P'S OF MARKETING

We would be remiss if we were not to cite the foundation of basic marketing. Developed in the late 1950's The Four Ps of Marketing (aka the Marketing Mix) endure today, and they are:

I.   Product – refers to goods or services
II. Price – the cost consumers pay - list, sale, wholesale, luxury, affordable or static
III. Promotion – marketing / consumer drivers
IV. Place – delivery and distribution

So, if we are to analyze the Four P's as they apply to music, we might discover the following characteristics;

Product – it is essentially you, your music, live performance, and merch. So, a top priority must be to continually focus on creating and developing your band, business, or brand.

Price – One's popularity, demand, and stature dictate a threshold of how much a fanbase will sustain. With regard to dynamic ticketing, merch, ticket prices and Patreon, price is quite elastic. Price as it relates to subscription services, physical goods, and the music itself is quite static. A subscription music service is ten bucks a month, physical goods such as EPs and full album CDs / LPs sell online and on merch tables averaging in price between $10 – 25 per unit. Pricing for developing artists is rather static so the initial objective should be to concentrate on building fans to increase plays, merchandise sales and tickets sold.

Place – fundamentally this too is quite static in music. The Majors, the indies and the digital music distributors all do a very good job at essentially the same thing; at getting your music out to all the streaming platforms worldwide. So, in music, one way or the other, place (delivery and distribution) are provided for. If you're signed to a label, your distribution is predetermined and predicated on the label's distribution partner. If you are self-releasing, it will be up to you which of the digital music distribution companies you select.

Promotion – your strategy in getting noticed. This can be particularly challenging with little or no budget, but it is possible to create a "buzz" around your release or event utilizing grass roots, digital and word of mouth and eWOM (electronic word of mouth) marketing. The age-old essence of the slogan, *it takes money to make money* is true – save some money (no matter how large or small) to promote your project to gain a wider audience.

There have been numerous attempts to update the Four P's, but none have been received without criticism. Some nominations have included *purpose, performance, personalization, and participation.* The point being many marketers agree, the Four Ps remain a concept to be embraced and explored when releasing a new product into the marketplace. In summary, a simplification of our analysis, it becomes abundantly clear that in music we need to predominantly focus on two of the Four P's – Product and Promotion.

There may be several goals you have in mind in releasing a single or an EP, however for our purposes, the primary objective will be to identify, develop and build your fan base. Forget the notion that you can market to everybody – you simply can't! You don't have enough time, money, or resources. Therefor you must focus on identifying and spending your time and energy marketing to the demographic and psychographic make-up of those who will become your core audience. *Effective marketing is targeted marketing to a specific few.*

GEOTARGETING

Let's start with the most obvious fan characteristic - to simply recognize one's local market and focus on developing fans in your geographic area. Marketing in a geographic circumference within a specific radius to your hometown, tour market or next show is the practice of geo-targeting. This focused marketing activity can be accomplished both digitally and physically. Social media posts, boosts or ads focused on a specific neighborhood or zip code would be an example of geo-targeting. Purchasing an ad in the free local alternative paper, postering, passing out flyers in the vicinity of an upcoming club date would be examples of physical geo-targeting. This is relatively straight forward, if you are a developing artist in the city of Chicago, it would be logical and financially prudent that you would initially target potential fans living in the city or the Chicagoland area.

Geo-targeting is particularly effective in promoting a local club date or when promoting a tour. Conversely, we also must be aware that when we upload music for distribution through CD Baby or Distrokid for example, that you are offered the choice of territories in which to release your music. You could for example, just release your music in North America and omit the rest of the world, but why would you do that? We know that a hip-hop artist from Chicago can generate a significant number of plays from female fans in Japan, with the artist never having toured or performed there. By selecting 'all,' your music is distributed throughout the world within hours. We are a globally connected society with access to music and the consumption thereof is indicative of this trend. Based on historical trends a developing metal band may book a tour of Europe as this audience has traditionally embraced this genre for generations. For centuries jazz musicians form the US have either chosen to live abroad or tour Europe annually as the audience there is more receptive to jazz than here in the states. You can also conduct research on favorite music genres by city or state. If you represent or are booking a Latin artist, you will focus on booking dates throughout Texas as that's the #1 genre in the state. Metal is big in the middle of the country, classic rock in the mid-west and alternative and pop on the coasts.

Keep in mind your goal is to target people who can make a difference. Let's say you have a show coming up and your main objective is to get fans out to your show. It should be quite obvious that you should target your marketing efforts to potential fans and club goers who by their physical location would have the ability to travel and attend the show. Focusing on a specific zip code, city or suburb would all be examples of geo-targeting. In the physical world, this can be accomplished by handing out flyers at a show of an artist in your genre, or outside of the venue where you have an upcoming performance. Although old school, this type of marketing can be cost effective and obviously highly targeted. In the digital world, this can be accomplished through social media posts and ads that only run in the geographic area you select and target.

Elite global brands which appeal to the masses (McDonalds, Coke-A-Cola, GM, Toyota, and mobile carriers) have little to no reason for the marketing department or their advertising agency to focus on segmenting their market. They're marketing stuff for everybody, and they have massive advertising budgets with which to do so. That may be a much easier strategy than the micro marketing approach that will be necessary for you to employ in your marketing journey. Assuming of course, you don't have a 'massive' marketing budget at your disposal. So, we've taken geography into consideration and have identified our first marketing segment – geographic segmentation.

You've probably heard of but perhaps not spent much time thinking about demographics and psychographics and how those consumer traits might influence your decisions in formulating a segmented marketing approach to your career. Your probably thinking, what exactly are demographics and psychographics and why do I need to know and understand them... and most importantly, how can they help in building a career. Let's take a look.

DEMOGRAPHICS

The 7 widely adopted characteristics of Personal Demographics are;
- Age – the most obvious and popular characteristic
- Gender – presumably fans of a metal band for example, would skew male
- Ethnic background - ideal for specific genres such as Latin, Gospel and Urban
- Education – interest in podcasts, new and current events
- Income – wealth or lack thereof may designate a genre preference
- Occupation – what field or line of work are they in – blue or white collar?
- Marital status – specific marketing for cruises, all-inclusive resorts, etc.

For the time being, try to make some general assumptions about your fans. Separating them by age is the most obvious and popular. Are they Gen Z (1996 – present), Gen Y (1977-1975), Generation X (1965 – 1976) or the Baby Boomers (1946-1964)? Determining age, ethnicity and income is known as demographic segmentation. This most basic form of targeted marketing will help you connect to your fans more accurately. Utilizing demographic segmentation provides not only a keen focus on a group of people but also provides cost savings in your marketing spend.

PSYCHOGRAPHICS

In the past, marketers focused predominantly on demographics and geographics, and while still important, are less important than identifying the hobbies, fashions, and trends of your fans. Today, marketers focus far more closely on the psychographics of their consumer or fan. The 6 widely adopted characteristics of psychographics' are;
- Personalities – is your typical fan playful or fun, serious, outgoing, or introverted?
- Lifestyle – what do your fans do day to day, where do they hang out?
- Interests – hobbies, do they attend concerts and festivals, skateboard, or cook?
- Values – does your music align with your fans sense of right or wrong, their beliefs?
- Opinions – conservative or liberal thinking? Are they committed to a movement?
- Attitudes – developed from both mental and emotional characteristics derived through experiences

Today, marketing is far more complicated and segmented than simply targeting to an age group. Today psychographic modeling is far more important than demographics in determining who your fans are. Some important questions to consider are: What are your fans hobbies? What do they like to do? What kind of a personality do they have? What are they into besides music? Where do they shop and what brands do they wear? Unlike demographics which focus on physical and quantifiable results, psychographic segmentation focuses on less obvious traits. Try to understand your fans as real people, trying best to comprehend the world they live in. Conduct research and communicate with your fans to understand their personalities and lifestyles. Through focus groups and surveys, you can begin to develop quantifiable metrics that identifies your fans activities, interests, opinions, and values.

Ideally you are hoping to make a deep connection with a select few of your fans, sometimes referred to as 'super' fans.' They are the people who are most enthusiastic and dedicated to you, your music, and your brand. Like an influencer or blogger, focus on communicating with them. These people can connect you and your music with others. They will tell their friends, post on social media, and spread the word about you and your music.

Malcolm Gladwell describes these "information specialists", or "people we rely upon to connect us with new information" as *Mavens.* They accumulate knowledge, especially about the marketplace, and know how to share it with others. ... As Gladwell states: "Mavens are really information brokers, sharing and trading what they know." [Source: The Tipping Point]
1. These early adaptors or mavens can assist you two-fold in the viral marketing of your project; They will take great pride in their quest to continuously seek and discover new music from you and,
2. They gain great satisfaction in sharing this knowledge of new music with friends and anyone they might influence.

Beginning at stage 1 of developing a fan base, get to know them, follow them on social, always respond to comments and questions and communicate with them one-on-one.

In order to have a chance to be successful, you need to begin by communicating with the audience you presently have regardless of size. Then keep them engaged. You can do this by constantly creating content. Give them something unexpected. Don't aim for the mainstream but make music that is true to you and aligns with your fans. Pick a lane. Be specific with your music and with whom you are wanting to engage.

> " The only way to be special is to not be average and the only way to not be average is to ignore almost everybody" – Malcolm Gladwell

Once your market segments have been determined, the next step is to engage with the target market. Choosing a segment(s) which will enable you to market to most effectively is known as *target marketing*. Assuming you understand the importance of determining your audience, the next big question is, how can you afford to market to them. The simplest answer is to invoke a social media strategy to promote your new release. Consumers spreading your message on your behalf is known as viral marketing. Interact with your fans to create a buzz and get them to spread your message. If you can conceive a story that will resonate with your fans, or potential fans that is easily remembered, easily shared, and speaks to you as an artist … you'll be on to something. Creating a narrative that helps you communicate your message is termed *storytelling marketing*. Try to identify something about you or your band that fans can relate to or be intrigued by. If you are even remotely familiar with the artist 50 Cent, it's likely you know something about him: fans or not. The fact that 50 Cent had been shot nine times is the story that was shared extensively early in his career. His music spoke to a segmented market which related to him as both an artist and a person. The genre of music he was creating, was ideal and highly targeted for his fan base. This legendary persona added an element of intrigue and curiosity to the story. 50 Cent is also one of the world's wealthiest rappers, thanks to his stake in a vitamin water company. Many have found his story inspiring . . . that someone could climb out of a lifestyle of dire circumstance and elevate themselves to evolve into achieving global recognition and success. Early on in her career, Taylor Swift was able to cultivate a fan base primary comprised of young girls. Cultivating a group of mavens early in her career that would then act as ambassadors' and spread the word to the masses was the end result. By apparently staying true to their artform, in recent times, Billie Eilish and Olivia Rodrigo have seemingly done the same in building a base of segmented / word of mouth marketing.

OUTBOUND V.S. INBOUND MARKETING

Assuming we have a general idea of how to build out your fan base – then, how do we then sell 'em stuff? If your goal is to earn a living in music, your objective will be to create music often, build your fan base, and ultimately – sell them stuff. There are a few ways to ask for a sale

– one would be personal selling. Try to meet face-to-face with your fans and promote your music through your appearances and your brand. Your goal should be to aim to inform and encourage the customer to check out your music and eventually make a purchase. Another idea would be to create a sales promotion by creating sales incentives. Typically, these incentives include a limited time discount at your merch store. It could be a 30% discount to sell off obsolescent inventory such as last year's tour t-shirt. Postcards and advertising pieces sent via the mail, as well as infomercials on tv were one of the earliest forms of Direct Marketing and both remain in use today. All the above would be what is known as "Outbound Marketing" where one literally pushes the product in front of the consumer. Things like contests, coupons, sale pricing, trade advertising would all be considered Outbound Marketing. In Outbound Marketing, the marketer is in control of the message - the where, when, and how the product is advertised. Traditional media buys such as print advertisements, billboards, television, and product sale priced and positioned in a retail environment would all be examples of Outbound Marketing.

Marketers today strive to create incentives to pull people in. Rather than pushing your message out, create inbound activities which encourage people to come to you. Working to get found should be your primary objective. Enticing a fan to sign-up for a newsletter, check out a new video, download a white paper, attend a streaming concert: all would be examples of Inbound Marketing. Pulling people in, where they choose to join you. This is primarily accomplished through content marketing activities targeted to potential fans, ultimately creating interest in you as an artist or a brand. Utilizing direct-to-consumer, less intrusive marketing techniques such as email, text (SMS), and social media is with-out a doubt the recommended and preferred method of communicating with fans. As the artist or brand, you need to constantly create incentives that bring people to you. Create reasons to be found or get discovered. If they follow you on social media or were motivated to provide you with an email in exchange for an exclusive of any kind – your Inbound Marketing initiatives were a success! Having the consumer come to you rather you annoyingly getting in front of the consumers face is by far the most effective and desired marketing strategy employed today. It's estimated that most marketers today are spending 10% of their resources on Outbound Marketing and as much as 90% of their resources invested in Inbound Marketing strategies. Creating marketing activities that motivate your fans to find you, like you, follow you and discover what you may be able to offer them such as a remix of a track, or a subscription to a newsletter is the end game. In essence, Inbound Marketing is all about building relationships.

An exemplary study of a successful inbound marketing campaign is Taco Bell's, *The return of Nacho Fries comes a spicy plot twist to the faux movie campaign that has accompanied each iteration of fries since they first debuted on menus back in 2018. For the first time ever, Taco Bell's Live Más productions co-created the storyline together with its biggest fans. The virtual writers room began earlier this year as Taco Bell called for submissions via the "Taco Bell's Nacho Fries Challenge" and invited fans to submit their original ideas for the next Nacho Fry commercial via Twitter with the hashtag #FriesChallenge.* [Taco Bell]

Analyze your local market and understand what is happening within your genre within your community. Which artists are having success and why? What are they doing to build fan engagements? Observe, study, and learn on both a national and local level. Can you identify any unique characteristic that they have capitalized and built upon? Perhaps it's a distinct look, a successful video, a remix, or a cover version of a song.

In an exercise, conducting no research, think about your perception of and define some demographic and psychograph attributes (biased or not) of the following music genres;
- Country music fans
- Metal fans
- K-Pop fans
- Gospel fans
- Latin fans
- EDM fans

Intentionally or not, heuristics and biases contribute to our understanding of basic generalizations and assumptions of an audience. Although far from scientific, certain traits become quite obvious, and are not biased, but rather factual and can provide a basic understanding of segmented (targeted) marketing.

Aside from making some basic assumptions, some of which, such as age are easy to identify, ask yourself, how can you best ascertain that your assumptions are correct? Conduct a focus group, talk with your fans, create a MailChimp survey, email a questionnaire to your fans, ask questions on social media. Be specific / drill down in the questions you ask to ultimately create a "model" customer/ fan. Rather than assume you know who your fans are, let them tell you by creating tangible metrics to confirm or modify your assumptions. Geo-targeting, understanding, and marketing to one's segmented demographics and psychographics of fans, while employing inbound marketing strategies should be your focus.

Resources:

Seth Godin - How to Get Your Ideas to Spread - Nordic Business Forum
What Demographics and Psychographics Mean for Small Business Marketing
How to Use Psychographics in Your Marketing: A Beginner's Guide
HubSpot Inbound vs. Outbound Marketing

6

PUBLICITY

UNDERSTANDING PUBLICITY

In the previous chapter we explored the definition of marketing and began to explore and understand the marketing component of customer segmentation. Next let's explore the definition and strategies of implementing publicity into your marketing campaign. The definition according to Merriam-Webster describes Publicity as *a) an act or device designed to attract public interest, b) the dissemination of information or promotional material.* Simply put; Publicity is the dispensing of non-paid promotional information with the intent to increase public awareness of a subject. From a marketing perspective, seldom will publicity alone 'break' an act. Yet it can provide an effective complementary component to the contributions of a successful project. Think of publicity as one vitally important component of promotion and marketing.

It would be typical for a major label artist to have the services of a publicist on retainer. Alternatively, an independent publicist is typically hired by a label for a 3–6-month publicity window on behalf of an artist. A good publicist is worth their weight in gold; however, a good publicist or publicity firm can be quite costly. Typically, a music publicist focuses on one genre where they have developed relationships with reviewers, critics, bloggers, television shows and tastemakers across multiple media outlets.

So, what does a good publicist do? If brought in during the early stages of artist development a good publicist may be instrumental in helping create or refine an artists' image. They may have relationships with fashion boutiques where wardrobe clothing for photo shoots may be 'rented' for the day. Although typically not on the 'team' a publicist can be a valuable resource in selecting a photographer, identifying the location of the photo shoot, and selecting the right publicity pictures. Like a skilled producer utilizing their experience, a publicist can be an outside, independent voice in making critical decisions in presentation and imaging.

A publicity campaign should be thought of as a necessary or required complementary strategy to your other marketing initiatives.

HOW TO BE YOUR OWN PUBLICIST

Think about yourself, what is your unique selling point or USP? Are there events in your life and career that make you stand out from the crowd which can be part of your story, your quest? It's difficult for a publicist to create a story of interest based solely on exceptional talent if they have no awards, accolades, or achievements to provide credibility. In other words, it's quite difficult for a publicist to create a compelling story simply by telling publicity outlets what an amazing guitarist their client is. Not everyone has a story, especially in the early stages of career development, but don't gloss over this. Take a moment and think if you can create a story. You may already have a USP, just by being yourself, or you may find it necessary to create one. What about partnering with a brand, a local micro-brewery, partnering with a charity, a local fashion brand in development as are you. Do some research, find local business that share the same customer segmentation as you. Reach out to them, meet, and see if together, as two entities you can create one single story much stronger than two stand-alone stories.

Find an angle. As your own self-publicist, it will be necessary for you to write creative press releases, blogs, social media, and website content, all of which is known as *content marketing.* As a publicist, your objective will be to have non-paid promotional messages written by the media in all formats (digital, hard-copy print, radio, television). Therefore, your message should be unique and interesting - think creatively. Ultimately the end game is to have multiple positive impressions targeted at music consumers, converting them into fans. Our psyche is such, that often we need multiple impressions of a product, whether that be cars, clothes, dining, or music. An effective publicity campaign is one way of garnering one of the multiple impressions that might be necessary to motivate a consumer to make a purchase, sign-up, or stream your content.

You'll want to provide you publicist (presumably you) with *digital assets* and tools that will enable them to do the job most effectively. A publicist's tools may include;
- The Artist's image – hair, make-up, wardrobe, shoot location or set, etc.
- Photo Shoot – selecting the proper two to three images
- Artist Bio - a concise, one page read written in 3rd person narrative
- Press Release – announcing a new single, EP, tour or tour date, showcase, etc.
- Artist's Website – should reflect the same artists' image, and general vibe
- EPK – (electronic press it) may be a video recording with the artist discussing the project
- Music – physical CDs remain essential for some press you may wish to service. The digital files should be made available in hi (WAV) and low res (mp3) file formats
- Photos - jpgs available in color or black and white and in hi-res file formats
- Video – the Artist's YouTube channel
- Social Media – stay consistent with your messaging on your platforms of choice
- Quotes – notable quotes from a formidable artist(s), influencer, et al.

As your own publicist, you will not be selling anything, rather you will be 'pitching' a story. The idea is first to persuade them to read your bio (or press release) and listen to some music. The ultimate objective is to convince someone to blog about you, attend a show, write about you, or book your band. Ideally, over time you might develop and maintain relationships with key writers, bloggers, influencers, and talent bookers in your genre (or mood) that you can tap-into when appropriate.

THE BIO

The big publicity machine starts with the most basic of tools - a well-crafted biography that provides a window into the artist's persona and distinguishes the artist from others. What sets you apart? Include your background, education, accomplishments, interests, and hobbies. What and whom are your musical influences? Include a quote from yourself. It is imperative the bio be written in 3rd person narrative. Clearly talk about the unique qualities of the band, brand, release, event, or tour. Tell all the facts that would be interesting to writers and other media recipients you may choose to send the bio to.

A professional publicist would request and conduct a one-on one interview with you in which to learn about you, get a sense of your being and take notes. Should you not have the luxury of hiring a publicist or writer, another option is to ask a friend who is a good writer or pursuing journalism and have them interview you. If nothing else, ask questions about yourself – what messages would you like to convey to someone just learning about you? Think like a journalist - discover all the facts – find those things will be make an interesting read and create a compelling angle to your story. Find an angle. Then incorporate all of the above into one concise story the length of which is not to exceed one full page. In writing this, recognize that in all probability, this bio will be included on the *About* page on your artist website.

Think of who your readers of this bio will be – speak to them in a fashion that is relatable to them and reflective of your persona as well. Keep in mind, nearly everything you create as a publicist will be repurposed as a digital asset online and on your website.

Take the time to search for and read other artists published bios. You can find inspiration from others more established than yourself when seeing how they are being presented in their bio. Look at comparable artists of the same genre as yourself and consider the format that has been used in creating the bio.

WHEN AND HOW TO CREATE A PRESS RELEASE

Press Releases are standard tools of a publicist. A press release is created to announce and publicize news and events. Press releases can be written to announce;
- The new release of a single, EP or album
- To announce a concert or tour
- To announce a showcase
- To announce the achievement of a significant number of streams or chart position
- To announce a partnership
- To announce the nomination for or winning an award

So, what are the elements necessary to create a compelling press release?

First, you need an attention-grabbing headline.

Get right to the point – make the news you are announcing abundantly clear. A press release should be written with the most important or impactful information at the beginning. A Press Release should be no more than one page.

Print the words "FOR IMMEDIATE RELEASE" in the top left-hand margin in all caps. Follow this line with relevant contact information: name, title, address, phone number, email.

Now create a headline that will grab people's attention.
Then at the start of the 1st paragraph in the body of your press release in all caps, indicate the city and date (i.e., CHICAGO, IL – April 24, 2022).

Start with a strong lead sentence, such as *this is the debut of, a new single or a showcase.* Make it clear what you are announcing.

Place the most important content in the first paragraph. Be sure to address the 4 Ws, the *Who, What, Where and When* in this paragraph. The writing should be short and concise. No filler copy. Only write what is absolutely necessary. Avoid the urge to write copy that is like a sales pitch. Keep it professional so that your press release will be considered credible.

In the 2nd paragraph include more detail about the artist, band, brand, or announcement. Include some select details about the act – who have you performed, opened, or recorded with, your influences. Is there a guest or feature, where was the project recorded, who produced it? Entice the reader, instill their curiosity not only to inform but to tease.

In the 3rd paragraph provide any facts, statistical information, sold out shows, social media numbers, streams, or quotes.

After the final paragraph, it is customary to include these marks, ## #, signifying the end of the press release

Following this, at the bottom, by inserting your boilerplate, and you're done!

Here's an example of a press release. The format should be consistent and in accordance with this example or something quite similar.   By following this format, you will make it easy for recipients to understand this to be a press release and not a bio or any other piece of editorial copy.

PRESS RELEASE   For Immediate Release

TGM Recordings
Contact: CONTACT NAME
CONTACT PHONE NUMBER
CONTACT EMAIL

Release Date: November 19th, 2021

TGM Recordings Announces New Single: Lurid Young,

(Chicago, IL - December 17th, 2021) **Lurid Young** by **Saint Romanov** feat. **Wolfgang Hunter and the death season**, premiered Friday, December 17th, 2021, on all music streaming platforms. The reminiscing, alt-rock love song was created in both the U.S. (Chicago and Dallas) and Brazil (São Paulo), with engineering and production by **Estúdio Fusão** engineer, **Pedro Canaan**, at **Kalindi Music's Studio**.

With vulnerable vocal performances from Saint Romanov and Wolfgang Hunter (frontman of **Fishing in Japan**) accompanied by haunting yet dynamic instrumentation from Brazillian-metal band, the death season, **Lurid Young** is similar to sentimental, rock ballads like **Everlong by the Foo Fighters** or **Say Yes** by **Elliot Smith**. **Lurid Young** was co-written by Saint Romanov and writing/producing group and band, **the Groovy Motherfunkers**, in Chicago (where Saint Romanov also recorded his vocals with **Producer Grind** team member: **Ethan Deetz**), before heading south, first to **Helmet Baby Records** in Dallas (where Hunter tracked vocals), and then to the death season at Kalindi Music's Studio in São Paulo.

Lurid Young follows recent singles from both Hunter's solo release: **Molly** and the death season's lastest track: **Minus** in a lead-up to their **Kalindi** EP. Saint Romanov will celebrate the release of **Lurid Young**, and his debut single, **Billy Boy**, by playing a small tour of his home state: Michigan, in January of 2022. The tour will coincide with the release of his debut EP **Left Handed Cigarette** and his own cannabis brand (also named **Left Handed Cigarette**) with Michigan growers, **Fresh Off The Farm**.

TGM Recordings has taken the streets of Chicago and Sao Paulo by storm, quickly developing a reputation for their versatile artist roster, engaging releases, and their vivacious live shows, that have become the talk of nearly every college campus in Chicago. Founded by artists, for artists, TGM Recordings is comprised of a diverse collective of young creatives, seeking to change the world, one groove at a time. Hungry, unmatched, and up-next, TGM Recordings is changing the future of music.

© TGM Recordings

CREATING A BOILERPLATE

A boilerplate is a standardized paragraph that begins with your positioning or mission statement. This is a single concise sentence which describes your artistry, band, brand, or company and what makes it unique. Typically, the boilerplate copy begins with the artist or brand name in bold text. Items of interest to journalists might include; where located, any unique value proposition, what you're offering your target audience. What's your secret sauce? Brevity is key. The closing sentence should be a CTA (a call to action) such as *for more information visit:* the link to your website.

When creating your boilerplate, think of it along the lines of an elevator pitch, or a short blurb that can be included in online venue calendars, endorsement deals, and metadata required for your social media, digital uploads, etc. The boilerplate should be a concise 3-4 sentence description about you, your band, or brand.

EMAIL MARKETING

Although email has been eclipsed in large part by SMS (texting), you may be surprised to learn it remains the most cost-effective form of marketing. That's right, you read this correctly. You cannot afford to ignore this free tool that you can utilize for converting potential fans to active consumers and for relationship building. Yes, there are other ways of communicating with your fans, but none have the impact of a well-crafted email in communicating a message or generating a transaction. No matter what stage of your career you are in, email provides you with the power to reach your fans 24/7. Email is the third most powerful and effective small business tactic in communicating your message, just behind social media and digital advertising [Statista 2019]. And best of all – email is FREE!

Topics which are ideal in generating and distributing in an email;
* To announce a new show,
* To tease the release of a forthcoming single or EP
* To announce or introduce a new video
* To announce a sponsorship or endorsement deal

If you were to partner with a third party (such as a micro-brewery or a *Taste of Chicago* or similar street fair in your market for example), you can broadcast their brand, township, or charitable organization to your fans. Assuming you set-up a reciprocal arrangement, they will be doing the same for you – promoting your performance on signage and to their database. Similarly, one of the CTAs, (calls to actions) at the end of your message may be to encourage your fans to share your email with any of their friends' they determine may be interested in your message.

According to Statista global email marketing in 2019 accounted for 3.9 billion users and is expected to increase to 4.3 billion users in 2023. A well-crafted email can also serve the purpose of educating or informing your fans on subjects outside of music that are of interest to you that you would like to share with them.

Need more convincing that email is a viable marketing too – here's some statistics for you to consider
- 293.6 billion emails were sent and received each day
- Average expected ROI is $42 for every $1 you spend on email marketing. [DMA 2019]
- Nearly nine out of every ten marketers use email marketing to distribute content organically
- 81% of small businesses rely on email as their primary customer acquisition channel, and 80% for retention
- The average open rate for a welcome email is 82%
- 49% of consumers would like to receive promotional emails from their favorite brands

So, what are the advantages, what do you gain when a fan joins your email list?
- They may share your music on their own playlist, or to social media,
- You can notify them about a live stream, in which you can invite them to join,
- Perhaps make them aware of your new Patreon account and encourage them to join
- Promote a sale at your merch store,
- Obviously, you can promote a new release, and
- A show, etc.

Of all the above statistics, what seems most impressive is the idea that for every dollar you invest in email marketing, the ROI potentially being $42 is simply stunning.

It's worth noting that the Average Open Rate for Music and Musicians is 21.88% which is slightly higher than the Average Open Rate across all industries at 21.33% [Source: Email Marketing Benchmarks and Statistics, Mailchimp]. This once again demonstrates why more than 85% of all marketers use email marketing to communicate with their users. With compelling analytical information such as this, do you not feel motivated to make email marketing a consistent component of your over-all and ongoing marketing efforts.

THE MONTHLY NEWSLETTER

Earlier we had referenced how typically an artist puts all their effort and resources into making the record and little or no thought with zero dollars to be allocated towards the marketing. The *Newsletter* is another such culpable and often overlooked effective brand building marketing tool.

First of all, it's free. There are several bulk sending email platforms, such as Constant Contact and MailChimp which is free up to the first 2,000 contacts. The freemium version provides automation, subject line helper, and multichannel tools such as social posting. The basic email templates allow you countless options in customizing each email for newsletters, surveys, a calendar, and integration with your favorite apps. The analytics they can provide will help you to better understand the value of your relationships with your readers. Referred to as reach and engagement.   Reach is the number of people who are exposed to your marketing message. In the case of our newsletter, you might think of this as the open rate. Engagement is the number of interactions; replies, comments, forwards, and shares.

Think about the continuity and relationships you can build with your brand if you were generating a monthly Newsletter. A friend or fan of yours will not be upset if you provide them with a monthly update on your happenings, but rather, would be upset, if they weren't a recipient of such and being kept in the know. The main purpose of the newsletter is to inform and entertain. The selling should appear to be a subtle offer. Realize that a monthly newsletter does not restrict you to sending only one bulk email per month, but rather allows you to create multiple brief emails about new shows, releases, merch, etc. Because we're addressing only the monthly newsletter, the focus should be insightful and about you. It's possible to create a 'book club' amongst your fans by sharing your latest reading, share a recipe, review a new restaurant, share what you've been listening to, your insight and updates on the local music scene, a rehearsal photo. What about the idea of each month featuring a spotlight on one member of your band or on your team members? What about the idea of monetizing your newsletter, (be it daily, weekly or monthly)? There's even a platform for that – Substack.

The topics, events, news along with the occasional issues you care to address may be valuable content in motivating a casual fan to become a patron or paid subscriber.

THE DATABASE (CRM)

Second only to networking (the industry relationships you make), the most valuable tool a publicist has is their database of contact information. As your own publicist or by engaging someone on your team to act as your publicist, this will be a critical research project for you to take on. Begin locally by researching and finding contact information for local entertainment critics, music reviewers, bloggers, college radio, local newscasts which feature local artists, etc.

In the corporate world Customer Relationship Management software (or CRMs) is licensed for employees', particularly salespeople to utilize in keeping track of their business relationships. CRMs track and manage a company's staff interactions with current and potential future customers. Essentially, a CRM is a sophisticated platform for database management. The #1 CRM platform in the US is Salesforce with prices starting at $25 per month per user. And if that's too steep for your budget, you should explore some less robust yet far better than no CRM, free options. The one CRM that is "100% free, and always will be," is offered by HubSpot providing inbound marketing sales and service software. There are other 'always free' free software offers you may choose to explore such as Mailchimp's CRM and Benchmark One.

A good CRM will assist you in delivering the right message while providing you with analytics on customer behavior too such as replies to emails and tangible results such as open rates, clicks, etc. If you were to include your fan base contact info into one of the segments you create in the CRM, it can help you analyze sales and conversions on your merch for example. CRMs can include all contact information including social media, email, voice calls and keeps track of the frequency and message of the communication. And if this is all too complicated, or you have your own ideas, although not as ideal as a CRM, you can create a database in Microsoft Excel. The drawback to Excel is all information will have to be entered manually, but it is a feasible alternative to a commercially available CRM. So, before you take on the idea of creating your own database that acts like a CRM, Google now offers Streak - "a fully embedded workflow (CRM) and productivity software in Gmail and empowers you to manage all your work right in your inbox.

When done properly, creating, and developing a database will necessitate an investment in your time to conduct relevant research which will ultimately be to your benefit. Initially work on the quality and not the quantity of the contact information you are seeking. Of course, a great deal of this research will be found online, however it may also necessitate telephone calls to obtain a reviewer's information. Don't be apprehensive about calling. Media companies field calls all day long from others seeking information as well. Anyone working in the music business either as an artist or on the business side of things can benefit from having a quality database. The contact information you should attempt to seek out and obtain would include:

- name of the company or organization
- contact name
- mailing address
- email and
- phone number

Keep in mind you are not going to create a comprehensive database in one afternoon. Rather, think of it as a constant work in progress as you build each and all new relationships. Start by focusing locally on your city or town and segment by category. Create several segments and focus on conducting your research on one segment at a time in collecting the information. Specific fields may include:

- Venues and Talent Buyers
- Music reviewers and writers
- Local college radio and record stores, music retail
- Free local entertainment television segments, newspaper, or magazines,

Conduct research nationally focusing solely on influencers and bloggers that have only shown an affinity or aptitude to your genre, or your style.

Now should you remain apprehensive about the necessity and idea of creating a database for fans and industry contacts, realize this, you own none of the contact information on social media, the platform does, and they have control over it. By creating your own database (CRM) you will own all the contact information and will over time begin to develop relationships with tastemakers and decision makers in your community and in your genre. As for fans - start with friends and family. You will constantly be building this database by having a sign-up on your website and at your merch table at live shows. Promote your sign-up sheet on social media and begin to build your database.

Resources

CYBER PR – The Ultimate Guide to Music Publicity
the indelible
Substack – The home for great writers and readers

7

YOUR DIGITAL HUB

Unequivocally - what destination do you drive all your online traffic? The correct answer is - your website. Sure, you can utilize social media to do the same, the difference being, it's far more difficult to accrue emails and market directly to your fans. Your website is where you can establish your image with; photos, music, and videos, post your live performance calendar, and host a blog. You own it. It makes you look professional, you're in control, you can gain valuable analytics, and you can sell directly to fans. So, if you don't already have a website, now's the time to fix that. In the event you already have a website, well done. With or without a website let's make sure we establish a basic understanding of the advantages of various content management systems (CMS), and the three types of Google categories as they pertain to traffic and media.

Think of your website as an extension of yourself and your music. The website should be a visual representation of your persona for visitor's providing clarity and insight about you, your band, or your brand. The objective of your website is to attract visitors, bloggers, and tastemakers (or superfans) while building your own custom community. Conceive a plan to create a digital marketing strategy. Utilize a calendar – for content creation - five days per week for a month, establishing continuity. This is accomplished through communicating with fans through email, posting on social media, and consistent blogging. Embed the links to your most recent blog post into your social media feeds. It's far more beneficial to post a story on your website and then share to your social media pages than the other way around. When the embedded link is clicked on, the user will be re-directed to your blog page, where they can interact and leave a comment. The goal of course is to entice your visitors to click on the home page or any other page of your website that may be of interest to them. Once a user has interacted and explored some content on your site, ultimately the end game is to convert them into making a purchase from your ecommerce store. Realistically, many first-time visitors may not be making a purchase, but more importantly, provide an opportunity to sign up for your newsletter or join the fan club. If your user takes the initiative, the process was a success, you collected one additional email for future direct marketing.

ASSET PACKAGE

Creating a website will require compiling the necessary elements in assembling an asset package. Your asset package should include:
- A logo
- A header image
- A profile photo
- An embed with links to the streaming platform of choice for your visitor
- Photos, images, and videos
- Tag line / slogan / boilerplate
- Pages / links or components should include;
  - A calendar
  - A blog
  - A media page
  - A bio
  - A contact page
  - A merch store
  - Outbound links to your social media platforms
  - A CTA (sign-up to my newsletter pop-up)

The importance of your website can best be illustrated when understanding the concept of driving traffic (via search, social media, blogs, and newsletters), to build a list (your database), to communicate with fans, and sell them stuff. Ultimately, this is done in the interest of making a profit.

Aside from making music, your primary job is to create and distribute relevant content to attract and acquire a clearly defined audience. The consistent creation of publishing media to break through the clutter with the art of communication, having the objective of driving fan engagement is known as *content marketing.* Recognize that content marketing is an ongoing process that should be a key component of your overall marketing strategy. The essence of this strategy is the belief that your ability to deliver ongoing valuable information to fans will ultimately reward you with fan loyalty. Keep in mind, content marketing is not about personal or direct selling, or shouting about your new release. Rather it's about providing the tribe you have curated with information they will find insightful and of interest.

Metadata provides information that summarizes basic text for the discovery of your online property. Website meta data is the text seen by Google as the description of a site. For this reason, including keywords in your meta description and pages throughout your site are vital for returning favorable search results. Now think like a user; what keywords would potential fans be entering in a search engine when searching for, or seeking to discover a new artist or band in your genre? Begin with 3-5 relevant keywords and include these tags in your home page editorial. These keywords might include the market you reside in, your genre and other adjectives that describe your music. SEO is an acronym for "search engine optimization." It is the process of generating traffic from the "free," "organic," or "natural" listings on search engines. Therefor if you want to boil down internet marketing to a single starting point – optimal keywords are the answer in making your website discoverable in the secret sauce that is SEO. Place appropriate keywords in the title and text fields of your website pages. When a person conducts a search Google crawls a multitude of sites looking for matching keywords, therefore you want Google to crawl your site as often as possible. The best thing you can do to make Google crawl your site more often is *content marketing* - producing fresh new content and publishing with regularity and frequency. Tag or provide captions for your images, Google doesn't recognize photos or images unless you do so. Be sure to connect your website to Google Search Console to view numerous analytics that will be beneficial in making changes to your site.

Another feature Google offers is AdWords, - which is a keyword advertising system in which you as the advertiser choose keywords and create a short one or two-line text ad which is displayed on the results page of a search. With Google AdWords, you're able to set a budget for advertising and you only pay when people click on your ads. The order of the ads is determined by the amount the advertisers are willing to pay Google for a user to click on an ad, (as well as relevance and click through rate). The benefits of online advertising are many: it's targeted, quantifiable, and cost effective as pay per click has revolutionized digital advertising.

Give some thought to highlighting your website's goal; what is your primary CTA, (call to action)? Is it to have someone sign-up for your newsletter, sell a ticket or merch, play a video, or listen to a track?

Take the opportunity of a fan visiting your website to make them aware of your active social media platforms, (hide the others). Ideally, you are seeking long-term engagement with your fans by developing a relationship to build loyalty and ultimately to sell em' stuff. If a fan visiting your site recently purchased a tour shirt and then wears the t-shirt to your next show, you have won twice! Once with the profit from the sale and the second, perhaps more importantly, the word-of-moth marketing this fan has created on your behalf. One thing you can and must be sure to do is – interact. Respond to every question and comment, thank them for signing up or making a purchase. Stay connected and keep your fans engaged.

3 TYPES OF TRAFFIC

Traffic is determined by the total number of visits to your site. Traffic, as defined by Google is designated to three categories;
1. Direct,
2. Organic and
3. Paid

Google Analytics defines direct traffic as website visits that arrived on your site either by typing your website URL into a browser or through browser bookmarks. Other examples would include traffic from your email marketing campaign, traffic from offline documents (such as business cards and QR codes). In accordance with recent trends, Direct Traffic is the key traffic source to being discovered. Organic traffic is defined as visitors who come to your site from unpaid, natural search engine results. And paid traffic is precisely what you might expect – traffic as a result of an AdWords campaign, CPC (cost per click) or social media advertising and boosts.

3 TYPES OF MEDIA

There are three types of media;
1. paid,
2. earned, and
3. owned

Paid Media channels such as Facebook / Instagram boost, Google AdWords, YouTube ads, web banners and offline adds like magazines and billboards would all be examples of paid media.

Earned Media is free but must be enticing to bloggers, brands, customers, and fans. Trade shows, business cards, likes & follows would all be examples of earned media. Earned media consist of channels you don't control; but you would like to influence or be included on. All earned media occurs with 3rd parties, such as a television performance, a music review, a mention, think any type of press. This is where your database and knowledge in creating an effective press release come into play.

Owned media. The primary and most valuable commodity you have would be your website. This you own and along with your social medial channels (which we all know we don't own, but we do for the most part, control). Think about uniqueness when creating owned media, things such as your newsletter, a white paper, a lyric sheet, a welcome video, your blog, and your merch stores (both physical and digital).

CONTENT MANAGEMENT SYSTEMS – (CMS)

If you have a website then you presumably are partnered with a CMS (Content Management System) to assist in building, and perhaps even hosting your website. A CMS allows you to edit, modify, organize, and maintain control of your website from a single dashboard. Content Management Systems can be edited by anyone, you need no coding background what-so-ever. Examples of CMS include; WordPress(.org), Bandzoogle, Hostbaby, WIX, and Squarespace.

WordPress is an online, open-source platform that is the most dominant CMS on the market empowering over 60% of the CMS market. Clients include the likes of NBC, TED, CNN, and the NFL. It is an excellent platform and can be adapted for artists, bands and brands and has numerous benefits and is extremely flexible. The downside, it is somewhat complex in how each theme is manipulated, edited, and managed – however it's arguably the best CMS. A viable alternative for any artist or band looking to build a website from scratch or to update your existing one, would be Bandzoogle. It is fully optimized in its responsive design, has an integrated social media connect, 'print on demand' merch store, the ability to sell show tickets, a built-in tour calendar, crowdfunding, fan mailing list tools, subscriptions and more.

Here's a basic list of the categories and capabilities you may wish to consider in selecting your CMS and building your artist website in accordance with Google Search Central.
- Blog
- Home for search
- Social channels
- About / Artist bio
- Events / Tour calendar
- Gallery
- Music
- Videos
- Contact info
- Integrated Database – or email client with an integrated 3rd party
- E Commerce store
- Ability to sell tickets
- Integration with Google Analytics

So, gather your digital assets, do research on the most appropriate CMS for you, watch some video tutorials for guidance to build, and realize your vision of a poppin' website for your artist, band, or brand.

RESOURCES

Creative Blog - 40 brilliant WordPress tutorials
Bandzoogle
Getting started with Bandzoogle
The HubSpot Blog's 2022 Web Traffic & Analytics Report [New Data]
HubSpot Website Grader

8

BLOGGING & BRANDING

THE IMPORTANCE OF BLOGGING

OK, so you were a bit skeptical about email marketing, how receptive are you to creating and maintaining a blog. While blogs may not be as vital as they used to be in promoting artists and their music, they are still relevant today. The benefits of blogging are substantiated with multiple statistics that highlight reasons why it is still a good idea to engage in this activity as a part of your marketing plan. The most compelling reason may be that from the outset, a blog keeps your website current and relevant with content marketing material. As a result of blogging, Google will index your site more frequently while producing higher-ranking results.

The "Blog Era" of music occurred from the late 2000s to early 2010s. Many artists careers were launched due to the influence bloggers had on music discovery for fans. Hip-hop artists in particular were able to build communities of fans who were turned onto new artists & music by following credible blogs. As a promotional tool, blogs were significant because they pre-dated the mass use of social media platforms that now provide multiple outlets and modalities to share information, engage in discourse, and build communities.

Traditional blogging has had its ups and downs since we began tracking corporate blogs in 2008. This year, public facing corporate blogs have demonstrated an increase in use for the fifth time since 2015. In fact, blog usage has more than tripled since its all-time-low was recorded in 2015 at 21%.

This year 387 (77%) of the Fortune 500 are using their blogs during the 2020 pandemic. [Source: Center for Marketing Research / UMass Dartmouth

A blog is a platform for you to delineate your thoughts and ideas and share them with your followers in a diary type style format. Here they will gain insight into your song writing, tours & shows, recording and mix sessions. However, you may find you derive more comments and feedback when you discuss your hobbies, personal activities, and interests. Blogging is a key component of content marketing. If the top Fortune 500 companies in the world recognize this, shouldn't you take notice? Content marketing is predicted to generate in excess of $400 billion in the next five years.

What's your message today or this week? Put your thoughts in writing and create an insightful message. Think of your blog as an alternate stage – a platform from which you can communicate your ideas, thoughts, and experiences. The best blog posts take in excess of 4 hours to create. Are you surprised to discover that the average bloggers income is $38,440 annually, [Source: Zip recruiter]. Supplement this income with live performance and merch fees, music publishing etc., and you're on your way to a six figure annual earnings as an independent artist. Bloggers who post with regularity get the best results so post frequently and in accordance with a calendar. Create a schedule and adhere to it (stick to it). Daily, weekly, twice a week, at minimum - once a month. Building a following through your blog will not happen overnight, or in a couple of months. Be consistent – commit to one blog post per week, or even a month and over time, if the topics and content you are posting are found interesting and relevant to your readers you *will* build an audience. It will take longer than you expect but stay committed - to build this audience of like-minded people interested in your thoughts and perspective.

So how do you monetize your blog posts – the simple answer is to be sure the Content Marketing Platform (CMS) you select is in compliance and compatible with AdSense. Then integrate Google AdSense into your website dashboard. AdSense integrates relevant ads onto your website pages by displaying targeted ads on your website. Now ads will appear on your website and when clicked on, you make money. Another idea is to endorse a product and include a link in your blog to a product or service for sale on another site. When someone clicks the link on your page and it goes to the product you have endorsed, you will receive a commission. Perhaps you've heard the term *Affiliate Marketing* – this is exactly what was just described. Another idea, once your online store has been created, you can include offers from your blog page which will link them to your ecommerce offering. Other ideas include a monthly subscription fee or charging for online courses (like songwriting sessions, guitar, or vocal lessons, etc.)

Be thoughtful in creating your posts. This is a tall order but think about this, if you were to post daily the statistics show you may generate 5 times the traffic of the other band across town that doesn't blog.

Set up properly, with frequent blog posts, you will be indexed higher than your competitors in Googles search results. Just like creating music on your DAW, blogging puts you on the same level playing field as your competitors who do blog. And if they don't have a blog, take advantage of this opportunity, and see what happens. Other than time, it will cost you nothing to blog. Conduct research on popular bloggers in your genre or field, follow them, comment and if feasible, create a personal relationship with them.

Blogging is a channel you control, where you can be susceptible, and open about your thoughts and ideas about music, civil rights, politics, or sports. A blog is an opportunity to reveal a different side of oneself outside of music. Create engaging headlines, think like a publisher – understand a blog is not a commercial for your latest single or video but rather your perspective on an issue that is meaningful and important to you. Your blog is not an advertisement but rather a forum for you to offer your perspective on issues in music or outside that spear altogether. Provide a glimpse or an insight into your daily activities. Talk about your passions, social issues, and topics you have an opinion on; politics, climate change, fashion, and food.

Have a compelling title. Typos and grammatical errors are unacceptable. A well-conceived blog post is not one paragraph. The sweet spot for your blog post is somewhere in the neighborhood of 1,500 words. Also, Google will reward you for referencing your sources with outbound links. The end game is to gain credibility and conversely increase the number of readers. Thinking optimistically some of your 'readers' may ultimately evolve into paying customers. In a few words, your blog should enrich and entertain your fans, friends, and followers.

Find an angle. If your drummer is a vegan, reach out to a top vegan blogger to create a conversation. Explore the idea of asking them to be a guest blog on your own blog. If someone in the band or on your team is a video game junkie, a yoga coach, a guitar shredder, a metal maven – reach out to these bloggers to create synergies and tap into their audiences.

The key to creating a blogging strategy is to do it consistently, once weekly, or monthly at a minimum. To keep your audience engaged, don't always discuss music. While it is fair game, from time to time- think about writing about something else. Insight into your personal life, ideals, and happenings. Having said that, successful bloggers develop a reputation of being experts in their field.

As a publication, a blog needs to have specific focus. Let's say for example, you know your blog will be about music. That category is far too broad, so next drill-down and repeat until which time you have found your specific area of expertise and interest in music (for our example). What do you guess will be the primary focus of the blog? Is it about hip-hop, song writing, music business or your music? Start out catering to a specific few. Now envision your blog post a year from now. What do you envision the specific perspective of the blog you have developed to be? Pick a lane and decide you're going to give blogging a try.

The statistics are compelling to say the least. The corporations that derive benefits from blogging are indisputable. The benefits of blogging include your website being higher indexed in Google searches and you may make money.

Need further convincing, here are some stats.
- 77% of internet users read blogs (Social Media Today).
- From 2021 to 2025, the global content marketing industry is expected to grow by $417.85 billion (ReportLinker).
- Companies that publish at least 16 blog posts per month receive 3.5 times more traffic than those that publish fewer than four posts. (HubSpot, 2020)
- Websites that also have a blog are shown to have 434% more indexed pages. (Optimonster, 2021)
- Nearly all bloggers today promote their blog content via social media sites, whereas two-thirds of them are using email marketing. (Statista, 2020)
- The number of bloggers in the U.S. is estimated at 31.7 million in 2020 (Statista).
- Blogging is such a scalable and affordable approach that it's the third most common content marketing strategy for business. And marketers that prioritize blogging see 13-times the ROI of businesses that don't. (HubSpot, 2020)

- Blogs have been rated as the 5th most trustworthy source for gathering online information. (Optimonster, 2021)
- Bloggers make the vast majority of their income from ads, affiliate products, sponsored product reviews, their own products, and online courses (RankIQ).
- More than half (55%) of marketers list blog content creation is their top inbound marketing priority (HubSpot, 2020)

If this is not convincing evidence that you need to have a blog component of your website, you're missing opportunities to be indexed on Google. Ultimately a blog will be beneficial in developing your fan base, turning casual fans into connectors, mavens, and salespeople. Remember, we warned you from the outset, that digital marketing would take a commitment and a substantial amount of your time to implement. Like your newsletter and blog, many of these responsibilities will necessitate a great deal of time to implement. One of the most widely read music industry blogs and email newsletters is *The Lefsetz Letter*. A WordPress blog published multiple times per week, where his sometimes-outspoken opinions and perspective as a music industry analyst and critic are met with approval and push-back. We know this because Bob smartly republishes all his letters to the editor, with no editing and full transparency for all subscribers to see. The controversial opinions expressed on breaking news within and occasionally outside of the world of music makes this a vibrant subscription-based blog many in the music business follow.

In essence, blogging is all about the creation of a brand and the development of a community. It all dovetails with social media blogging. For example: Jeff Tweedy (Wilco) uses Substack well not only as a tool to communicate but also as a revenue generator as he charges his community to receive some of the content he offers there.

Remember, to delegate – to fellow band member, or a member of your team and have them own an ongoing duty. After a period of time, they will become experts and will take ownership and pride in their responsibility that will evolve in their newly discovered area of expertise.

THE IMPORTANCE OF BRANDING

What exactly is a brand? As defined by Merriam-Webster, a brand is: a public image, reputation, or identity conceived of as something to be marketed or promoted.

We interact with brands all the time. It's estimated that the average person is exposed to more than 5,000 advertisements per day. These outbound message filter into our lives through logos, symbols, names, and tag lines all representing brands. All of which are intended to promote a brand to stand out from the competition. Think of the sheer number of brands one is inundated with by simply entering a Target store or a local market. A stop at your local coffee shop is a conscious decision to interact with a brand. As impressionable humans we are deeply impacted by both form and function. Most all of us are passionate about some element of design and function - in clothing, electronics and in dining. It's also logical we all have a penchant for a particular brand albeit in fashion, musical instruments, or sneakers. Branding can be passionate business. Think: Mac vs. PC, or Logic vs. Pro Tools. So, if you have started your career in the entertainment business you already have a brand. The question is, how much time have you spent crafting and creating this brand?

Your brand is predicated not only by your music but how your dress, how you act, your personality, and even your views on the world that may be communicated in your music and on social media. Think of a unique characteristic that distinguishes your brand from another (think Boy George, Lady Gaga, Katy Perry, Lil Nas X, Prince, Doja Cat and Lizzo). You may already have a brand, and if not, give some thought to creating one for yourself, or your band. Your brand is how you're perceived in the media and most importantly by your fans.

First create a brand image. If you don't have a logo create one NOW! We subconsciously connect the dots linking a brand to a trademark (a logo or symbol). All businesses have a logo – and as a friendly reminder, you *are* operating a business. If you don't already have a logo, do it yourself, hire a friend, or engage a graphic designer to create one for you. No excuses get it done - damn it. Your logo is the fundamental, starting part of your brand. Having a creative logo that reflects your brand is imperative. Once created, if you're smart, you'll file a trademark application with the *US Patent and Trademark Office*. Once approved, you are ensured ownership and use of that name and logo in perpetuity. The country group formerly known as Lady Antebellum, and the Los Angeles based blues singer Lady A lawsuit is a perfect example of neither party doing so.

Now that you have a logo - think about next composing a concise marketing message. The intention of which is to create a positive image of your brand with your fans. Whatever distinguishes or sets you apart from your competition is your tag line. The value and benefits of establishing your brand (your logo for example), will add intrinsic ($) value to your brand. Strong brands are authentic and real. In the case of *Chance The Rapper* his intangible brand is aligned with the common good of his community and his fans. People will discuss you and your brand by your artist or band name and that will conjure memories of live shows, videos, chance meetings, etc.

ENDORSEMENT DEALS

Drill down to the brands that producers, musicians and artists find compelled to embrace like: *Pro Tools, Fender, Gibson, Shure, Yamaha, DW* drums, these are all brands we know and recognize in our business.

Are their music, fashion, or lifestyle companies that you perceive to be exceptional and would like to align your brand with and score an endorsement deal? If so, is your brand strong enough to reach out to this manufacture (or company) to explore the possibility of an endorsement deal. The answer for now may be no. Major endorsement deals may offer a signing bonus, free or discounted gear, cartage, and provide free backline on tour. Now think on a local level. Is there a local luthier, a boutique music instrument manufacturer, or a fashion designer in your market? Think of what you can offer them in exchange for an endorsement. The initial stage of an endorsement deal typically would include the sales of goods at wholesale cost or less. Think about and explore small local companies be it a clothing designer, a guitar or amp manufacturer, etc. Located in Chicago, *Lakland Basses* started out as a small boutique shop. Founded in 1994, their instruments have been embraced and are the instrument of choice by some of the finest bassists in the world. Today the endorsement arrangements between the company and each artist are a win / win situation for both parties. ... Ideal, highly targeted branding. Think small, not big, until which time you get your fist endorsement. If you're remarkable, brands will be seeking you out. In order for that to happen – you must first build YOUR brand.

Sometimes it's all about timing. Gaining the attention of a label at the opportune time is another example of building your brand. Signing with a label is an endorsement deal. Signing with a major label is significantly more prestigious than that of an indie. The major label deal represents more prestige and a higher level of financial commitment, hence - endorsement.

Once you've settled on the branding of your artist or band, and assuming you've accumulated any critical mass, the next thing to do is to seek out an Artist Endorsement deal. Endorsement deals within the music industry may be the first partnerships to explore. A guitar manufacturer, a drumstick or cymbal company, a string manufacturer, can lend incremental credibly to your brand. And although the typical deal for new or developing artists doesn't include a monetary advance, you'll most likely have the ability to purchase your endorsed brands product at cost. More importantly, what you'll gain are the bragging rights that you have an endorsement deal with one of your favorite brands. Perhaps the most intangible benefit derived from an Endorsement Deal is the creditability it lends when including your product's endorsee's logo in your digital and physical marketing efforts and posters. It's the "holy s@#$ I didn't know he had a deal with XYZ, he must be bad a@#," effect.

SPONSORSHIP DEALS

Signage on the stages and throughout a music festival would be examples of sponsorships. Corporate brands pay a fee to post their signage (logo & tagline) to a targeted audience in the hopes of making a deeper connection. If you have a substantial database and have considerable reach a sponsorship deal may be feasible. A brand logo on your Sprinter van or tour bus, signage on stage, on a tour poster or t-shirt would all be examples of sponsorship. Again, think small, think regionally. Can you identify a comparable sized company or brand that you might be able to approach to explore the idea of sponsorship?

CO-BRANDING

Co-Branding is a strategy where two brands form an alliance and work together to combine the two audiences with the objective of creating one larger audience than either of the parties individually. With the right brand partners, you can expand your audience, add credibility to your brand, and create strategic marketing opportunities that would otherwise not exist. We all know of multi-million-dollar fragrance, cosmetics, water, and fashion endorsement deals from mega-stars, but scale this concept back. Adjust your expectations. Think on a local level. Recognize we interact with brands all the time. Identify local or like-minded small brands that align with your vision or share the same demographics or psychographics as you. If you're in a rock band, think about creating a partnership with a micro-brewery or other brands that partnering with could result in the perfect synergy. Arrange to play a show in their parking lot for example. Their patrons discover you and likewise. Everybody wins. Think regionally, give it consideration, and act upon it. Local brands will be open to meeting and receptive to your ideas of cross-promotions. Reach out to them.

What you are wanting to establish is brand recognition. If a friend asks, "have you ever heard of the *The Lawn Chairs*?" and you have and that resonates with you, that's positive brand recognition.

As a brand you should actively communicate who you are, engage and interact with your fans. Keep your branding consistent across all platforms, i.e., social media and website, newsletters, Spotify profile, your YouTube channel, etc. Think about the idea that as a brand you might develop a strong emotional connection with your fans – after all that's what *McDonalds* has successfully done for years. Now think on micro-terms: share a story, make a deal with a local vendor, make a meaningful connection with your fans and potentially new ones.

Corporate brands, large or small want to tap into the deep connections with artists. Examples of this include *Red Bull,* branded stage sponsorships to the PROs at *Lallapaloosa* and other festivals, *Formula One, Red Bull Records,* etc. Again, think small. Your music creates an emotional connection with your fans so think of brands that may want to tap into your fans and your database. Seek out and create a brand partnership resulting in both parties finding broader awareness and combined, discover a new, bigger audience. If you're planning to shoot a new music video, you might be able to offer your corporate partner their product featured (maybe more than once) in the shoot. Realize that marketers are looking to develop a strong music strategy. For them, partnering with an artist or a song can generate and create a buzz around their product.

CAUSE MARKETING

Lastly, we would be negligent if we were to not address the understanding and benefits of *Cause Marketing*. The idea that one aligns their brand with a charitable cause can generate goodwill and be compelling to both media and fans. The added result being exposure to new fans committed to the same cause. Identify a cause that you believe in such as climate change, Black Lives Matter, LGBTQ+, Voting Rights, etc. Seek out a non-profit (501c) organization and pitch them the idea of you providing services (a performance) to support their cause and mission. Offer a reduced fee for a live performance for your band at their next event (a marathon, at a farmers' market). "Cause Marketing" works because all parties benefit from the endorsement and beliefs in each other's organizations. There should be a focus on giving back to the organization and supporting the "cause."

THE ARTIST BRAND PROFILE (OR DECK)

An artist band profile (or Deck) is 8-10 slides that provide a brief presentation of the artist for a potential endorsement or sponsorship deal to a business, organization, or corporation. Be sincere and only pitch products you companies you believe in. The deck should highlight your fan reach and engagement, streaming and demographic / psychographic stats. Do you share the same target market? Essentially the deck should be a custom pitch of why you are an ideal fit with the brand and alternatively, what the benefits are that you might provide the brand in return.

Understand that sponsorship and endorsement deals only work if you have some scalable streaming stats or YouTube views for example. Of course, there are other types of metrics which you might include in your Artist Deck such as; sold-out shows, social media numbers, usage of your database, etc.

It should be pointed out that securing a deal will be largely predicated on the size and reach of your audience, your metrics and level of touring. In any case, should you have the opportunity to enter any kind of sponsorship, endorsement deal or strategic corporate partnership, put it in writing. Engage the services of your entertainment attorney in the negotiating process.

RESOURCES

3 Ways to Differentiate Yourself: Artist Identity, Vision, and Intention | Music Business
Ted Talks How symbols and brands shape our humanity
How To Get sponsorship For Musicians, Whether Corporate, Clothing Or Other

9

SEO, CMS, GOOGLE SEARCH CONSOLE & CPC

"**Digital Analytics** is the analysis of qualitative and quantitative data from your business and the competition to drive a continual improvement of the online experience that your customers and potential customers have which translates to your desired outcomes (both online and offline)." Avinash Kaushik

Do you have any kind of clearly defined digital marketing strategy? Probably not, it's a grey area for many companies both large and small. You might respond I'm doing it myself or we hired a social media guy but we're not too sure what he's doing. Instead, create a plan, put it on a calendar with alarms. A reminder *this week's blog is due in two days,* to update your calendar, interact with those that follow you. Create content for them such as your weekly blog. The marketing challenge today is how to connect with fans, engage, and communicate with them. They have opted into you - you have access to their emails or can message them directly and even post to groups. Ultimately the endgame of this initiative is conducted in such a way as to create a connection, then engage with them, ultimately resulting in a reason to buy – this is the new business model.

As an independent artist there is one critical destination in which to drive your traffic, and it's not your social media channel of preference, but rather your website. You own it. You control the image, the message, and the offering such as your most recent video, tour photos or new music. Sure, you can utilize social media to do the same, the difference being, you will be confined to that platform(s) while not accruing emails to market directly to your fans. So, if you don't already have a website, now's the time to fix that. And if in the event you already have a website, first, well done and second, never forget, we can and will always be learning. There is always room to improve what you're doing. This introduction to SEO, CMS and Search Console will provide some clarity, insight and ideas which will prove to be relevant and pertinent to your website. Ultimately, there exists a reverse architecture of participation whereby we aggregate fans via 3rd party channels (social media and YouTube), to ultimately drive this traffic to our branded website.

WHAT THE F#*% IS SEO AND WHY IS IT IMPORTANT TO ME?

SEO is an acronym for *Search Engine Optimization.* Essentially it boils down to keywords. SEO is the process of generating traffic from free organic search, i.e., Google. Payment isn't involved. SEO is about how Google and other browsers work, attempting to deliver relevant results for what people are searching for. We all know this, we do it every day. Give some thought into the keywords people might enter into a search seeking to discover or find you, your band, or your brand.

Metadata is the text Google recognizes as a description of a relevant search. Think of incorporating words into the editorial copy of your website that users or potential fans might search for when attempting to find you. Google algorithms first search for more broad keywords such as 'gospel artist', then you would be well advised to include your market (i.e., Chicago) to take advantage of Google's algorithms. Thus, you would be delivering relevant results to the user. Score!

Keywords are the secret sauce that enables Google to find you. Although there are studies, even entire books and white papers written on SEO, in a nutshell it boils down to 3-5, 5-10, or 20-30 *keywords* that potential / new fans might search for when looking for you. If one was to distill internet marketing to a single word – keywords would be it. These are the words fans might enter in a Google search to find your website. Select some keywords with broad terms such as genre and others with specificity (your market/city). It's not that complicated, if you're in a metal band, from Lansing, MI, you would and should include the words *metal band* and *Lansing, MI* in the short description on you home page. If you're a wedding band from Chicago, you should include, *Chicago, wedding band* performing *pop hits* as well as specificities such as *performing Motown classics* in your keywords. Repeat this process throughout your pages when indexing your website. Check out your competitors. What keywords do you find on their pages?

Ultimately your objective is to drive traffic, to build a database to communicate with and sell them stuff to make a profit. Learn, you are operating a business with expenditures and revenues that need to drive a profitable return on investment, or ROI. Unless your registered as a 501c3 organization, you are not running a charitable business but rather a business which needs to continuously create and cultivate revenue sources.

You are the master of your craft . . . your music. You now have a new responsibility of being a content creator. *Content marketing* is the process of continuously creating digital content with the goal to market yourself and your music. A blog your posting, new music, an uploaded cover tune or video are all examples of content you are producing and are all elements of your content marketing and subsequent branding of your business. Content marketing is a tangible dedication to your constantly creating, publishing, and distributing relevant content. Content marketing should be viewed as an extension of your artform, the ability to communicate with your fans - minus the direct intent of selling them anything. However small you might start, remember fans have opted into you (via your opt in sign-up) and they want to hear from you. Don't let them down. You are no longer interrupting them; you have an obligation to connect and engage with them. Instead of pitching them the sale of a hoodie in your merch store, think about educating them, provide you own perspective on current news, other music business transactions, artists, etc. The essence of a content marketing strategy is the belief that by delivering consistent, relevant, insightful, and interesting content you will create a legion of *super fans*. These super fans will prove to exemplify the 80/20 Rule in marketing. Whereby these 20% of your fans will drive 80% of your revenue. Focus on building this elite, committed groups of fans. Talk to them and engage with them. [Note: content marketing is applicable to any artist, business, or brand – with no exceptions.]

What you want to do is have Google crawl your site. Search engines use programs called *crawlers, spiders, or bots* that gather information from websites. Nothing turns Google's algorithms off like your blog or a calendar that hasn't been updated in six months. The best thing you can do to make Google crawl your site more frequently so that you can be found in search results is to develop content marketing ideas and implement them.

The message here is simple, engage a clearly defined and understood target audience with the objective of ultimately driving a profitable consumer sale. Think about this - if you are truly an artist, your strength lies in the ability to create. Think of content marketing as another outlet in which to express your creativity.

GOOGLE SEARCH CONSOLE

Google Search Console is a no-cost service which will provide you with the tools to optimize, tweak and improve your website strategy. It also is the gateway to Google AdWords. Hence it will be necessary for you to connect your website to Google Search Console. Upon doing so, Google will provide you with a Google Analytics tracking code which you will integrate into your website. Once you have access to the many free 'webmaster' tools Google has to offer you will gain the ability to refine and optimize your website.

GOOGLE ANALYTICS 4

One of the most powerful and free tools to monitor, track and analyze your website traffic is Google Analytics – the most recent release being Google Analytics 4. In addition to the number of visitors or sessions in any given period (day, week, month, or year), you will gain access to the number of page views, average session durations and bounce rate. *Bounce rate* is defined as single page session (your visitor did not click on a tab or open a new page). Bounce rates are calculated as a session that triggers only a single request to the server and then exits. Presumably a visitor landed on your home page – and bailed. Don't panic if your bounce rate is high – anything around 70- 80% range is average. The lower the better. Google Analytics 4 has enhanced security, machine learning capabilities, and in addition to the obvious demographic, and geographic information now include lifestyle and segmentation reports.

As a reminder, *traffic* is the total number of visits to your site in a day, a week, a month, or a year. Connect your website to Google Analytics to gage an understanding of the traffic visiting your site.   Within Google Analytics traffic is divided into three categories.

Direct Traffic would be defined as visitors that arrive on your website by typing the exact or specific website URL into a browser or a bookmark. A click through on an embedded link from your newsletter for example. Visits from an outside links such as from your social media channels are also considered direct traffic.

Organic Traffic is simply the people that arrive on your website because of a Google search. Search engine results and paid traffic because of pay-per click ads from Google's search engine would also be examples of organic traffic.

Paid Traffic – is the traffic you purchase though the Googles AdWords platform.

GOOGLE ADWORDS

Google AdWords is a platform you should seriously consider. AdWords is an advertising system in which you can advertise your cover band in a select market search field and set a bid for a click through from a potential employer, a party planner for a bar mitzvah, a wedding reception, or anniversary party. Let's assume *The Lawn Chairs* is an 80's cover band from Milwaukee. They would benefit tremendously by utilizing Google AdWords paying only for click throughs for interested parties in the specific geographical radius of Milwaukee, seeking a cover band of 80s hits. Let's say for example we have a wedding band in Chicago, IL. The keywords we would place into our AdWords account would obviously include Chicago and wedding band. Because you designated a geographic circumference around Chicago, in which to run your adds, no one in LA or outside your designated market will seem them.   You've likely seen these ads many times. These are the sponsored ads returned to you from Google in the top of the search field. The beauty of Google AdWords is you only pay when your ad is clicked upon. This is referred to as *cost per click,* or CPC. The most relevant and highest bids will be shown at the top of the search results. You control the cost of the bid, by designating the top price you're willing to pay for a conversion. For example, if you were to offer .20 or $2.10, as your bid, you would only pay on a click through, and if you offered the highest bid of $2.10 and were to book a gig as a result, that would prove to be a remarkable RIO. Spend $2.10 to book a gig paying $1,200. The ROI is off the charts! The benefits of Google AdWords are many.

Consider this, you can set a daily or weekly budget on your AdWords bid, and easily digest the analytics. Is your AdWords' campaign working? If done correctly, they should deliver an easily recognized ROI.

For example:

Bid: $.50
1 click at $.39
1 click at $.40
1 click at $.43
1 click at $.45
1 click at $.48
Total cost of $2.15
The average CPC = .43

Is this example doable? Investing forty-three cents to acquire a new fan? It may cost more, it may cost less, but you may discover AdWords to be an integral part of your marketing expenditures. It can be a modest approach yet highly cost effective. Experiment with it. AdWords may prove to be one of your best marketing tools.

GOOGLE ADSENSE

We've introduced AdWords, but what about integrating *Google AdSense* into your website. If you're a blogger, this may be *your* primary source of income. AdSense is designed for website publishers to display targeted ads on their (or your website) pages. Earn money with website monetization with Google AdSense. Google will provide you with a code and they will optimize your ad sizes and placements to be seen and clicked. When a user views or clicks the ad, you get paid. Google even has a new easy-to-use automated platform that makes smart decisions placing ads on your behalf – with a moniker of Auto ads. Should you develop your blog to have a significant number of subscribers, AdSense could evolve in becoming a vital or even the primary revenue stream.

OPTIMIZING WEBSITE CONTENT & DESIGN

Determine your primary site goal. Typically, this would be offering a visitor the ability to seamlessly sign-up to your newsletter or fan club. Other ideas might include trading an email for an unreleased "cover song." Decide on your primary call to action (CTA) and make that apparent when one first visits or is about to leave your site.

With the exception of your blog (which should be robust), all other pages should use effective and succinct editorial content throughout the website. People scan a website for content of interest to them so consider creating lists, including photos, and embedding videos. Think like a publisher. Google Image search is not as comprehensive as a traditional Google search. Therefore, tag or caption your images for optimization.

One other thing Google likes in SEO is outbound links. Even better, reciprocal links. For example, you have an endorsement deal with a guitar string manufacturer, the idea being that you would both share embedded links from your website or blog to the string manufacture, and they in return would do the same.

We realize this all sounds quite boring and not on your priority list, but do this once, optimize your website with keywords and you will be doing yourself a favor. It should be obvious but it's imperative your website has a responsive design, meaning the site automatically reformats your pages for various screen sizes whether, mobile, table, or desktop. Be sure to socialize your site so that people can follow you on your preferred social medial sites, and link to them so that fans can follow and like you. Nearly all CMS provide a simple interface for doing so. Whatever you do, don't ignore outbound social links with dead links.

The long-term objective of your website should be engagement. This is accomplished by developing long-term relationships with your fans. Your monthly newsletter, your weekly blog, uploading new videos and music. Ideally you want to engage and create sharing through electronic word of mouth or eWOM. Interact with your fans, allow replies and comments, and always, always reply – good, bad, or indifferent. This is *your* platform to take a stance, whatever subject that may be: sports, politics, social injustice, whatever subject you choose to write about.

This basic introduction to content marketing, SEO, Google Search Console, and CPC should provide some type of clarity on the possibilities and tactics used in SEO. This chapter is meant to be only an introduction and is designed to provide you with a general understanding of SEO. Should you wish to delve into any of these strategies further, there are many other more detailed resources you can seek out for further clarification. Whatever you do, build a website, optimize it, and constantly create content marketing for SEO.

RESOURCES

Optimizing your band website for SEO - Bandzoogle
How to Add Your WordPress Site to Google Search Console
Verifying Your Site With Google Search Console

10

BOOKING, MARKETING SHOWS & TOURS & THE PANDEMIC DID NOT KILL THE LIVE ENTERTAINMENT BUSINESS

Following a 100% closure from the Pandemic in 2020, the concert industry is back in 2022 – in a very big way. Demand for live music tickets is skyrocketing, and artists are touring now more than ever. If you think that there was pent up demand for fans, consider the artists. More than 80% of an artist's revenue comes from performing live and they were unable to do so for 18 months or more! For the next couple of years, the audience will be drinking from the firehose of live entertainment.

The quantity of tickets sold is not the only indicator that fans are showing excitement to be back at shows; it's also the price they are paying to see the highest demand acts. When extracting larger concerts across the secondary market during Q1 2022, fans are spending an average of over $300 per ticket when evaluating sales that occur three months or more from the event. In the same comparison for Q1 2019, tickets sold at an average price of only $142 per ticket! And the prices for sold tickets in 2022 are back to within 3.8% of those sold in 2019.

In addition, touring has now grown beyond just simply live music. Live events are now made up of ANYTHING that people will pay to see live. Ticketed performances for comedy have exploded with artists such as Kevin Hart, Amy Schumer, John Mulaney, Sebastian Maniscalco,

Jim Gaffigan and others are selling out arenas, while many promoters are seeing 20 to 30% of their business represented by comedy. In addition, there has also been the inclusion of podcasts, authors promoting books, actors promoting their television shows and movies shown with stars from the film commenting afterward.

So, the dark days of the pandemic do appear to be behind us, and the pent-up demand is showing itself via ticket sales. The fact that - Live Entertainment is returning should not be taken for granted, especially when you consider the post pandemic movie theater business. Domestic box office grosses for the movie theater business were down approximately 61% from pre-COVID 2019. The Pandemic had revealed cracks in the armor of the movie theater industry. People preferred watching a movie from home, especially after producers made it possible for them to see first run movies. In addition, the quality of home flat screens and audio systems have made the home experience a tough opponent for the movie theater industry to fight. Whereas the attempts at streaming live performances into people's homes failed. Fans want to get out. Fans want to socialize. And fans want to see live entertainment and be together experiencing the performance.

A BRIEF HISTORY OF LIVE MUSIC VENUES

Back in the day, radio stations, like sports and music venues, were primarily privately owned businesses. Radio station DJs could spin any new release single they had discovered. There were no mandated playlists. Artist could break first regionally out of Philly, Detroit, or Chicago. As there was for the most part, no corporate entity involved, local radio stations could add the new single with no push back. They after all were family owned or a small business. In 1996 Bill Clinton signed into law the *Telecommunications Act* which was intended to diversify the ownership of media companies. In actuality, it allowed them the ability to snatch-up countless radio and live music locally owned small businesses, i.e., radio stations, concert promoters, and venues. What ensured is what is referred to in the business world, as a *roll up*. In a roll-up, a major player / a corporation buys all their competitors. Offering each a one-time significant cash payment and stock options - a very tempting offer and subsequent decision for a small business owner. And with few exceptions, small business owners of both promoters, radio stations and independent music venues took the cash. Creating an oligopoly – whereby few companies control the vast majority of market share.

You cannot overstate this impact on radio consolidation. That simple moment in time when Bob and Elizabeth Dole took their free rides on the *Clear Channel* private plane and then eventually delivered the votes that allowed large corporations to own large quantities of radio stations in America. Ultimately giving you the generic music, which is purveyed today. Homogenized and served to you like a choice at the *McDonalds* drive through. It not only impacted the music that you listen to, but it also gave a single group control over the news that you listen to. Yes, music and the media discovered that ownership of perception could mean maximizing profit.

This consolidation was the beginning of the sameness of all things in many ways. No longer could you break songs locally (in your hometown for example) and develop it regionally. You couldn't have a hit in Atlanta or Baltimore alone. You couldn't have a song that started as a hit in Denver, catch on in Chicago and DC and blow up across the nation. Now, adds to formats were defined by one or two groups (or individuals) and "recommended" (in some instances mandated) across the country throughout their network. It's all about control, consolidation, and profit for these publicly traded companies. A sameness that took place in radio, much in the same way that a sameness took place in many aspects of our lives (Denny's, Outback Steakhouse, Walgreens) took place in the concert and ticketing sector of our business. Again, the corporatization of America. Was this good for us or was it bad for us? That's for you to decide.

THE HISTORY OF CONCERT PROMOTION

In concert promotion, there is a fifteen-year window when the business changed COMPLETELY. It all starts with Ron Delsener and *SFX*. SFX is the precursor to the company that you know today as *Live Nation*.

Here is a brief overview:

1996:
SFX Broadcasting buys concert promoter Delsener/Slater.

1997 (this is the 1st big year of change):
The *SFX Entertainment* division is founded; In a deal valued at $230 million and one that creates one of the industry's largest promoters of live entertainment, SFX Broadcasting acquired

four of the nation's leading promoters, including *Bill Graham Presents*, the Northern California firm bowed by the legendary impresario in 1965. *Contemporary Group*, the leading concert producer and promoter in St. Louis and in the surrounding areas of Missouri, Kansas, Nebraska, and Oklahoma, was acquired for $90 million. SFX also paid $15 million for *Concert/Southern Promotions*, a key promoter in Atlanta and the Southeast. To round out the buying spree, SFX paid $70 million for *Network Magazine Group* and *SJS Entertainment*, a provider of research, programming and production services to the radio and record industry. Among its holdings is *Album Network*, a 20-year-old music industry tip sheet.

1998:
SFX Entertainment, Inc. is spun off; an exclusive deal with *Ticketmaster* is signed.

1999:
The company completes its first European acquisitions; the *SFX Sports Group* is formed.

2000:
Clear Channel Communications buys SFX Entertainment.

2002:
SFX Entertainment is renamed *Clear Channel Entertainment.*

2005:
The company is spun off as Live Nation, Inc. on the New York Stock Exchange.

2010 (this is the 2nd big year of change): Ticketmaster Entertainment and the world's largest concert promoter, Live Nation, complete their merger after agreeing with U.S. antitrust officials to divest some assets. Ticketmaster also owns *Front Line Management*, the leading artist management firm founded by Ticketmaster Chief Executive Officer Irving Azoff. Its roster of 200-plus artists includes the *Eagles* and *Miley Cyrus*. The new Live Nation Entertainment now owns more than 140 concert venues globally, sells around 140 million tickets a year, promotes 22,000 concerts annually, and represents over 80% of all shows booked in America.

The US Government antitrust division decided that this is NOT a monopoly. With control over all these aspects of the ticketing business, Live Nation Entertainment has major control over ticket prices. Live Nation markets add–ons such as; service fees, promoting fees, and processing fees (which average 27 percent of the ticket cost) as an extension of the ticket price.

There is a lack of transparency regarding the true value of concert tickets, yet customers can't really turn to another ticket selling company because of Live Nation Entertainment's industry dominance.

There is little or no doubt about it that as an artist you need to be in the public's eye and consistently maintain a profile and image. Given the growth of social media and the internet, there has never been a better time for a band to get its music heard. You MUST maintain a strong digital presence. Gone are the days when you can just be a musician. You must have a strong sense of who you are and how you are seen. You must control perception via your online existence.

Aside from digital marketing, this essentially all boils down to live performances. To put this in perspective, live music revenues eclipse those of the recorded industry by more than two times. As a developing artist, it may be difficult to find paying gigs. Be creative in your strategy and tactics. Attend open-mics and jam sessions. Sit-in where you can and importantly, make yourself known amongst the other musicians in your community. Find alternative venues such as a coffee shop, a restaurant, a microbrewery, a record store, etc. where you can perform. But most important, listen to the voice of the God who sold millions of shoes (Nike) and JUST DO IT! It's unlikely that you can negotiate a performance fee (or guarantee) with a venue, but then again, they may be only offering the door. Take it! Believe in yourself. Take EVERY GIG. Another idea is to work with a few other bands and negotiate a "buy-out", whereby you rent out the room for one flat fee. Typically, you act as the promoter, you set the ticket prices, you retain the door or ticket sales while the venue keeps the bar. Think creatively in generating money; utilize a tip jar and definitely set-up a table and sell merch at your shows.

THE KEY PLAYERS

Four key players in the concert promotion industry are;
- The Promoter
- The Manager
- The Agent
- Social Media and PR Manager

THE PROMOTER & THE BOOKING AGENT

A *promoter* is any individual or company that is responsible for organizing, promoting, and selling tickets to a live performance. It is the promoter's responsibility to provide the venue, promote the show, sell tickets, hire security, and meet all the requirements of the *Performance Agreement* and *Technical Rider*. Promoter's contact *Booking Agents* directly, or vice versa, whereby an *Agent* may contact a promoter for an opportunity or favor both having long-standing relationships in pairing like-sized rooms with comparable artists with the goal being - everybody makes money. This again is another example of the importance of having and maintaining relationships in the music biz. Club owners start thinking about what band should open and headline New Year's Eve. The city or township explores how well your band might draw for a street fair or a municipal 4th of July food fair. Midday week shows are typically Wednesday and Thursday where a band is ultimately traveling to a major market for a Friday or Saturday show are deemed to be routing dates. Hence, routing dates, typically take place in a secondary or smaller market. Acts reduce their guarantee on weekdays while en route to the larger venue weekend shows. Agents and Talent Buyers / *Venue Owners* have a history and a rapport and therefore attempt to pitch, and book shows that are a win / win for all parties involved. The idea is to book an artist or band in an appropriately sized venue in comparison to the projected ticket, bar, and merch sales. Legacy bands, comedians, developing artists on the cusp of breaking can book a 1,200 - 3000 seat venue, while superstar artists can play festivals and stadiums. Either way, once there is a 'hold' on the date the performance moves to a written, negotiated, and signed Performance Agreement. Once management and Artist have green lighted this tour, it is the responsibility of the promoter and the agent to negotiate the deal. Upon doing so, the agent generates a Performance Contract with the accompanying *Rider*. Once the deal has been negotiated and signed off on, there is typically a 50% deposit due. This money is placed in an escrow bearing account until which time the performance ensues. It's customary for the agent to release the deposit while the other 50% balance is paid to the performer or designated representative – typically the Tour Manager, just prior to the performance.

The performance agreement would include the obvious; the date, time and place of the performance, the fee, the number of comp (complimentary) tickets, etc. It would also stipulate the promoter is responsible for payments of all *Performing Rights Organizations* (PRO) fees. Accompanying the Performance Agreement is a *Technical Rider Agreement, a Tech Rider* or simply a *Rider* – which provides the sound and light requirements, mic input list, stage plot, hospitality, ground transportation, and may include a percentage of revenue from merch sold.

Mid-size national acts typically list the specific brand and model of drums, keyboards, and amps which are to be provided by the promoter. This equipment is typically rented from a sound equipment rental company – and is referred to as *backline*.

There are essentially 7 types of concert venues, and they are broken down as follows:
1. Stadiums – the largest facilities for concerts. Typically, these are sports stadiums which require extensive set-up to convert into a music venue with cartage required for everything from stage to sound to lights.
2. Amphitheaters – outdoor theater seating venues which typically accommodate 5,000 – 30,000 and have installed stage, sound, and lights.
3. Festival Sites – such as Chicago's Grant Park which once a year is completely transformed into Lollapalooza, with streets of the city being temporarily closed down.
4. Arenas – another multi-purpose facility which most often is the facility of a professional sports team. Capacity is between 7,500 – 25,000.
5. Theaters – can easily be converted into a music venue having a permanent installation of stage, sound, and lights.
6. Mid-Sized Music Venues – indoor concert facilities designed with a permanent stage, sounds and light. Only backline may be required for the artist. Capacity 1,000 – 2,500
7. Small Music Venues & Clubs – same as mid-sized venues having a permanent stage, sounds and light. Typically, the artist, band, or DJ, are responsible for bringing in their own personal backline. Having a reduced capacity of typically less than 600.

LIVE EVENT BOOKING

Engaging the services of a reputable booking agency would be ideal, however, if your guarantee is non-existent (playing for the-door), then in all likelihood you won't be particularly attractive to a booking agent. Understand that 10% of nothing is nothing. A guarantee of a few hundred or even a couple of thousand dollars may not meet the agencies' criteria in taking you on and adding you to their client roster. It's a good idea to get on their radar, but the first question asked from the Agent to your Manager is "how many fannies can they put in the seats?" If the answer to the question is too embarrassing to answer, chances are your act is not yet ready to add The Agent to the Team. Should that be the case, for the time-being you may find it necessary to act as your own booking agent. Start out by doing research on the various suitable venues in your market. Do not call the clubs before you have explored the various venues' websites, if for no other reason than to ascertain which clubs are appropriate for your band at your current level. If you're not going to draw a sizable crowd, then avoid pitching venues too large such as *The House of Blues* for example. Identify and pitch the clubs that would be appropriate for the size audience you draw. The strategy is to play smaller rooms, increasing your audience size, with the objective of then moving up to the next tier of clubs and ultimately, to the biggest venues in your market. Many live performance venues provide information on their *Contact* page as to where you can email them with a succinct message and a link. When emailing, include a short yet concise message with all the necessary info; including an introduction message along with a link to your website and media. Include any pertinent information that would be critical in influencing the talent buyer's decision as to hiring your band. Have you opened for any bigger bands, sold out any smaller rooms, have an impressive number of streams or views, or planning a tour? Check the club's calendar and see if there is a comparable, yet bigger band in your genre that you could open for and suggest that to the promoter. After you've sent the email, wait several business days. If in the event you have not received a reply, resend it. Be persistent, but don't be obnoxious. Always be polite. Ideally you will want to establish a rapport with the talent buyers who know you, like you, and know you're dependable and on time. In the same way it no longer matters if you are on a major record label, it does not matter if you have a major booking agent. Many great bands were and are booked by smaller agencies (Bon Iver, Arcade Fire). What matters is if you can deliver tickets sold in that market. Start small and grow in every market you play in. And above all, enjoy the journey. Like anything, it's not about getting there, it is about the journey. And oh, ask for some cool stuff on your rider, like a day bed and a place to do your laundry.... You'll see!

TOUR BOOKING

Once you have established yourself or better yet conquered your hometown market, the next logical step will be to increase the radius of the circumference in terms of miles in which you can or have already begun to develop a buzz. If you're in a major market or mid-size market, and you have built a considerable following in the city proper, play some gigs in the suburbs and see how that translates into an attendance. Once you can fill venues of any given size in these markets it's time to look elsewhere, to the next neighboring city perhaps. Once you begin to book dates that require an overnight stay, you should then conceptualize that you may in actuality have the first date of a mini tour on the calendar. Think about building around that booked date. Instead of thinking about the first secure date on the calendar as a gig out of town, think of it as the first night of a tour. Once you book two consecutive nights in a row and come home with a net profit you have completed your first successful tour. Obviously, this can be embellished in numerous ways; you book 2 dates over a Thursday, Friday or Saturday of the same weekend or variations thereof.

At this point, it's fair to assume that you have at least one additional individual traveling with you, they may be doing sound (FOH -front of house), managing your merch table, driving the tour bus, etc. They may not yet be the official tour manager, however at this juncture you should be in a position to bring a tour manager on to your team. Once you have added that member to your team, you will be able to delegate some tasks as they pertain to live shows. Does your tour manager have additional capabilities in which they can lend additional experience? Can they provide double duty so to speak?

Additional responsibilities might include:
- Mix front-of-house
- Provide tour accounting
- Manage the merch
- Drive and/or arrange for ground or air transportation
- Book hotel rooms

Once you have built a successful tour in a few select markets the next objective will be to repeat it. At minimum you should play these markets two to three times per year, each time with word of mouth bringing a bigger audience to each performance.

LIVE EVENT MARKETING

If there's a free rag (a local free entertainment publication like *The Reader* or *The Illinois Entertainer* in Chicago for example) DON'T consider taking out an ad in it. Your best and most effective advertising is social media in all forms. The only way to consider advertising in a local weekly is via either their online presence or their social media. In all your advertising and existence on socials, be aggressive, be smart, and be FUN, or no one will care. And, do MORE than just sell yourself.

Reach out a week or two in advance of a show to local morning TV or college radio to promote your show, play your record, or even interview you. Look for local radio, online entertainment sites, and especially regional or local music blogs. Find a way to be seen.

Don't forget your database/contact list. This is, after-all, why you are building it. Email both tastemakers and fans. Get your gig posted on live music event calendars. Offer a free pair of tix to a blogger or anyone that can make a difference in your career; offer them VIP seating and a backstage pass. And obviously, promote the show on your website and social media pages. Consider spending a relatively modest amount on social ads (or boosts) or any other platform of your choosing. If there's another act on the bill, create a pdf of the show and cross-promote; then share on both acts' social media pages and websites.

Well before the summer, check local municipalities' websites in your market – they may be accepting submissions for bands for street festivals and outdoor events.

Another idea, think if you can create any incentives for fans to attend your live show. The first; [name a number], get a free autographed poster, slice of pizza, a beer, or a CD.

Even if you are a 'solo' artist, it will be incumbent for you to have a band to tour with. Live music is such an integral and necessary component of building your brand and fan base.

Are you curious to learn what percent of your revenue may emanate from touring? As an example, Billboard's annual Money Makers report listed the band U2 as the highest-paid musical act of the year in 2017. Of their total earnings, about 95% came from touring while less than 4% came from streaming and sales.

In another example, Drake purportedly gets paid between $400,000 to $2 million for a single show depending on the audience, length of performance, and other factors. His estimated fee for features on other songs is reported to be around $100,000 per verse. When it comes to club appearances, he charges around $200,000 per hour.

Various other resources cite national recognized Hip-Hop Artist performance fees of $20,000 - $100,000 per show. These figures exclude superstar artists who can command in excess of $500,000 - $2 million for a show.

Although these figures are presumably far greater than where you are in your career, what it does, however, is provide insight into the importance and potential of live performance and touring at any level. Too often an act is so laser focused on the "music" that they lose sight of the actual visual performance they are presenting. In other words; at rehearsal and at every show work on not only improving the music but the overall performance - the show. Regardless of genre, was the performance entertaining on any level? Did you get the audience reaction you were seeking? Again, not only thinking about and working on music, work on and think through your live performances – rehearse portions of the shows.

It would be remiss for us not to forewarn you, that if you're not already aware – touring, life on the road is not for the faint of heart. This is particularly true in the building process of a developing act. Your first few tours may be in a Sprinter with 4 others and the gear being pulled behind in a trailer. And in all likelihood, you will double up with two per hotel room... if you even get hotel rooms. Many times, you will sleep in the van. It will be necessary for you to make a concerted effort to eat well, stay healthy, and workout. Although the people on the road may be your bandmates and friends, traveling and co-existing 24/7 with anyone can be trying at best. At this point it is not the glamorous life you had envisioned. Things can and do improve – you move up to touring on Prevost buses – luxury travel for 6-8 while on tour. However, there exist one identical similarity in the two types of touring coaches - the mileage and the number of hours spent on the road. Upon examination one will come to discover that very few have made it as an "overnight sensation". Of course, there are exceptions, but history shows us more-often than not, acts put-in years and years of touring, until finally getting a record deal and making it big. Some bands become regional acts – playing the top local festivals, State Fairs, etc. while a select few evolve into globally recognized icons. Everyone's journey will be unique and unto themselves. It will be incumbent upon you to consistently analyze your situation: is your career growing, are your making money, is it your full-time gig?

Looking in from the outside touring on a million-dollar coach may seem like the glamorous life, traveling and seeing the world, but many find after a few tours, months, or years on the road, away from family and friends it is not exactly the lifestyle they had envisioned. Keep in mind, there exist countless jobs within the music business that do not require extensive touring and constant traveling.

LIVE STREAMS

One area of live performance which was exploited by the pandemic was live streams. Live streams can be broadcast from a venue or your living room. The set-up costs can be minimal, and you can reach fans throughout the world. Determine a goal in your hosting a stream; is it to make money, gain new fans, do you / can you sell tickets? If so, there's a platform for that at Songkick. There now exist a number of platforms in which you can conduct an online live performance and hang. These platforms include: YouTube Live, Facebook Live, Instagram Live, TikTok Live, Twitch, Twitter, Amazon Music and check out Restream. Although we have returned to live in-person performances, if you attended or conducted a live streaming event within the last couple of years, there's no reason you can't continue hosting a periodic live stream for both your fans and as a money generator. Don't restrict a live stream to only being a live performance. Expand your concepts to include a home studio tour, a masterclass, Q&As, or turn your fans on to a hobby of yours (cooking, skateboarding, fashion, etc.).

Resources

Tour Management 101- Roles, Titles & the Touring Family Tree
Promoter 101 Podcasts

11

MAKING MONEY WITH MERCH

According to Panic! At the Disco's manager, Bob McLinn, 30 percent of the band's profit on its most recent tour came from merch. "Ever since CDs started going by the wayside, everyone was like, 'How are we going to make more money?'

THE VALUE & OPPORTUNITY MERCH PRESENTS

Perhaps you've given little or no thought about merch. You're thinking about creating music, right? Recent analysis tabulated that making it in the music biz may now be comprised of 50% marketing with only 50% of an artist's time spent on music. Are you aware major artists and successful developing niche artists that get it, focus on the various revenue streams we have introduced thus far? If done properly, one of the most significant components of revenue is making money with merch. This revenue will be generated from both your online merch store and your live performance merch table.

Don't dispute nor discard this notion what-so-ever. If you're not into merch or if you don't understand what an asset and opportunity your online merch store and live gig merch table represent, well then you have overlooked not only a significant revenue stream, but also an opportunity to build your brand. Making money from merch is a part of the business side of music. Your merch sales offer and provide a significant revenue generator having the potential of 150% - 400% mark-up! Compare that to the revenue of a 10,000 Spotify plays and you will quickly realize it's a fine idea to be in the merch business. The merchandising business generates more than $3 billion dollars a year representing the equivalent of approximately a fifth of the recorded music industry revenue, [Source: Rolling Stone]. This means that this merch stuff, if you do it right and market this to your fans and at gigs could equal a significant percentage of your income. Think about that.

When calculating return on investment, or ROI for a tour, tour accountants project the line item of merch to be 10-35% of their total revenue to compliment and supplement tour revenue. In the case of the very biggest names, they can bring in $300-400,000 of merch only – all in the space of a few hours.

Recognize, people make merch buying decisions with their hearts, not with their heads. As an artist, you have already made an emotional connection with your fans. Now sell 'em stuff!

If you can afford only one item at a show, the research has shown, it would undoubtedly be a black t-shirt. And in if you can carry only 2 shirts on tour, research shows you should have 2 black t-shirts: 1 high-priced, 1 less expensive.

- So, order 50 colored t-shirts @ $11.70 per shirt and sell for $30 for a $18.30 profit per shirt representing a total net profit of all 50 shirts of $915.00.
- Let's say you order 300, inexpensive 1-color white-Ts at a cost $6.00 per shirt (including shipping), and you sell them for $15 representing a $9.00 net profit per shirt. Assuming you sell two-thirds (200) of the white-Ts on that leg of the tour, you would have generated a net profit of $1,800.
- Alternatively, let's look at the same Profit and Loss (P&L) but this time ordering a high priced, 4-color black-T. If you were to place an order for the same quantity of 300 Ts, the difference being a black T with 4 color art at a cost $10.70 (including shipping) per shirt, which you can then sell for 30 bucks represents a $19.30 net profit per shirt. Now assume you sell the same 200 of the black-Ts on that leg of the tour, you would have generated a net profit of $3,860.

Which inventory would you rather tour with, the cheap Ts or the expensive ones? Keep in mind that several factors should be considered in determining the success of your merch sales. The data exists to help understand demand for merch by your fans/audience and the costs associated with it. The genre of music you create/perform, the type of merchandise, location, and size of venue can all be factored in.

Now think about the economics and logistics of touring with 600 Ts on tour. Can you accommodate carrying both the cheap white-T and the higher priced black-T? If so, that would be ideal. However, if it's practical to take only one-T on the road, if you have only one option research shows us that you should carry the higher priced black-T.

Top selling items of 2019 (*atVenue* insights)
- 1 T-Shirt $35.00 50% of all items sold
- 2 Long Sleeve $46.00 5%
- 3 Hat $34.00 4%
- 4 Pullover Hoodie $61.00 4%
- 5 CD $20.00 4%
- 6 Koozie $6.00 3%
- 7 Poster $31.00 3%
- 8 Sweatshirt $55.00 2%
- 9 Zip-up Hoodie $60.00 2%

It will be necessary to keep a pre-show and after-show spread sheet to reconcile the inventory. Aside of making sure you're not getting ripped off, the other benefit is to learn what stuff is selling and what isn't. And if you have only one 1 black T, what size is selling the most?

According to 2021-year-end statistics from atVenue, "more fans are buying merch now than in 2019. The average per head merch investment has increased from $5.54 in 2019 to $7.04 in 2021. The average price of a t-shirt is now $35.

Convincing bigger bands to wear your gear (whether through being cool enough for them to notice, or possibly by begging them) can result in an immediate spike in sales. Note: Miley Cyrus wearing a Billy Idol T-shirt.

PRINT ON DEMAND

Creating an online merch store does not have to require an investment, other than your time. Do research. Create an account with an online print on demand merch store that meets your needs. Find one that is compatible with your CMS and offers you the flexibility in merch assortment you're looking for. Think of your fans; what are they wearing? If you discover its hoodies and tie-dyes for example, make them. Mimic what the tends in fashion and style are with your fans. Make stuff for them. Upload your logo and order samples.

Print on demand stores will also provide you with analytics such as:

What is selling (t-shirts, hoodies, or caps), and;
The price point (sweet spot) your fans are willing to spend

These analytics can help you determine what you might want to order and stock when you tour or play shows. You may determine that your fans are expecting a more upscale hoodie and willing to pay for it? But again, if you are unsure of what item to stock, it is an indisputable fact, that if you offer only one item at a show it would be a black t-shirt. End of discussion.

As a general rule, you will want to sell the item at 2 - 3x the wholesale cost. A major artist selling out the United Center or Madison Square Garden can earn $300-400 thousand dollars in a four-hour span, think about applying these metrics to you or your band, subtracting zeros. Can you make $300- $400 bucks a night or from your online merch store? Playing a live show, make a note in the set list to remind yourself to mention your merch store from the stage at least 2 times during the set. After the gig, don't disappear, you're not a rock star yet. Promise your fans and deliver by showing up at your merch table. Don't be bashful; make it apparent you have stuff to sell, and you'll be at the merch table after the gig.

Online and at the gig, make some inexpensive stuff. You can have buttons, patches, stickers, koozies and stuff having a wholesale cost of .60 that you can sell for three bucks with a markup up 300-500%. Stickers, patches, magnets, guitar picks range from .20 - .60 cents and have a 400-750% markup. Plus, you can give away cheap stuff in exchange for an email.

Should you integrate an online print-on demand merch store, it won't be necessary to try and determine how many of each size shirt (or whatever) you will need to order. With print-on-demand you won't be left with unsold, obsolescent inventory from your t-shirts in small and

XXL. Determining the proper number of small, medium, large, XL and XXL T-shirts and huddles is a no-win scenario. We'll provide some guidance in the following "Merch Table" section.

Think outside the box, what are some new items to add to your online mix that you think are cool? Leisure wear and home decor are popular consumer trends and would include such things as sweatpants, framed lithographs, blankets and pillows, a coffee table book (-w-rehearsal, studio, and tour photos) all of which involve no upfront fees and represent ancillary income both online and at the gig.

Due to the Covid-19 pandemic and resulting transitioning to working from home, society has only continued in their quest for casual wear. The popularity of what is deemed leisure wear exploded over this time-period and only further emphasized our penchant for casual / comfortable clothing. After all, if you're on a Zoom call who knows if you're wearing exquisitely pressed slacks to match your suit or a pair of sweats. The point being you would be wise to offer some leisure wear in your merch clothing assortment. A few ideas for leisure wear and related lifestyle items might include:
- Pajamas
- Sweatpants
- Underwear
- Socks
- Bathrobes
- Candles
- Rolling papers
- Incense

It's totally understood that many of these suggested items may not fit the demographic or psychographic make up of your ideal fan, but with print on demand you can conduct some A/ B research to better understand what does and what doesn't work. Which points out the obvious, with print-on-demand you can create countless items, projecting a larger-than-life online presence for your fans while generating incremental revenue. The offshoot benefit of which is the analytics provided for you to determine what items sell and what don't. Through this online statistical information, you can better understand what specific items are worth the effort to carry on tour. Your online merch store allows you to evolve with fashion and trends. A Tour Manager for a "Legacy Band" out recently for four dates said, "They carried 5 boxes of Black T-shirts; Large, X-Large and XX-Large on the tour and sold 4 of the 5 boxes in four shows. In its most simplistic of forms, this is an ideal example of knowing and understanding your demographics. In this case, they are all large, overweight, and over 50. No need to carry small or medium T-shirts. It's not worth it. The moral of the story is that if you understand who your fans are, and you create and market your merch to your fans both online and off, you can build a brand, gain fans, and make money!

> According to the recent NPD Group research, 31% of total apparel spending in the US is forecasted to be leisurewear. These items would include sweatshirts, sweat-pants, sleepwear & socks

OK, are you ready for this, Forbes has called the Tote Bag "the new must have luxury item." This is fabulous news, make a tote bag! You can make a cheap one and sell it for 5 bucks or a high-end end for $20. Either way your merch consumer / fan left with their purchases in a branded tote bag as opposed to a disposable, non-eco-friendly disposable plastic bag. This is such a brilliant marketing idea, as your band or brand logo will be carried as a lunch bag or reusable grocery store bag to work and/or school. It's eco-friendly, profitable and a brand building opportunity.

Surprisingly, you should offer some high-end stuff too such as a leather jacket or jean tour jacket. You might carry one of each size or simply tour with one large and if that's not the right size you can take a deposit and place a custom order. Better yet, create a strategic partnership with a local clothing manufacture / designer and create an event. A runway show / you provide the music. It's all in the name of merch. You could have the opportunity to create some custom-branded merch.

Remember, if your fans are at your show, on your website, or listening to your music, you've already made a connection with them. Fans often make decisions with their hearts not their heads. Fan loyalty and purchasing merch is a perfect example of cognitive vs. emotional buying decisions. They are looking for a reason to buy. Offer a limited edition, end of inventory sale item at the gig and online. Make buying merch simple, customizable, and seamless . . . these are all essentially marketing activities.

Major established artist's that have a guaranteed number of shows booked on a tour and can guarantee several shows per year and number of attendees are offered an advance in anticipation of representing their merch on a tour. The major labels all own their own merch companies. Universal Music Group (UMG) has *Bravado* and Sony Music Entertainment has

Ceremony of Roses. If you sign with a major label, there is a strong likelihood that your merch partner will be predetermined – a wholly owned merch company of your label / distributor. A major merch company advance all the upfront costs, and the artist is compensated with a 20-30% royalty. These types of deals are offered to major artists. So how do you as an indie artist capitalize and maximize your revenue from merch sales?

First of all, accept credit cards. Now this is obvious as it pertains to your online merch store, but make sure you can accept credit and debit cards at your merch table. Another idea is to place a tip jar on your merch table; see what happens (experiment). It may sound old school, but have a legal pad of paper, an iPad or clip-board with a sign-up sheet at your merch table so that fans can join your fan club. It's free. If there are fans that don't have a budget for merch, ask them to sign-up and give them something inexpensive. There is no downside. And what-ever you print, free or otherwise, don't forget to incorporate your branding strategy and have your url on it.

OK – so let's take deep breath and think about what we have discussed thus far. In essence, it's all about creating a brand around your music/artistry, promoting it, and ultimately monetizing the brand with fashionable merchandise. Having a strategic plan to generate revenue with merchandise can greatly complement your career initiatives.

Again, here's where you can get creative. Your website, your merch table, and your merch store are all an extension of your artist and brand, and they all need to attract attention. Find ways on all platforms to draw people in.

> The global custom t-shirt printing market size is anticipated to reach USD 7.57 billion by 2028. Increasing preference towards fashionable, customized, and unique clothing, as well as rising disposable income within the young population, are major factors driving demand for custom t-shirts worldwide. Customized t-shirts are primarily targeted toward the young population as it allows them to design clothing matching their style, personality, and preference. [Source: Businesswire}

THE MERCH TABLE

Here's the deal – at the gig, at a live performance, it is your obligation and responsibility to do 2 things. One, unless you're already a rock star, mention your merch table and announce you'll be there after the show to say "hi", etc. This merch strategy obviously is not applicable to all, but if you're in a baby band, a developing artist trying to find super fans, the best place to do that may be at the merch table. Two, mention your merch table at the end of the gig and announce you'll be there momentarily. Done well, this tactic will provide an opportunity to identify with and make a very special type of connection with fans, or potential super-fans.

In the music business timing is critical. If you choose to make this a nightly routine following a show or after a gig, make sure you get to the merch table quick, within 5 minutes of finishing the show. Don't disappoint. You can celebrate with the band and crew after, and only after you have met your fans at a meet & greet or at the merch table.

Your presence at the merch table is the opportunity for you to turn a stranger into a lifelong fan. Your fans are familiar with you, or they wouldn't be there. In person, at a show at the merch table, you will have the opportunity to connect with some of your most important and influential fans. Even if they don't' buy anything this is your chance to meet them, share some information, and collect an email.

As a general guideline when placing an order for clothing items it's necessary to determine a specific quantity for each size. If you need 100 t-shirts, it's recommended you select the following quantities:
- 10 Smalls,
- 25 Mediums,
- 30 Larges,
- 25 XLs, and
- 10 2XLs.
- Depending on the shirt style and audience, you may want to add a few 3XL and 4XLs too. [Source: Printperfection]

BUNDLING MERCH

This is a very simple yet effective concept. Think about a fast-food chain and how they include bundling in their marketing. If you were to order, say one cheeseburger, fries and a medium soft-drink. Purchased separately these items would cost more than a bundle, can you say Happy Meal, Family Packs, or the combo. The concept with merch is the same - if you have a CD priced at $10 and a t-shirt at $30 – sell them as a bundle for $35. The idea of bundling is to increase the average per transaction price point from one item at full price to 2 or 3 items collectively purchased at a discount. Most online stores provide a provision for bundling. At the gig, the contents of a bundle must be clearly signed and priced accordingly.

MEET & GREETS

Upon achieving rock star status, artists can hold a 50-100 person meet and greet, pre-show or after show and charge $100 - $500 bucks or more per person. Think of this scenario and opportunity on more of a micro scale. Can you "sell" meet and greets for nothing more than gaining a new super fan? Does there exist an opportunity to sell a pre-show meet and greet for a nominal price point that might include a backstage photo with you and your guests, and even a t-shirt?

So, we're all aware that this is a viable source of additional money for a major artist, charging anywhere from $250 - $1,000 + for the opportunity to take a photo. As a new/up-and-coming artist you need to consider what you have to offer.

Take a lead from the Rolling Stones; they only do meet and greets before the show. It's far more organized, and everyone looks more presentable. What can you offer? A backstage pass prior to a show to 10 fans, each including a digital photo you can email plus a signed tour poster they can take home with them. Think small, this too could be another previously unfounded revenue stream. At the very least, it's an opportunity to build good-will with current fans. Consider including meet-and-greet opportunities with a fan club membership.

YOUR ONLINE MERCH STORE

It's your website and your brand, they have opted into you, they're curious and they want stuff.

It's absolutely imperative that you have an ecommerce component / an online merch store. Your online merch store can offer numerous possibilities, many of which are impractical or not viable in physical merch. Create a 'Store' tab. You can have more stuff to sell than you can imagine. Print on demand is the coolest thing to revolutionize merch. With print on demand, all you simply need to do is create an account, upload your logo, and creates any of the virtual print on demand items they might offer. Imagine this, you can offer all of this at no cost to you. You can offer numerous possibilities, including things that would be difficult or impossible to transport in a physical environment. Here you can offer and sell the same physical stuff you've been offering plus new digital only items and experiences such as:

- LPs (these are quite heavy and cumbersome to carry on the road + they melt in heat)
- Outtakes & Cover Tunes
- Acoustic and Alternate Versions
- Bundles / Merch packages
- Cassettes / USBs
- Sheet Music, Transcriptions & Guitar Tabs
- Handwritten Lyrics
- 1 on 1 - Zoom Private Instruction Lessons
- A Private Concert (w/ a radius clause)
- 30-minute Zoom hang with the band
- Artwork, lithographs of EP cover art
- Jewelry – leather bracelets

Many items can be created online at a print on demand merch store at literally no upfront cost to you. As mentioned, simply create an account, upload your logo and images, and begin to create everything from coffee mugs to t-shirts. They in turn, when an order is received, print, package and ship the item to your customer / fan. Obviously, the margins are reduced as each order is a one-off, but there remains a formidable net profit for you on each item you create and is in turn purchased from your online store. Equally, you have a new fan wearing your brand!

There are unlimited options beside Shopify and Printful, but before committing to one, ask yourself
- How easily does the store integrate with your CMS?
- Are there any upfront fees?
- Do they print on demand?
- Pick, pack & ship?
- What are the margins?
- Can you sell bundles?
- Do they pre-make banners and advertisements

Also consider Crowdsourcing or Fan funding, and keep in mind all these items will be relevant and can act as fulfillment articles to you contributors. If you're smart there are always ways to make money with merch.

When you sell a t-shirt for $25, let's just say after printing, packaging, and shipping you net an $11 profit as the store owner. If all you had to do was upload an image, that's a good use of your time. With this business model of essentially drop shipping, you can put 100% of your investing money directly into advertising through Instagram/ Facebook, Google Ads, etc. The automated store takes care of itself, the only thing you need to concern yourself with is doing your main job of creating music and driving traffic to your store. Interesting to note: of any of the nay sayers, now you can create a merch store with multiple offers with no upfront costs to you. It should now be quite obvious that your online merch store can be a major component of your revenue streams, both online and offline. Focus on it. Develop it.

Resources

For Merchandise:
- Printful
- Weneedmerch.com
- Merchkitched.com
- Bandsonabudget.com
- Mycustombandmerch.com
- Intunegp.com
- Stream Elements
- Shopify (Shopify Plus)
- Dizzyjam

- Culture studio (Chicago)
- Manheadmerch
- Merch.ly
- Bandsmerch

Make your website a virtual merch table
Intro to Shopify
ep 39: Tour Management 101: Merch 101

12

SINGLES/SPOTIFY & DISTRIBUTION

"The artists today that are making it realize that it's about creating a continuous engagement with their fans." Daniel Ek – CEO / Founder - Spotify

We're living in an age of singles. Like it or not, this is absolutely true. The days of an artist releasing a full-length, 10-12 track LP are over. Visiting the local record store to check out the other "album cuts", was a pastime of mere mortals and mavens alike. Eagerly racing to get their hands on these 2-sided pieces of vinyl (an LP). Albums back then provided depth and insight into an artist through images, artwork, and information, with passionate fan-bases digging far deeper into the project than the 2 "hit songs" the record often provided. Physically, an LP cover, which measures 12" x 12" (a far cry from the thumbnails we're accustomed to today), placed much more emphasis on the cover art. And for us nerds and aficionados, after dropping the needle on side 1, we would scour the liner notes. Tenaciously scanning for where the record was recorded, who engineered it, produced, mixed & mastered the record, who's the drummer, the bass player, keyboard player, et al. Then you could flip the album over and listen to side 2. It wasn't only about listening to music; it was about the immersive experience.

Despite the ephemeral history of recorded music, this is not the first time *"singles"* were the dominant format. The first "single era" was primarily due to the technological limitations of early recorded music. During the late 19th century and the first several decades of the 20th century, phonograph records (and their predecessor: the phonograph cylinders) were limited in duration due to the relatively crude disc-cutting techniques of the day. Prior to the LP, the standard mediums of the industry were the shellac-made, 78 rpm gramophone record (which could only hold up to 3-5 minutes) and the 7-inch single (which only held up to 4-6 minutes). These kept the standard time for singles at about 2-3 minutes (not far off from the standard of a pop single, today). Despite Columbia Records' chief engineer: Peter Carl Goldmark pioneering the development of the 12-inch-long play vinyl record (otherwise known as an LP) in 1949, LPs remained a secondary market to the short, snappy singles of the 40s and 50s. According to famed music writers Ann Powers and Joel Whitburn, it wasn't until the arrival of the Beatles in the US in 1964, that the *album era* unofficially began.

And quite the era it was, with many experts agreeing that the *album era* lasted from the 60s into the 2010s, with a steady decline throughout the early 2000s and the rise of the internet. We're currently in what writers like Jon Caramanica and Kevin Whitehead have dubbed: *the post-album era*. So how and why have we returned back to a singles era? Ironically, rather than the technological limitations behind the first *singles era*, technological *advancements* are the primary culprit behind the dawning of this new *singles era* (*the post-album era*). Many have suggested that streaming platforms, Spotify in particular, has made our music libraries, less and less personal. As a result, artists, producers, and labels are basing their strategies around singles and curated playlists rather than full albums. The recorded music business was started with the advent of technology that made it possible to record and playback sound. The music industry is forever tied to the technology that plays a role in the creation, capturing, distribution, sales, and consumption of recorded music.

In recent discussions with a highly regarded music executive, it was revealed that although they agreed to the general precipice of Spotify and Apple, (to eviscerate illegal file sharing) they warned it would result in the industry being morphed into a singles business. And geez if that isn't precisely the case today. People are realizing a viral sensation on TikTok could be significantly more effective than releasing an EP. With a viral sensation on TikTok translating to millions of plays on streaming platforms like Spotify, it could likely garner a record deal for the artist responsible.

This is possible, although statistically improbable. Creating a 30 – 60 second, viral, media sensation on TikTok, is at best, unlikely. You can roll the dice and hope your single resonates with a curator, meets an algorithmic criterion, or your video blows up on YouTube. All of this is possible, and you can strive for it. But to be brutally honest, it's unlikely.

The big question is, with all the music being released how do you plan for your single to get noticed amidst all the clutter? How can you cultivate, at the very least, a small cadre of devout, hardcore fans that will listen to your every release - guaranteed (permitting of course, that they've been informed about it)? If you don't believe in the track 100%, if the track is not compelling, if you have even an inkling that it might not sound professional, don't release it. Play the track for your closest family and friends. If they have little or no comments, if they're not genuinely enthusiastic about what they're hearing, then keep writing, keep recording, keep developing, and improving your songwriting and production skills.

Don't release a song if it is not to the highest standard that you are capable of. Or to be perfectly blunt, don't release it if it sucks. Remember the age-old adage; you only have one chance to make a first impression. Make sure everything you release has integrity, showcases your talent, and has an audience. If you're unsure if your track has achieved your vision, or if it's not properly engineered, mixed, and/or mastered, then wait and fix it. Don't embarrass yourself. Don't rush and release something you later regret. Continue to record, track, mix, master, refine and start over. Release only what you believe is great music.

Master the track. During mastering, the final mixed tracks of a song, EP or album have EQ, compression and field imaging applied to enhance the sound. Mastering levels are adjusted to be competitive with other commercial product and, in the case of an EP or LP, the tracks are mastered at the 'same' level to make for a more cohesive project. Mastering a track makes a difference; don't kid yourself. Major Labels deem the process so vital to the success of a project they typically spend $5,000+ for the Mastering Studio & Engineer, plus $3 grand for the Artist & Producer travel, hotels, and other expenses. Allocating 10 grand per album for mastering is typically built into the recording fund. Now, assuming this is not the best allocation of your 10 thousand dollars, you may be able to find a Mastering facility that will do this for $500, or you can do it for free with a plug-in, (obviously with diminished results, but it's far better than not mastering). The point being, don't overlook or minimize this step. Ultimately, you'll need to provide your distributor with a Mastered 44.1 kHz, 16-bit stereo WAV or FLAC file.

Once completed, you can then work on setting-up the release of your "Sergeant Pepper" masterpiece track. Have cover art ready for not just the first single but the second / follow-up single as well. Make sure that the cover art is 3000 x 3000, otherwise your distributor may reject it, or it may appear blurry. Take the time to make sure the picture is exported properly and that there is no quality degradation in transferring the document from the platform that you made it on, to your distributor. As stated earlier, this is a singles world we live in. Each single you release has the opportunity to be added to a curated or algorithmic playlist – an EP or LP for that matter does not. But individual tracks off of an EP or LP could. Many people drive up streams by releasing the song first as a single, then again on an EP. You can link the songs on platforms by re-uploading it with the same ISWC code (be sure that the track is pretty much the same, nothing more than a couple of mix/master changes, and no changing the track's time beyond at most a second), so that when the song is reuploaded on an EP, it already has all of the streams it's garnered previously as well as listeners and saves. This will not only help to boost the single's streams but will ultimately make the EP appear to have more streams upon release. Additionally, when you re-release it, it automatically is re-eligible for Spotify algorithmic playlists like Release Radar. Show up to gigs with a printed QR code (you can make them for free online) that leads to your Spotify page. Encourage people to simply scan the QR code and then to follow you and check out your music. Get creative with making this printed out QR code, add colors, pictures, lyrics from your songs, whatever you think will get people's attention. If there are other bands performing, leave the QR code somewhere near the stage or at the bar, somewhere that people can continue scanning it, long after your performance.

If at first the single doesn't resonate or find an audience, since you have a second single ready to go, release it sooner than you had anticipated. No need to wait.

Here's another idea. Many great singers are not songwriters. Find great songs. If you're a poet, find a songwriter and vice versa. This is called collaboration and it is key to success for professional songwriters. The buzz word on collaboration is quite apparent when analyzing the number of songwriters (3-7 or more) on a hit single. Do research, find songs that resonate with you. Record a recognizable cover tune; reimagine it and re-record it. Assuming your cover tune is well-known and recognizable, the SEO will reward you. Then record a small 30-60 second version of the cover that you upload as both an Instagram Reel and as a TikTok, these platforms LOVE COVERS! Perhaps shoot them in a cool location or wear a crazy outfit, something to help the cover stick out.

The industry is experiencing tremendous valuations in intellectual property such as copyrights, music publishing, and masters, all coinciding with the valuations of these publicly traded Majors increasing significantly. It's quite possible that the music industry will enjoy a renaissance in a few years and at this moment in time, it looks as though the streaming services will take us there. It's imperative you get into the streaming game.

IT'S A SINGLES WORLD

So, you've made this track and you now think it's your "Sergeant Pepper" or competitive with the recent hits and trends of comparable artists in your genre. You're so excited for the world to hear your art that you want to release it this upcoming Friday. Good plan, right? Wrong. You have to set-up a release. At least 60 days out, set a release date then upload the mastered track to your distributor, who will in turn have it considered for curated and algorithmic playlists. Ideally, the track should be made available at 4 weeks and no later than two weeks prior to the release date. If this is your first / debut release, you may work with your distributor in claiming your Spotify Artist Profile prior to street date. Get your cover art together for the single. Upload your WAV file and complete the metadata at least a month before your actual release date for Spotify, Apple, Prime, etc. Your distributor can assist you in making this happen. This four-week window provides the curators a chance to be made aware of and hear your track. Do not minimize this opportunity. Should your track be added to any curated or algorithmic playlist for that matter, you have just benefited tremendously by properly setting up the release of your single. Have the video ready to go with the release of your single. Upload the cover art to your blog, your website, social media, and generate an email to your database.

The advantages to releasing a single are numerous. It cost less to produce one track than a full album or EP. You have the ability of releasing singles more frequently which may drive the algorithmic streams (and to re-release the single when including it on an EP). Frequency is everything. You need to stay top-of-mind with your fans. Continually create so you have a consistent release schedule. The upside of releasing a digital single is you don't have to manufacture CDs or other physical formats. Instead of releasing an EP, it's best to release singles often, perhaps one every 30 days or spread out over consecutive months.

If you have not yet released a single it's imperative you do so, even if it's just to create your Artist Profile Page on Spotify. So, think about releasing an introductory track, save your best track and lead with a less obvious hit single. Think of the first release as an opportunity to plant your flag and claim your Spotify Artist Profile.

What about a feature, or featuring another artist? Is there someone at your level that you can co-write and record with? Including them as a feature on your track, with both artists promoting the release, you'll double your marketing and social media presence. If you can find an artist to feature on the song, then you'll be automatically reaching their audience as well. Figuring the song gets on Spotify's Release Radar, which will automatically notify your followers that your song is out, both artists followers will be notified, instantly reaching more listeners who are interested in your type of music. If the other artist were to blow up, it could increase your ethos in your respective scene. You may even see a direct correlation to the increases in your own catalog as the result of new fans scanning through your top tracks. Or, at the very least it could provide juicy fodder for your next press release.

The band, U2 went on tour playing a cover of Neil Diamond's *Sweet Caroline* as an encore. If you think you're above recording a cover you're missing the point. Reimagine a tune. Take a 70s or 80s track and breathe new life into it by rerecording it. Reimagine a punk song into a ballad or find a popular song from the 80s or 90s and deconstruct it. Reconstruct it. Don't discount remaking cover songs, many artists including Justin Bieber and Voalise gained prominence by doing so. It might just prove to be your big break. Remember *All Along the Watchtower* by Jimi Hendrix, *I Will Always Love You* by Whitney Huston, and *Hallelujah* by Jeff Buckley, were all cover songs. If it worked for them, it could work for you.

Here's a side note to think about: whenever you have the opportunity, record your live shows. It's ideal if you can capture the performance on a multitrack DAW or Pro Tool files. Try to capture and transfer the board stereo mixes, ask for them, listen to them, learn from them. Improve your musicianship. If board mixes are not an option, record it yourself with a Zoom Recorder or any recording app on your phone such as GarageBand. Playback doesn't lie. With the emotional energy of the audience, it may or may not be as remarkable as you remember it being. However, any source of recording is a valuable rehearsal, songwriting, and performance tool. Record your shows and listen back - you may be astonished at what you hear, both good and bad (ha).

DISTRIBUTION

At this point we should quickly get acquainted with the distribution companies collectively referred to as the Three Majors: *Universal Music Group, Sony Music,* and *Warner Music Group.* Each of these three publicly traded companies also own and operate so-called indie distribution companies. They are:

- Universal -w- Virgin Music Label and Artist Services & Signup
- Sony -w- The Orchard, and most recently AWAL
- Warner -w- ADA

These major owned *indie* distribution companies predominantly work only with indie labels and will occasionally make an exception to accommodate an "established artist." In addition to the distribution companies themselves, there exists a plethora of record labels owned by the Majors. Needless to say, if you or the label you are signed to have a distribution deal in place with either one of these distribution companies or signed to a label having a "pass through" distribution deal, then your distribution partner is predetermined. However, if you're an indie artist, the three majors and these major owned independent distributors are likely not an option for you . . . yet.

Assuming you have no offer on the table from label, and assuming that to be the case, it's time to explore your distribution options. There are a number of highly capable and affordable alternatives in providing distribution for you and your music (or podcast). It will be up to you to research the various digital distribution companies and select one as your distribution partner. They vary based on release fee, commission rate, annual fee, etc. In many ways they are all equally adept and fully capable of what they do including reformatting your WAV file to the required file format of the various MSSs (Tidal, Amazon, Apple, Spotify, etc.). There are numerous resources for comparison studies. Conduct your own research to determine which platform is best suited for you. [see RESOURCES].

One editorial comment – as all the distribution platforms perform a nearly identical function, and although there may be exceptions, we've yet to learn of an artist "making it" by attributing their success to their digital distribution company. At any rate, we will move on and discuss strategies with the various digital streaming services (DSS), namely - Spotify.

SPOTIFY AND THE OTHERS DIGITAL SERVICE PROVIDERS (DSPS)

Thanks to the numerous advancements in technology over the last couple decades, we can now enjoy the entire history of recorded music, immediately at our fingertips whenever we'd like (internet connection permitting). This capability is largely provided by companies referred to as Digital Service Providers or Music Streaming Platforms (also referred to as DSPs or MSSs, respectively). There are numerous consumer comparison studies available, based on fidelity, library, playlists, algorithms, etc. Like distribution platforms, they do what they do succinctly and with perfection, ultimately the choice of MSS is left up to the consumer.

As evidenced by consistent trends of the past several years, overall streaming revenue is increasing as streaming is undoubtedly the preferred choice of format for the casual music fan. Sony's recent 3rd quarter, 2022 results further illustrate this trend with the company posting an additional 1.3 billion dollars in revenue with streaming accounting for 37% of the growth over the same period in the previous year. Keep in mind this phenomenon of music consumption via streaming services is popular throughout the world. To further illustrate our point, the benchmark which has recently been achieved is somewhat astonishing. Collectively the Majors are generating over $1 million dollars an hour in streaming revenue. [Source: Music Business Worldwide]

There is one MSS platform that has created more artist friendly tools and is the benchmark by which all basic analytics are measured. And that streaming service is Spotify. Therefore, it's imperative that you know some Spotify basics.

One of the most important Spotify basics to understand is playlisting. There exist several different types of Spotify Playlists. The primary ones being:
* Listener Playlists
* Spotify Editorial Playlists
* Spotify Algorithmic Playlists

LISTENER PLAYLISTS

Listener or user-generated Playlists – are playlists that are user-generated which are curated by any individual, including yourself. Remember that anyone with a Spotify account can create as many playlists as they like. We make this distinction, as you, as an artist or brand should create at minimum two (2) playlists.

Playlist A – comprised of only your music
Playlist B – various artists

Spotify algorithms prefer a playlist with no fewer than 20 songs and no more than 60. 25-30 songs seem to be the sweet spot. Build a playlist around your musical interests. The playlist could include bands you've played with, tracks you've played on or bands you've toured with. Promote your friends' projects. Many playlists today focus not on a genre but rather a mood. You know the kind; jazz for a rainy afternoon, dinner party music, workout music, et al. Be enthusiastic about the playlists you'll make. Have a passion and take pride in your playlist. Update your playlists on a regular schedule. To make a playlist that's worth following, it should be dynamic and change over time. Otherwise, a fan will listen once and be done with it. Make the playlist diverse and interesting, with surprises. The Spotify algorithms will downgrade a playlist that is too heavily artist centric, so keep it restricted to one track per artist. Choose a day each week to make updates. If the updates are significant enough you may announce via SM, email, etc. Wouldn't it be great if you built an audience that returned every week, like your own New Release radar that is laser focused. When a fan adds a track from your playlist to one of their own, Spotify's algorithms take notice.

Change it often by adding and deleting tracks. Connect with the artists that you're putting on your playlist. Have them share it on their social media to gain more followers on your playlist and build a long-lasting relationship with their followers and community. This can allow you to build your own following as well. Be sure to sneak your releases into the playlist whenever they come out so the other artists' followers can add to your listener count. Once you grow your Playlist's following, you can then upload it to SubmitHub and make some extra, easy revenue. Keep in mind you can feature your playlist on your Artist Profile; more on that later.

SPOTIFY EDITORIAL PLAYLISTS

A Spotify Editorial Playlist is 100% human curated by the Spotify editorial team. Most are genre or mood specific such as Yacht Rock, Hot Hits, etc. Being added to one of Spotify's editorial playlists such as Rap Caviar, Fresh Finds, Viva Latino or Today's Top Hits is huge! If your track is selected for a major playlist your music is being introduced to potentially thousands (or millions) of like-minded fans.

Many of the editorial playlists, have a massive audience and placement on one of these most-popular playlists will have a direct correlation to a formidable increase in streams. Often these placements are established from connections with the editorial team through labels, publishing companies, PR companies, etc. However, any artist can pitch their songs to the general editorial team through their Spotify Artist Account. They prefer you pitch no less than a month ahead of the release. Though, the odds of getting selected are slim, it could be a make-or-break moment in an artist's career.

ALGORITHMIC PLAYLISTS

Algorithmic Playlists – are updated weekly and as they are algorithmically created. No two playlists are alike. Popular examples of these playlists are Release Radar and Discover Weekly. The playlist is curated by the algorithms based on an each individual's music listening habits, trends, artists, and genres. In the case of Release Radar, it's based on the artists that you're following, and you when they release new music it included in the playlist. Essentially, no two fans' algorithmic playlists will be alike. Each playlist is unique to that user.

Should your track be added to a user's Discover Weekly customized playlist, then you are on the road to music discovery by potential new fans.

COLLABORATIVE PLAYLISTS

You can create a new playlist or use an existing playlist to designate it as a *collaborative playlist*. Once you declare you have a collaborative playlist, you can invite others by sharing the link via app or messaging. They too can then add their favorite track(s) to the list. And when they do, there name will appear. It's kind of like making a group mixtape.

Streaming has and will continues to see greater growth in the coming years. Claim your Profile, add a Canvas, and get in the game to generate revenue and build your fan base.

PROMOTING YOUR SINGLE

Awareness is key. It's all about making the core fans from your database and social media posts aware of your forthcoming release. It's essential that you set this up within a week or two of public awareness and build anticipation. Curators and bloggers are only interested in breaking new music. They are the purveyors, and they provide "recommendations." Connect with bloggers through SubmitHub and then connect with other bloggers 1 on 1. Do a Google search for them and find their website and contact information. Leave them a message and introduce yourself. Include a link to your website, making it easy for them to check you out. Once you've established yourself on a select few targeted bloggers radars, send them music early: 2-4 weeks in advance of the release. It's imperative you provide them with music well before the release date. Bloggers will only write about new releases. Direct Message (DM) bloggers that you like on Instagram or Facebook or reach out through an email (the latter is much more preferred). DMs are likely more appropriate for much smaller blogs, don't slide into Billboard's DMs, you'll just look unprofessional. Don't reach out asking for something right away. Compliment their work, share their reviews on social media, send them other people's music that you feel would fit their writing style. Develop a relationship. Once you develop a relationship with a blogger, you can then expect better, more detailed reviews, and have them more frequently. Their audience will recognize that you've become a favorite of the blog and are more likely to follow you then they would if they had just written a little-effort post about some random musician, one time.

Create a Press Release to coincide with the release of each single. It's fair to assume that outside of your core fan base, bloggers and reviewers may not be at all familiar with you. Provide some insight and background about the track. Where was it recorded, who engineered and produced it? Aside from uploading it to your distributor, be sure to enter the metadata with your PRO, SoundExchange, and SongTrust (if applicable) and the MLC.

Once again, think about what you can do to get noticed in spite of all of the clutter. Utilize your database and email your fans and industry contacts prior to the release. Hold a listening party on Zoom, promote the single on social media, write a blog post about the track (which could mirror your press release). Arrange for an in-store performance at an intimate venue like a local indie record store or coffee shop, who may be appreciative and receptive to the idea (especially when trying to bring back traffic after Covid). Go out into a public place with a lot of foot-traffic and hand out posters, publicizing your latest single. Make sure it has a QR code on it so that it will be quick and easy to scan and check out. Play at a local house party, somewhere where people will be receptive and excited for your new music. Make a dance challenge for the single, by creating some choreography for the music, and uploading it to TikTok and Instagram. Make a contest out of it and have fans submit their versions or interpretations of the dance. Have a prize of like $100 (it doesn't have to be a lot) and tell people you'll pick and announce your favorite version. They can enter the contest by tagging you and posting the video on Instagram. It could allow for your song to become the next big thing on social media.

If you're making your own tracks, understand trends. There are no long intros. People are impatient and are one click away from skipping to the next track. Consider putting the hook out front, (the Beatles did it) and have a bridge. If you're making pop tunes, it's best to keep it under 3-4 minutes. Jazz and classical, gospel, house, etc. are the exceptions. A word of advice, only use expletives in your lyrics when necessary and appropriate. Anyone can release a track full of them. Expletives are not necessarily an advantage unless they are juxtaposed as part of the musical expression.

ARTWORK

Like at a major label, the artwork is often due before the Master. Do not think about uploading your WAV file without finished and approved artwork from all parties involved. A JPG or PNG file that measures 3,000 x 3,000 seems to be preferred.

SPOTIFY FOR ARTISTS

Let's give credit where credit is due. Spotify essentially eviscerated illegal file sharing of music and monetized on demand streaming. Who would have believed, one could possess nearly all the world's music, instantly playable on a smartphone, or any connected device? The downside is the controversy that exists whether Spotify is compensating creators properly (what is deserved)? While Ed Sheeran became the first billion-dollar earner from the streaming service, the vast majority of the music on Spotify does not generate enough revenue for artists to make a living. And yes, there are a few hundred, even a thousand making more than a million dollars a year, but the percentile is not altogether different from the income inequality in America.

A & R departments are constantly researching and monitoring an artist getting a million streams per week. They are few and far between, so it may be best to have less lofty goals. In nearly all instances, the artists themselves, not management if they had any, were not planning on this viral hit. All that you can do is create at the top of your ability, make music that you believe speaks to an audience / that has a community. Then mix / master, have your artwork and credits together, and upload your track.

Remember, before you can claim your Artist Profile on Spotify, you need to release a single. If you think you have a hit record, it may be best to hold that back and release your 2nd favorite track in an effort to first claim your Spotify Artist Profile.

Once verified as a Spotify Artist, think of this as your *homepage*. This is what people will see when they click on your profile in a search. Be sure to;
• Add a header image
• Add a short bio
• Integrate your concert calendar
• Embed a Shopify link and sell your top 3 merch items, and;
• Sell tickets

Artist Pick is where you have the ability to promote a new track, album, playlist, or concert for a fourteen-day period. Make sure you have a good picture to go with it (album/track artwork, a photo from your last show, etc.). Like all the picture options on Spotify for Artists, you will have to follow the exact specifications they require.

Spotify has even partnered with fundraising platforms including GoFundMe and PayPal.Me to provide a link on your Artist page to raise funds for your band, crew, cause, or organization you support.

Once you can claim your profile, you need to upload a profile pic (as well as the header image and image gallery), a brief bio, and integrate your calendar, social media, and merch store (with Shopify).

Now that you have a Spotify Artist profile, take the simplest of steps and embed the link to your new blog post, share on social media, and ask your friends to follow you on Spotify. Run a *Pre-Save Campaign* where you can alert your fans two weeks in advance to save your new single so that it hits their playlists on the day of release. This is a *Pre-Save Campaign*. And our best advice is to always initiate one. Your distributor may be able to provide further assistance in this strategy. Make sure you get people to pre-save your single. Artists constantly overlook the power of the pre-save campaign, but it is an option and it's genuinely helpful. Not only is this another excuse to promote your single prior to the release, but it also allows Spotify to know which new releases already have a lot of attention, even prior to their release. If Spotify sees that there are a lot of people waiting to hear the release, they're more likely to have their algorithm step in or add it to a playlist. Pre-Saves also notify people directly when it is available.

It may be obvious but ask your fans on social media to "follow" you on Spotify. In addition to plays, artist managers, labels, venues, and Spotify curators will look at your Monthly Listeners (as well as your social media, website, upcoming concerts, or anything else that you have integrated into the page). This illustrates the point as to the importance of having a reasonable number of Monthly Listeners. Get everyone you can to follow you on Spotify. Email friends and family. Copy and share an artist link or embed code in SMS to Facebook, Messenger, Twitter, et al. After a couple of weeks, or periodically, repeat this process – ask your fans to follow your Artist profile on Spotify via social media, emails, and texts. This way it's likely your fans will be notified of updates when you release new music.

Add the Spotify embed plug-in to your home page. Then ask your friends to follow you on Spotify. At a show, ask your fans to get out their phones and follow you on Spotify. Announce your own playlist and ask them to check it out and comment.

Have a link-tree to all MSS of your track or Artist Page on the homepage of your website. Post this Spotify link in your YouTube video descriptions, Twitter bio, the "about" section of your band's Facebook page, Instagram bio, and LinkedIn page. Encourage your fans, family, friends, and featured artists to share your own playlist containing your influences and new music discovery with their friends.

Don't be bashful, ask your friends, colleagues, and other artists to "follow" you on Spotify. It's the single most important thing you can do to help your streaming numbers.

So how do you get on a Spotify playlist? After you have claimed your Artist Profile in conjunction with your distribution partner, make the track available to Spotify 2-4 weeks prior to the actual release date. Don't concentrate on big numbers, only focus on building your play counts, followers, and monthly listeners consistently. Just like outlined previously, don't disappear from your fans. When you release a track, be prepared to follow it up with another within a reasonable amount of time. A window between releases of twelve, perhaps even six months is totally unacceptable. You can't keep a fanbase engaged if you are not releasing music.

If you're considering the services of an independent promoter to help you grow your streaming numbers or if you're approached by a promoter, proceed with caution. Especially if you're being offered a guaranteed increased in Spotify plays. Spotify as an organization has been vocal regarding its feelings about artists' hiring a 3rd party promotion company to increase plays. Spotify's Co-Head of Music Strategy, Jeremy Erlich, has stated: "I hate it. They're just scamming artists. There's absolutely no promo in the streaming world. We don't talk to any of these people at all. They're a scam."

SHOPIFY FOR SPOTIFY

Spotify has partnered with one of the most popular CMS retail platforms on the internet, Shopify. So even if you have a Bandzoogle website integrated with Printful, you should still build a Shopify merch store out to integrate your merch opportunities with Spotify. Once integrated you will be able to see and control the merchandise you are offering.

TICKET SALES VIA SPOTIFY

You can list concerts and festivals, if you are listed (publicly, not privately) on one of their ticketing platform partners including: Ticketmaster, songkick, Eventbrite, AXS, and StageIt. The integration is seamless and to your distinct advantage. Once listed, Spotify will send recommendation emails to fans based on their location and what music they're into.

CANVAS FOR SPOTIFY

Spotify for Artists \ Canvas allows you the ability to have 8 seconds of seamless looped video – in place of your static album art. It's album artwork on steroids. And the results are compelling. This could be a cool (relevant) picture, a snippet from a music video or live-show recap, or some trippy visuals (just make sure whatever you use, you're legally able to do so). Regardless of what you use, Spotify's algorithm will love you for it. This is a visual format, keep in mind there is no need to add captions or credits as that's already provided in the metadata for the user.

There's little or no doubt that adding a video roll / Spotify Canvas can increase shares, playlist adds, streams, and profile visits.

Your Spotify Canvas should meet these requirements:
* 9:16 ratio (vertical)
* At least 720px tall
* An MP4 or JPEG file
* 3s to 8s long (MP4 only)
* Choose a video from your camera roll
* Edit to 3-8 seconds

A STRATEGY FOR SPOTIFY

The most important thing you can do to influence the algorithms is to concentrate on having more fans follow you on Spotify. Make this your top priority in your strategy with Spotify.

Utilize social media, messaging, and embed the Spotify Artist profile link in your social media landing page.

Keep in mind that when sharing a link to a single, that fans will only hear that one track of yours and the algorithms will play a completely different artist next. Instead, send links to your Playlist A, made up of only your music.

Because playlists are so important in this process, identify a few playlists in which your music would be a perfect fit and that have a significant number of followers. Follow these playlists. Follow them on social media, leave comments, and read their blogs. Try to make yourself known to them and get on their radar. Consider contacting the playlist creator to see if they might be receptive to hearing your music and possibly adding it to their playlist. Once again, a Google search can be helpful. You'd be surprised what you can learn about a Spotify playlist in a Google Search. Approach them the same as you would a talent buyer with a polite, succinct message and the link to your track. If they pass on adding your track, don't be discouraged. What-ever you do don't unfollow them. It's about relationship building and good will. Approach them the next time you release a track. This time with the advantage of having a relationship with the playlist creator. You just might get added. Don't be bashful, ask your friends, colleagues, and other artists to "follow" you on Spotify. It's the single most important thing you can do to help your streaming numbers.

RESOURCES

12 of The Best Music Distribution Services in 2022
Best Music Distribution Companies – Full Comparison Chart – Ari's Take
How To Release Music on Spotify (Step-by-Step Process)
CD Baby RELEASE PLAN
Spotify for Artists

13

VISUAL & MIXED MEDIA

It may have all started on Twitter with a tweet from Justin Bieber or was it *Call Me Maybe, by Carly Rae Jepsen* that transported them and countless others into becoming YouTube sensations. YouTube launched in 2005 and the gold rush was on, with dozens of aspiring artists uploading videos of cover songs and their original compositions. We're all aware that Justin Bieber was discovered via a cover song on YouTube that caught the eye of Usher who then in turn signed a Management deal with Scooter Braun. In 2010 Abel Tesfaye (better known as The Weeknd) began posting R & B tunes which went viral landing him a record deal with XO, a Canadian label. At just 15 years of age, another Canadian pop idol, Shawn Mendes blew up with MTV naming him a *YouTube Sensation.* Others that started out their careers posting videos to YouTube which eventually got them noticed include: Soulja Boy, Ed Sheeran, Post Malone, 5 Seconds of Summer, and Charlie Puth. All of which illustrate that the visual media component can be paramount in building a career or at the least, complimenting your music strategy.

Visual media for music has existed well in advance of artists such as Elvis Presley and the Beatles. Technically the first music video ever recorded was just prior to the 1900s by the Edison Company. Once sound could be properly synched to film, numerous musicals, operas, as well as big band performances were documented, including the making of the 1927 movie, *The Jazz Singer* starring Al Jolson. Films were then captured in concert settings such as the 1962 *Newport Jazz Festival*, Ray Charles: "Live In Paris (1968), *Woodstock*, Bob Dylan's *Rolling Thunder Revue* (1976), and Led Zeppelin's "Live in Seattle 1977." Bands then envisioned conceptual pieces such as The Beatles "Help," Elvis starred in more than 30 motion pictures, with the ultimate music motion picture being Prince's, "Purple Rain." The big era of music videos were cultivated with the debut of MTV (a 24/7 music video format). The first video ever played on the network was *Video Killed the Radio Star* by the Buggles. The network created "video stars" with legendary videos from Michael Jackson, Duran Duran, Madonna, even Nirvana and then catapulted previously local L.A. hair bands (Poison, Twisted Sister, Motley Crüe) into overnight sensations. Artists, bands, and labels alike realized music video was a powerful medium for connecting with fans.

You may be creating visual media suitable for social media platforms such as Instagram or TikTok on your smartphone, or Go Pro. While not ideal, if shot and edited properly, it can be adequate. Filmmakers are shooting motion pictures on smartphones - so it makes sense that you should be able to do the same for your next music video. If, however you have a budget and a production crew of any size or budget to shoot a music video, our advice is to take the opportunity to not only create one (1), three (3) minute music video, but also to conduct filmed interviews on-set with the artist or band, the Director, and the crew. You can use this interview footage as a teaser film in advance of the release of the single and video. Once everything is properly edited and you have your three-minute music video, take the time to edit this down as well. You can edit the three-minute video down for a Spotify Canvas, an Instagram Reel, TikTok video, or a 60 second YouTube Short. In other words, rather than simply uploading the music video to your YouTube channel, you should edit the content to propagate all of your social media formats with consistent messaging and branding.

YOUTUBE

Although they offer one of the lowest if not *the* lowest rates paid to artists in the industry per stream, YouTube has made many strides in making an effort to be artist friendly. Our perspective is this: at one point, prior to the advent of social media and the music streaming services, YouTube had far more influence on music. Since that time, it has evolved into a platform for major established artists who announce their newest video to their fan base. For the rest of us it remains a challenge to break through the clutter of music, competing with big budget music videos, comedians, and internet personalities/influencers. Not to mention, competing with the sheer amount of content on the platform.

As of February 2020, more than 500 hours of video were uploaded to YouTube every minute. This equates to approximately 30,000 hours of newly uploaded content per hour. Talk about clutter. The amount of content on YouTube has increased dramatically as consumer's appetites for online video has grown. In fact, the number of video content hours uploaded every 60 seconds grew by around 40 percent between 2014 and 2020. [Source: Statista]

At one point, having a million YouTube views was meaningful. Today however, the service has morphed more into a platform for blowing-up views of established artists' newest debut video. There seems to be no clear-cut pathway for cultivating developing artists on the platform. Artists no longer "break" on YouTube. The platform itself has transitioned into a streaming platform (YouTube TV) offering 85 television networks, on demand video and cloud-based DVR as well as YouTube Music. However, this does not change the obvious, that you should claim your *YouTube Artist Channel* and utilize their servers as a repository for your video content. Claim and create your YouTube Artist Channel.

There's no advantage to housing a video of any kind on your server, whether a songwriting session, a guided tour of your bus, or a band members birthday party on the road, YouTube is your de facto video upload platform. The platform encourages likes, subscriptions, and provides code for embeds and sharing for your fans. Plus, if you embed it on your website, the total plays accumulate on YouTube.

There was a period in time in which labels and artists alike, invested significant amounts of money into video production (Guns N' Roses "Estranged" @ $7.6 million, Michael & Janet Jackson, Scream @ 12.7 million, Madonna, "Express Yourself @ 10.9 Million). This strategy seems to no longer be a key component of a track blowing up. In other words, don't invest much in the video, but do make one. The viral, cheap production may actually find an audience before the slickly produced $40K to $100K music video. Over time, you can increase your budget, to make higher quality videos. By then, you'll hopefully have garnered a large audience that will appreciate them.

The bottom line, no (or shall we say few) musical acts are breaking on YouTube, currently. It's a fabulous platform for major artists to rack up several million views, yet for the most part, the streams don't rival that of the other streaming platforms.

However, it's a great repository for an artist. – claim.

Your Artist Channel – which should include:
- Header image
- A profile / short bio
- Connect your social media feeds
- Embed a link to your website

YouTube is another platform that is a free resource in which you can upload media and potentially derive modest revenue.

TIKTOK

You may have heard the news that for the third year in a row, TikTok is the most downloaded app in the world. According to Statista, as of January 2022 TikTok had a billion users. To put that in perspective, Spotify has less than 400 million subscribers worldwide. Not surprisingly, TikTok's demographics by age group skew young with approximately 48% of the users under 30. It's also interesting to note that approximately 60% of the platform's users are female and the Gen Z audience has now surpassed Instagram's audience size. [Source: Statista]

Let's call it what it is, TikTok is BIG. You might recall, the first video to go viral on TikTok was a simple break dance. Today the content consists of everything from scientific experiments to the most random content you could imagine. Yet what remains constant is the music bed. TikTok creators often utilize music or soundbites to invoke their message. As an example, think of a broken-down truck on the side of the road, a man on a skateboard drinking Ocean Spray cranberry juice while lip-synching Stevie Nicks vocals to the music bed *Dreams* by Fleetwood Mac (originally release in 1977). Without the music, the video would be nonsensical. Before the video was uploaded, *Dreams* was averaging 49,000 streams a day. In the three days after the clip landed on TikTok, those streams rocketed to an average of 105,000 times a day (via *Rolling Stone*). Sales of the song went up by 184%, while Spotify stated that streams of *Dreams* on their platform had increased by 127% with a 242% increase in first-time listeners of the song. Apple reported a spike of 221% in the songs streams, while there was also a 1,137% increase in Shazam requests for the song.[Source: NME.com]

TikTok truly can be the perfect digital funnel in fan engagement.

As of February 2022, dancer Charli D'Amelio was the most followed content creator on TikTok, with 136.6 million worldwide followers. Influencer Khabane Lame followed closely in second position with 132.6 million followers and singer Bella Poarch ranked third, with a total of 88 million followers. [Source: Statista]

These numbers are simply staggering. It's estimated that the top annual earnings for TikTok video creators can range from $8-18 million dollars annually. Earnings include advertising revenue, appearances, as well as sponsored content. Additionally, many influencers are able to use their brand to advance into different businesses or facets of their career including but not limited to: cosmetic lines, clothing brands, TV Show/Podcast/Secondary Media channels, or even . . . a music career.

It's highly rumored that Major labels are paying influencers and TikTokers with big bucks upfront to include the music from an artist on their roster in the influencer's reels. So, assuming this to be true, it may be the most recent form of *payola*. You may remember *payola*, the banned transaction of cash and gifts in return for radio airplay or pay-for-play. TikTok cannot be ignored as one potential pathway to making money for the music business. It does seem to be, however, the luck of the draw. The infamous story of a guy whose band had been dropped from their major label only to discover Spotify plays increasing to numbers previously unforeseen when the album was initially released four years ago. The "culprit," a TikToker who incorporated the band's 4-year-old song as the music bed in his TikTok short. As is often the case, and following suit, the song was then shared and used in other TikToker's videos (often following a trend created in the initial video). This provided for even more exposure and corresponding streams on Spotify.

What's interesting to understand is the music which goes viral on TikTok does not necessarily have to be a new release. Creators are discovering these tracks whether they're brand new or have been in their libraries as favorites for years. Now there is an opportunity to create entertaining short form media with the music in the foreground. Across the entire platform, music is a vital component of creators' tools. Influencers, fashion, comedy, and entertainment incorporate music in their shorts, to the extent that 88% of users and top performing videos include music. [Source: Tik Tok What's Next Report 2022]

In speaking with artists and hearing testimony, one begins to understand the value of TikTok. Essentially, in a matter of days, the perfect viral video can propel a wannabe into an overnight sensation. The Major labels first utilized TikTok, (as they did YouTube) as a discovery medium for up-and-coming potential talent. Today, the Majors are even more shrewd in their strategic marketing with the platform, paying significant sums of money to influencers to include a specific track from a forthcoming release in their reels. As a side note, now even the little man (individuals or small organizations) can attempt to level the playing field utilizing SubmitHub's new "Influencer" option. Another strategy being employed by indie labels is to actually sign an influencer to the label roster; not for their musical aptitude, singing ability or talent but rather to gain access to the millions of followers of the *influencer*. Recognizing that the influencer is not a singer, they then engage and employ the talents of professional songwriters and producers to create a track that the internet sensation can then broadcast to their legions of fans. Let's assume, the TikTok star receives 5 million views of the song, a sizable portion of those fans then shift to Spotify to discover other tracks by said artist, only to discover there may be no other tracks, or in many instances, the other tracks are sub-par. Let's say a Spotify Playlister having 800,000 followers might consider adding the one track to their popular playlist, not necessarily on musical merit, but rather to gain access to a portion of that influencer's audience.

In the world of visual media, you're not just competing with music videos and concerts, but you're competing with attention from restaurants offering traditional pasta recipes as a commercial, Chipotle partnering with influencer David Dobrik in a paid marketing campaign, local business promoting their new location, product demonstrations set to music, and other whimsical, and/or entertaining content.

From Rome, Italy, *Manaskin* and Chicago-bred *The Walters* are just two of the artists who have skyrocketed to fame and signed major label deals as a result of blowing up on TikTok. So, what do their metrics look like in order for a TikTok creator to be noticed by a label. One case study we have looked into is that of a relatively unknown artist that blew up on TikTok, which then transferred into 300 million Spotify plays (nearly all of them on one track of a 4 track EP). A bidding war amongst six major associated labels ensued, with the artist ultimately being offered and signing a deal, with an Advance of a million dollars and a $500,000 recording fund. The "artist" had never even performed live. According to a senior manager of artist relations at Spotify, she estimates that over 70 artists have been signed by labels after going viral on the platform. [Source: Variety]

TikTok, however, is not without its critics. Take for example the singer songwriter, Halsey, who honed their craft prior to the advent of TikTok. Based on talent and serious obstacles and challenges she had overcome, and by sheer determination was discovered and signed to a major label. Then asked by the label to create a TikTok, she rebuked. There has also been speculation that the conversion rate of these so called TikTok "artists" signed to major label deals turning into full-fledged rock-stars may be ridiculously low.

Looking for comparable stats? After gaining a million followers on TikTok, Nessa Barrett was signed by Warner Brothers Records. Her social media metrics since that time are in the range of;

- TikTok Followers - 18.1 million
- YouTube subscribers - 1.05 million
- Twitter Followers - 2 million
- Instagram followers - 6.6 million
- Spotify: 3.4 million Monthly Listeners with her top song at 5.3 million views
- 120,000 video usages

So, assuming Warner Brothers paid her the going TikTok rate, an advance of a million dollars and a recording fund of half a million, was this a smart signing. Let's take the Spotify numbers alone and do the math. With over 2.5 million combined streams of her top 5 tracks at .005 per stream = $12,500.

Then there's Jenna Rain. Her story is that her father invested in his daughter beginning at the age of 12 spending three grand a month with a social media marketing firm. By the time she turned 17, she had a record deal with Warner Brothers, again with a million-dollar advance and a $500,000 recording fund and now managed by Scooter Braun.

The key strategy you should invoke and promote, is the "sharing" of your track for other creators. Accumulating five one week, then three the next. The key strategy is to get other "TikTok creators" to incorporate your music track as a music bed in their creation. This is known as a *usage*. The secret sauce to TikTok is it's all about the usages. Essentially the end game is to forgo synch licenses with the residuals being the discovery of the creator, translating into Spotify plays. Building a house or baking a cake on TikTok with your song in the background also counts as a play. This strategy is especially useful if the creator uses your song in a video sensation that becomes a trend, with your song being the key identifier of the trend when other creators do it. This could mean your song is in the background of a dance that becomes popular through TikTok or could even be related in a more random sense, such as the Cranberry Juice-Fleetwood Mac example we mentioned earlier. If someone drinks cranberry juice on a skateboard, the first thing people are expecting to hear is *Dreams*, otherwise the person would just look (I understand this will sound ironic but) silly.

Let's take a look at Jaymes Young, with an astounding 18 million monthly listeners on Spotify. How did it happen? He has less than 25,000 Twitter followers and 125,000 Facebook followers. Yet nearly 100 million Instagram fans. Interestingly enough, he has over 800,000 subscribers on YouTube. He created the Infinity TikTok challenge, and as a result, the song has 5.2 million usages! So, what might we attribute Jaymes Young's success to? How about TikTok usages. All of these combined metrics earned him an Atlantic Records recording contract.

Recently TikTok announced a wholly owned music marketing and distribution platform (to compete with CD Baby, DistroKid, etc.) called SoundON. The distribution service allows users to upload audio tracks and receive royalties (albeit a minuscule per stream rate). Now anyone can upload audio offering your track to anyone wishing to use it.

If you're interested in cracking the code on being a TikTok star, simply search Google and you'll find dozens of content creators who claim to have found the answer. In the fast-food franchise business, the consistency of burgers and fries in every restaurant in the chain is paramount. What you'll discover is this ain't Burger King. There is no fool proof recipe for TikTok or going viral.

INSTAGRAM REELS

Once you've discovered a TikTok artist and would like to learn more, Instagram seems to be the next most logical platform in which to explore and learn more about one's favorite topic, influencer, hobby, or maybe even music. Today, regarding music it has migrated to TikTok first. TikTokers who want to know more about someone, next migrate to their Instagram Profile to learn more about them. Although a great proportion of Instagram Reels' content are brought over from TikTok, or are rather just uploaded to both, don't under-estimate the power of using Instagram reels for growing your brand image. If you're a producer, make a 1-minute beat, and film yourself making the individual layers of the beat, in a creative way. Make a quick 1-minute cover or tease your next single with a short, acoustic, sneak peek. For many artists, Instagram will be the first-place people will look after discovering you (whether it be at a gig, on Spotify, meeting at a networking event, or at school, etc.). Having stimulated short form media, along with engaging images, will be important in building up your Instagram profile. The importance of Instagram in digital networking is huge. People in your digital network, might look through their Instagram when looking for an artist, producer, musician, or songwriter for a specific project. Showing off your skills on Instagram might just land you a gig, partnership, or collaboration. Additionally, it allows for another way for people to discover you, via Instagram's discover page and via algorithms as well.

WEB 3 AND NFTS

A hot topic in technology and certainly the music industry is the potential of the "future of the internet" or Web3. It refers to blockchain technology that could overhaul how the internet works in many ways including how and where information/data is stored, how its accessed, and who has ownership of it. Web 3 is decentralized and a blockchain is a system that records transactions made in cryptocurrency. A prominent cryptocurrency is Bitcoin, like physical currency has value from one user to the next. Each Bitcoin can be exchanged or traded for one another. An NFT is a non-fungible token. It works in the same way as a cryptocurrency however NFTs represent a real asset; essentially an original copy of digital file. The vast majority of NFTs are in the form of jpegs. As each item and transaction are recorded on the block chain, it ensures authenticity and ownership. NFTS represent a new way for fans to connect with artists with creators (both relatively unknown to the biggest names in music) creating innovative content on the blockchain. There is a great deal of intrigue, interest and perhaps even a bit of skepticism regarding NFTs, however.

Music artists have begun to test the waters with NFTs to distribute music/albums. In 2021, Canadian rap artist Tory Lanez released an NFT album, "When it's Dark" that was controversial due to technology issues related to transactions for the album and claims made by the rapper regarding its value. In 2022, Snoop Dogg acquired Death Row Records with plans for all future releases to be NFTs.

The real question is whether blockchain technology and digital assets such as NFTs are viable in the music industry. Many believe the opportunities are significant and we are now seeing the initial trials of the technology by artists and record labels. There are many examples but a notable one is crypto rapper Spottie Wifi. An early adopter of cryptocurrency and aspiring rap artist Mig Mora used his Cyberpunk NFT as the image for his alter ego named Spottie Wifi He released a seven song EP as an NFT limited to 2000 copies. Each copy had a mystery NFT which also included sync rights to the master recordings, or the ability to license those recordings for sync purposes in films, TV shows, or commercials and profit from those licenses. The album sold out in 90 seconds and earned over $190,000.

Keep an eye on how music artists and labels are using this technology and see if you can find a fit for yourself or the artists you may represent.

RESOURCES

YouTube Creators
TikTok: For Business
How To Market Your Music Online | How to Build a Fanbase from scratch - Adam Ivy
YouTube Music Certification
What Is Web 3? / Harvard Business Review
OpenSea - the world's largest NFT marketplace

14

THE MARKETING PLAN

Everything presented thus far in the book has been in preparation for developing a marketing plan. A marketing plan is an essential component to any new release. Whether that be a single, an EP, or a full album. As discussed earlier in the book, a lack of adequate thought going into the actual marketing of the release is often where artists fall short. Spending a significant amount of time, energy, and money creating music but then in-turn, releasing it to the world with little or no strategy. It's imperative *you* make people aware of your new release, via social media, email, et al. and encourage them to: listen / like / view / share. It's also somewhat unimaginable, if you haven't' given any thought to investing (spending) some money on your new single.

Here's a couple of typically conceived perspectives on releasing a single:

> *"My stuff is da bomb, that's all there is too it. Like I need a Marketing Plan. I'm going to upload this WAV file this Friday and the world will discover it and I'll be a viral sensation and make a million bucks."* OR:

> *"I've got a new track we believe in, we have a final mix, we have to master it, and I need some sort of a strategy or a plan before I can release this."*

There was a time when the brunt of the marketing and promotion of music was solely the responsibility of the record label. The music business hasn't worked that way in a long time. Today it's up to you to forge a pathway through all the clutter, and the best way to do that is to outline (write down) a strategy of getting from point A to point B. In business, a Marketing Plan is conceived and executed when launching any new product.

Accompanying the set-up of a Major Label release is a 10–14-page compressive marketing plan. These are highly confidential plans, yet delineate, the who, what, when, where and most importantly how to accomplish the targeted strategic objectives. The planning includes activities prior to, upon release, and 30-60 days after the release. The VP of Marketing at a Major Label is responsible for seeing that this doc gets created. The document includes a confidential list of contact information for the staff involved at the label as well as identifying the independent publicist, digital marketing firm, promotion firm, and other qualified designated / hired 3rd parties to assist in the promotion and marketing of the project. While it may not be necessary for you to create such a comprehensive document, at the very least, identify targets and objectives (KPIs), and create a timeline for the release of a single, an EP or a full album.

Be prepared to do some research in preparing your marketing plan. It may be prudent to research an artist in your market or a market of a similar size that is not yet a household name but has metrics which exceed yours such as higher sales or streams, larger live audiences, more social media followers or chart position. Think of this artist as your friendly competition. Your KPIs for this project should include goals that equal or exceed your competitor's metrics. Don't set yourself up for disappointment, thinking you can equate the success of a huge artist like Jay-Z on this release. In other words, keep it realistic.

Consider the following in your research:
* What are their top five markets?
* What is their social media platform(s) of choice?
* Check out their website design
* Do they have a fan club?
* What are their YouTube subscribers and views?
* Check out their playlists
* What is their number of monthly listeners?
* Do they have financing?
* Are they making money, and how?
* Are they a viral sensation, and if so, what platform?
* What size of venues are they playing?

Use the information you gather and consider it when developing tactics for your own marketing plan. While much of what is presented in this book is meant to aid you in formulating strategy to achieve your goals, there is also an emphasis on exactly how you will achieve these goals.

1. Think of the marketing plan as a detailed plan that involves specific KPIs, target audience and strategy.
2. Then describe the specific tactics you will implement in achieving those goals.

The former is *strategic marketing,* and the latter is *tactical marketing.* Aside from a necessary timeline, state the individuals on your team, their contact information, and their responsibilities. You may be approaching your project on your own or with little support – and if this is so - find a team, or at the very least a partner or two.

Construct a marketing plan to address the following:

- Goals - based on realistic expectations including: activities, statistics, any publicity, advertising spend, shows / touring, social media advertising, etc.
- Consider utilizing grass roots techniques that can be realistically executed or implemented. Flyers or handouts announcing any live performances or direct messaging your contact list
- Creativity and thinking outside the box are a big +
- Budget: (however big or small) You determine how much you need, but remember you are hoping the project will be financially successful, so only borrow what you think you can pay back
- A break-even analysis. Determine how much revenue you need to generate to recoup the money spent on the project. Identify the point at which you will breakeven.

What's your plan? This is your road map. Formulate, create, write, and share this marketing plan with the people in your inner circle. All of whom will benefit from having a written document to gain a better understanding of the calendar and each person's or firm's role in the marketing of your release. Utilizing demographic and psychographic segmentation, coupled with geo-targeting focus only on relevant customers – then create a strategy to target them. What are you KPIs?

Topics to address in the marketing plan might include:

- PROJECT OVERVIEW
- TRACK LISTING
- CREDITS, METADATA & DISTRIBUTION

- MARKETING GOALS AND OBJECTIVES
- THE TARGET AUDIENCE / ANALYTICS
- SOCIAL MEDIA MARKETING
- THE VIDEO
- PUBLICITY
- ADVERTISING
- THE TEAM
- THE TIMELINE
- THE BUDGET
- A PRACTICAL APPROACH
- SINGLE RELEASES
- ASSESSMENT
- FOR CONSIDERATION
- ADVANCE YOUR CAREER
- RESOURCES

PROJECT OVERVIEW

It's fair to assume that all on your Team have previous knowledge, insight into, a friendship or acquittance with the artist and the music (or band or brand). An edit of the artist bio should be succinct and sufficient as a place holder for the Project Overview. Then address the details of the release, the concept or message. What's the title of the project? The *street date* or release date? What is the scope of the release? Is there a video and tour dates? Include a product overview. What physical formats (if any), are you planning on manufacturing, vinyl, or CDs? What's your pricing plan for physical products and what quantities will you need? What distribution platform do you plan to utilize?

TRACK LISTING

Self-explanatory. Include the publishing information and track times.

CREDITS, METADATA & DISTRIBUTION

Specificities;
- Recorded at:
- Producer:

- Engineer:
- Arranger:
- Musicians / Singers / Other
- Mix Engineer:
- Mastering:
- Publishing:
- Distribution:
- Executive Producer:

Who is your distribution partner?

MARKETING GOALS AND OBJECTIVES

What is your basic objective, what do you hope to accomplish with this release? This plan is your strategy to achieving your goals, however modest or optimistic you might perceive them to be. This is your opportunity to address the objective of the project and put it in writing. Identify some specific KPIs that are important to you. Be realistic with feasible goals. KPIs might include a quantified number of increased streams, YouTube views over a specified period of time, a percentage increase of monthly listeners and new followers on social media, etc. Tangible goals will allow you to analyze what's working with your plan and when its necessary to pivot and adjust.

THE TARGET AUDIENCE / ANALYTICS

At this point, through surveys and market research and by making comparisons to similar artists of your genre, you should have a good idea of the demographic and psychographic make-up of your fans. Declare your target audience, create a positioning statement. Address the audience you are planning to focus on. Remember, you can't afford to market to everyone, so drill down so the Team has a clear understanding of the who, what, when where and how you will be spending your marketing efforts and dollars. Focus only on relevant customers. How do your fans think? Where do they get their news and pop culture info? Where do they attend shows and parties? Now create a strategy to reach them?

SOCIAL MEDIA MARKETING

This topic has previously been addressed. Please refer to Chapter 15 for a comprehensive look at social media marketing.

THE VIDEO

Having an accompanying video to the track provides numerous additional marketing opportunities and increased potential audience exposure. Although not 100% essential, it's ideal and highly recommended the audio and video have simultaneous release dates. There's a thought that one can release the audio and follow-up with a video a month or so thereafter. This is flawed thinking. Understand, that what-ever your budget the video will cost the same to produce prior to as after the release. If your budget is a concern, another option is to produce a less expensive, *lyric video*. Either way, the point being, make an accompanying music video to maximize the impact of your release. We're all creative people right - then figure out how to make an affordable video for your single. A video enables fans to 'see' your brand and can often be one of the key marketing drivers for a project. Quite possibly, working backwards, think about the delivery date of the video determining the actual release date of the audio. Once the video is shot, synched, and edited, how do you plan to announce the debut of the video? Obviously through social media, a new release email, securing a placement on a blog or influencer tweet, etc.

PUBLICITY

Outline the actionable publicity targets for the release in the marketing plan. As publicity is the non-paid message intended to inform, at minimum you will want to generate a Press Release and distribute that to industry tastemakers, bloggers, etc. Think creatively about an event or performance you might be able to secure. College radio and local television interviews/ performances are typically tied into promoting a calendar event. Prior to reaching out to pitch local networks and vlogs for a performance, have a show or event to tag with the interview and performance. Alternatively, connect with people on your media list in an effort to secure a story or interview about your release, your artist, or whatever is newsworthy as an alternate means of disseminating information for the project.

ADVERTISING

You would be well advised to set-aside a modest budget for a social media ad campaign. Strive to amass a modest social media advertising budget to equal a nominal daily spend. If you think this is beyond your budget, we will implore you to skip coffee at Starbucks every morning – get your priorities straight. Is marketing or coffee your priority? The benefits of investing as little as a few dollars per day in a social media advertising campaign can provide profound effects in your marketing efforts. Social media advertising is ideal for geo-targeting; to promote a local show, an in-store appearance or performance, or an event. Think of this spend as an investment in your career. Remember the age-old additive, *it takes money to make money*. You may find this to be the case. Invest wisely and monitor your spend in real-time analyzing the tangible results in terms of Likes, Shares, Followers, Plays, Monthly Listeners and Views. Social media advertising may provide a path in your finding a larger audience. Assume you were to invest two dollars a day for 30 days equaling a $60 dollar total monthly spend. Did you see a bump in streams, views, tickets, merch sold, etc.? Decipher your analytics. If the cost of conversion per new fan was $3, and that new fan was motivated to attend a show and purchased a ticket @ $10-20 bucks, your digital advertising investment and subsequent ROI is off the charts. By analyzing marketing trends of this type, you may begin to understand that it is far more beneficial for you to experiment with $10 or $15 per day in your spend rather than two bucks a day. If done correctly you may discover this strategy - in exponentially building a fan base, may result in found money (revenue) in the form of new ticket sales, merch sold, followers, streams and additional emails gathered for the database.

THE TEAM

Listing the names of the Team members and their contact info not only provides the obvious but also designates the few individuals who are responsible for working the record. Ideally this list contains no fewer than three, and up to 5 - 7 individuals. Assembling a strong and trusted team with networking skills will ultimately provide all involved (most importantly the artist) with credibility.

THE TIMELINE

Consider the duration of your marketing plan activities leading up to your release and after the release or *drop date*. Your timeline should be comprehensive and as detailed as you can make it. Be specific about dates and timeframes for each and every activity. Be sure to include appropriate *lead times*. These are the complete timeframes from the beginning of a process to its completion. For example, if you are trying to get a news article in a local paper or monthly magazine it will be necessary for you to reach out to a writer sometimes weeks in advance of the publication. This will allow the reviewer enough time for them to write the story and for it to be published. In doing so, the review will run strategically right before or month of release. You cannot expect a last-minute request for media coverage to be accommodated. Lead times will vary depending on the type of media and the particular publication.

Think of your Marketing Plan as a roadmap and calendar which delegates who is responsible for activities beginning at least 6-8 weeks out. Applying full-court pressure as the release date approaches increasing activities peaking up to and a few days after the release. It shouldn't stop there. The full-court press should continue for 2-4 weeks after street date at minimum.

THE BUDGET

How much money do you need to reach your goals? Your budget should be built to cover all the activities you've indicated in your plan to meet your objectives. Your budget should be an itemized accounting of these activities that indicates dollar amounts for each line-item. Do research in advance to determine the specific amount required for each line-item in the marketing spend.

If you have a team or assistance in implementing your Marketing Plan you should designate individual responsibilities. Consider who is:
- overseeing the Team? you? your manager?
- finance – who's responsible for providing and allocating the budget
- overseeing the video
- handling social media marketing: FB, Instagram, Twitter, Spotify, etc.?
- generating a press release and managing publicity activities in general?
- registering with a PRO, SoundExchange, SongTrust?
- developing your website?
- responsible for getting gigs and booking live performances?
- overseeing manufacturing and building your online store to sell merchandise?
- responsible for managing the merch table at shows?
- Acting as the production coordinator responsible for the manufacturing of physical goods (CDs, LPs) and merch for your new release party?

- Arranging digital/physical distribution of your music?
- Exploring synch licensing opportunities

A PRACTICAL APPROACH

Do you need a pie in the sky marketing plan that is more of a wish list? Of course not. That's a waist of your time. Assuming you have good music, it's all about strategy. You are better off creating a concise 2–4-page document which outlines *your* Marketing Plan that will be useful to you rather than overthinking each of topics listed and creating an unfeasible plan to implement. The Major labels have a cadre of people assisting in developing detailed and confidential marketing plans. Gain input, thoughts, ideas, and suggestions from the Team you have. Most importantly follow your timeline and do your best to hold your team, (or better yet your manger) accountable for executing the deliverables on the due dates you establish

SINGLE RELEASES

As stated previously, today the music industry has returned in many ways back to a single driven business. Apple iTunes which launched its download business by allowing consumers to download single songs from an album without purchasing the entire album set the stage for increased demand for singles. Now with streaming service and the ability to easily create playlists of random songs, singles are significant for artists as primary product and not just a tool to drive album sales. When releasing singles, a comparable amount of care should go into the marketing plan for them. Agreed it's not necessary for you to create 12-page robust marketing plan for the release of your single, however, it would be prudent to delineate the "who, what, when, where, why, and how". Again, we're not talking about creating some excessively elaborate document to satisfy the higher-ups at a record label, but rather a useful document for the select few members (trusted friends with the best of intentions). With a plan in place, all on your Team can participate in and gain experience in the industry for themselves while promoting your (or your artist's) music and career. Start six weeks out – and while we're not going to tell you what to do day by day, think methodically. Make a move every couple of days. Put your actionable items on a calendar and design a roadmap for the release of your single and the 2-4 weeks ensuing. Adhere (stick) to this plan. If you have the aptitude to create a more robust marketing plan to share with your team – kudos. If you remain a solo artist with no team, create at the very least a new release calendar for yourself to follow.

ASSESSMENT

It's all about analytics, right? Well, if you believe that, and you should, a marketing plan is analytics on a calendar. After 8-12 weeks you should begin to analyze the metrics and begin to understand what worked and what didn't. Did you drop the ball on anything? Maybe you neglected to send the 2nd follow-up email about your release to your Mailchimp database, or whatever. Now, with the forthcoming release of your 2nd single – begin again, 8 weeks out and replicate what was effective and substitute new ideas and tactics to refine the approach. Over time, you will begin to perfect the strategy of dropping a new track. Although it may take one, two, or even three years, you should, by this time be making progress in artist development with increased metrics both in terms of streams, views, merch and tickets sold. Once you have the ability to headline a sold-out show in all likelihood, you may find yourself on the radar of an indie or major label. And a record deal may be forthcoming. It worked for the Smashing Pumpkins at the Metro in Chicago and for numerous other bands being discovered in clubs and venues across the country.

FOR CONSIDERATION

The editorial we have provided is under the assumption that you have an abundance of talent or are a musical prodigy. The genius of Beethoven, Mozart, the Beatles, Stevie Wonder, and the likes of Jacob Collier is undeniable, yet these talented individuals are few and far between. As we mentioned from the outset, this is another reminder that there may exist many numerous pathways for you carving out a career in the music business outside of being an artist. Being a part of the team, an entrepreneur and a tour manger are all part of the ecosystem of the music business. The opportunities, jobs, and gigs are too numerous to mention. Come to the realization that perhaps your career in the music business resides in a sector outside of artistry. Not everyone is an artist. Your strength may be in recognizing your ability to discover and align yourself with talent.

An "Artist" by a loosely held idea is a creative, gifted individual. Typically, they are not aligned with, nor interested in the business. There are far more people working in various aspects of the music industry versus the artists' themselves. This is where you must find your niche. Are you the individual that can identify and engage a team? If this is so, there's a likelihood you're fully capable of assuming ownership in the formulation, creation, and the writing of the Marketing Plan on behalf of the act. Should this be the case, there's a strong likelihood that you may have a career as an artist manager or in marketing. If you can create this road map, or marketing plan easily for an artist, you should consider a career as an artist manger. Very few artists are capable of self-management just like very few artists (except for Stevie Wonder) are capable of self-producing. If you have the ability to be a leader, organize, have your Goggle calendar well managed, "love" the business, then consider all the alternatives to being an artist. Being an artist is not all it's cracked up to be. Come to terms with your strengths, understand your limitations, and focus on your music business passion – whatever that may be; sound engineering, booking bands, live mixing, artist management, tour, or venue management.

ADVANCE YOUR CAREER

Who in your orbit might have a relationship with other individuals or organizations they can introduce you to in furthering your career? Don't lose sight of the fact, that perhaps an even more important initiative than making music or marketing, may be NETWORKING. One piece of information that we can pass on, with few exceptions, one's career path in the music business will likely not be what you expected or envisioned. Be open minded, likable, reliable, on time, respectful; and network. You will find a career in the music industry.

RESOURCES

Marketing Plan Template

15

SOCIAL MEDIA MARKETING [WELCOME TO THE JUNGLE]

Sorry to say this, but seldom does good music alone prevail. Don't forget, it's all about the marketing stupid, and social media is a proven and necessary component of marketing.

For a new artist, social media can at times, be the equivalent to being lost at night in the jungle equipped with only a flashlight. In which direction do you go to find your own pathway through a never-ending paradigm of posts, captions, graphics, stories, reels, and tweets?

On the surface, social media and post creation appears to be quite mindless (food and cat pictures for example) with little or no thought going into a strategy. This is not the case if you are working to build an audience for you, your band, or your brand. There exists a direct correlation between social media and your popularity and success. Thinking through and developing a social media strategy can prove to be extremely beneficial to your career. At present, it's nearly imperative that you have an Instagram account, perhaps a TikTok profile, et al, and assuming you do, what is your strategy?

Questions to ask yourself may include:
- What do I have to say, what's my message?
- What can you comfortably share from your personal life?

- Inform fans about upcoming events,
- Do you have a social or sociological movement to align oneself with?
- Can you participate in a cause marketing event with a non-profit organization?
- What are your content creation assets (photos, reels, music)?
- What is the perceived personality or impression you wish to convey?
- Which 2, maybe 3 platforms should you focus on?
- How much time (20, 40, 60, 120 minutes) should you dedicate to social media per day?
- When and how to inform fans about upcoming events, and;
- Determine, how does this strategy benefit my music career and not dilute but rather enhance it.

Yikes......this could feel a bit overwhelming with so many questions to dive into, and you might be thinking about tackling social media ad hoc. On the other hand, this could be perceived as another challenging yet vital component of your total marketing initiative. For some, self-promotion is inherent, having no reservations in promoting oneself. While for others, many of us, are a bit quiet or shy and have our reservations and hesitations about being transparent. You can learn to post in a quiet, discriminant way, about a cause, a news event, a movie, or a book – others outside of your followers will find you based on your chosen subject matter. It's true that consistent, well-conceived social media posts are time consuming. Yet if constructed properly, they can pay unrequited dividends. This is quite apparent with TikTok sensations' views translating to Spotify plays, ultimately resulting in a Major label deal.

This ain't rocket science – we're all creative people, make it fun, inquisitive, and unique. This is the digital alternative reality of your life and career! Social Media is an art and how you go about creating that art establishes your brand and your voice. It's about the strategy and frequency rather than the off the cuff pics of your lunch today (unless "Lunch Pics" has become a consistent and beloved segment of your normal social media routine). Being authentic and true about your life and career is what will drive algorithms, engagements, and shares. Your content can't just exist, it must *engage*! Your audience shouldn't just be viewing your social media, but rather, they should be active and regular participants. This will not only be favorable to algorithms, but will help build a passionate fanbase, that will follow your brand religiously.

Ask yourself, what do people care about when it comes to "my" social media channels? How do I cut above the clutter? What makes people so incessant about scrolling through their Instagram feed each day? What are these people looking for? This is a rhetorical question, there's no right answer, but do your best to figure it out.

Think about it, while scrolling, we're all looking for something remarkable, insightful, educational or, to be entertained. Look for and recognize these events in your daily life and incorporate them into your posts.

ONCE UPON A TIME

Before Facebook, Instagram and TikTok, there had always been various forms of "social communities." Take for example, classmates.com and SixDegrees.com which catered to friends of friends and associates from school. But well before that, (pre internet) The Grateful Dead, cultivated a nationwide community that would gather around their tour markets with fans initiating tailgate parties, camping, and music. The announcement (the message) was spread through monthly newsletters, tour support ads in free local publications, and word of mouth that provided fans information about tour dates, gatherings and news regarding band members and "Deadhead" community members. Soon thereafter, caravans of fans traveled throughout the country following the band. Fan clubs, newsletters, and meetings would take place in the late 1960s and early 1970s from the band's headquarters in San Francisco. This was the advent of social media and the "superfan," a person who has an extreme or obsessive admiration for a particular artist, band or brand. Recognize two things; 1) all of this happened, pre-internet, and 2) this grass roots marketing remains cost effective today, it's targeted and highly effective (minus the internet).

Imagine a world void of the internet and social media. Our modern global society existed quite well prior to the advent of such for centuries. In lieu of social media, music, social and political awareness was purveyed /distributed and discovered in print publications such as *Rolling Stone, The Village Voice, Cream, Billboard and Tower Records* in-house magazine *Pulse*. This is where you discovered new music, artist interviews and insights, it was simply how one gathered music news. Next on the scene, was a 24 / 7 music television station - *MTV* with VJs and music videos that connected us all. Other than FM radio, there existed few music 'silos,' and for certain – MTV was the panicle of these silos. The internet was launched into the public domain in 1993. If one had seen or been on the internet in the late 90s, chances are you were viewing it on a dial-up modem over a telephone landline. Pages loaded so slowly it's nearly incomprehensible today. Broadband and wireless internet was widely adapted in the early 2000s. In August of 2003, a new social media company emerged onto the scene and took the world by surprise. It was called Myspace.com. It was the first social network to reach a global audience and had influences in digital technology, pop culture and of course, music.

Myspace was the first real social media site, (founded by a musician) that catered to musicians and bands. Between 2005 and 2008, Myspace was the largest social networking site in the world. Myspace was so popular and prominent that there was little or no need for an artist centric website. That would be like an artist today saying that there is no need to have a web-site because of their Instagram, (note: both are critical). *MySpace* lost all relevance in a few years' time and in April of 2009, MySpace was acquired by Rupert Murdoch's *News Corp* for $580 million. In June 2009, the company laid off 30 percent of the workforce and reduced it to 1,000 employees, and today remains online but for what-ever reason has no relevance or visibility in comparison to the other more recent emerging social media platforms. Concur-rently in 2004 from a college campus at Cambridge, MA a little known social media site called *Facebook* launched by a then college student Mark Zuckerberg emerged. Facebook started out as a social media campus experiment, whereby you had to have an .edu to log in. Then, in September of 2006, they opened it up to the general public and the floodgates opened.

Twitter, a San Francisco based company, also launched in 2006 and evolved into the preferred platform for established superstar artists, entertainers, celebrities; ultimately inventing the 'influencer.' *Instagram* emerged next, and Facebook acquired them shortly thereafter. *ByteD-ance*, a Beijing China company launched *TikTok* in the US in 2017. By 2018, it began taking off and is today arguably, more popular than Google Search and is one of the most downloaded apps in the world. And now where do we find ourselves? We're all overwhelmed with the choices, the plethora of social media, branding and communication platforms that exist, never mind being mindful of the next emerging social media platform.

The pathways to social media are voluminous – *Twitter, Twitch, Facebook, Instagram, Tik-Tok*, et al. The bottom line is you can't be everything to everybody. Once again pick a lane. Delve into the two (2) social media platforms you're most comfortable with, and that you believe aligns with your fan's demographics and psychographics. Which two is up to you. The thinking is it's nearly impossible to maintain a current profile amongst 3, 4 or 5 social media platforms by yourself, so pick your two favorites and become an expert on them. Begin devel-oping a community across the two platforms and monitor your growth (make sure it's easy for followers of one social media to become followers of your other social media), acquisitions and most importantly – engagements. Understand and follow those who are mavens and influencers in your orbit. How can you engage with their brand and audience, to grow your following? What brands or individuals have they collaborated with?

You may think, your songwriting, performances and production are getting better with each track, you're encouraged about the notable progress you are making – thinking that if the music is great enough, that alone will ensure success (whatever one deems as success). And while it's true, you are becoming a much more skilled artist – and there is marked improvement in your music, have you noticed that others' less talented than you, seem to be gaining broader recognition. So, what's the difference? How do you level the playing field? The answer presumably might be, they are spending less time creating and more time marketing.

Are you aware that it has recently been calculated that "successes" for an artist now relies approximately on 20% talent and recording, the other 80% is marketing? We have discussed and explored various types of marketing thus far, from publicity, database management, blogging, finding, and identifying the 'mavens,' the gatekeepers and the bloggers. All of which is a form of social media marketing.

Beware of getting trapped in the vicious cycle of record, release, record, release always realizing the same general outcome while ignoring the marketing component. Remember: it's not only about the music stupid. It may not be the music but the ability to connect with and build relationships with your fans, so they get to know you as a person. Whatever you do, don't be the cliched artist who like a rat on the proverbial treadmill always finds the same end result. If it's not working, if you haven't explored it – don't discount it – but rather explore it. Be enthusiastic about the two platforms you will ultimately select – with the end goal of being an expert on the platform. Should you do so – it may pay compounded dividends.

Facebook / Instagram have some pretty effective advertising tools in which to target your audience by market (geo-targeting), and incorporating such obvious demographics traits as age, race, occupation, interests, etc. Watch tutorials, lean to understand the basic opportunities and parameters of 'boosting' a post. Advertising a post is slightly different, there you can drill down into what you believe to be your core demographics. Smart, cost-effective marketing can be realized with a minimal investment of $1-2 dollars a day. Dip your toe in the water – experiment. Begin to understand what works and what doesn't. Artists', bands and entities that have established their 'tribe' have learned how to invest (spend) hundreds to thousand of dollars per event, to realize a 200% return of their investment. In other words, if you develop your social media following, fans and likes, a possible scenario may be to invest $5,000 in social media advertising to promote a show thus resulting in a ROI of $10,000 in ticket sales, netting you five grand. Of course this example can be extrapolated utilizing investments of anywhere between $50 - $500.

THE SOCIAL MEDIA PLATFORMS

FACEBOOK

It's an older demographic. However, since *Facebook* acquired *Instagram* you have the ability to seamlessly connect the two accounts. Facebook Boosts are highly cost effective, and with little risk, may drive new fans. The beauty about a Facebook for Business ad is that in can be integrated with Instagram ads with the ability to geo-target. Ideally, within a radius of a mile 2-5, 10-15 15 -30 miles, or any prescribed driving distance to a show. Then select the targeted age group, occupation, interests, etc. Check it out, learn to work with, refine and become an expert in Facebook / Instagram advertising which can be highly cost effective in delivering a positive ROI.

TWITTER

If you're an Influencer or a pop star, this is the social media format du jour. You have the ability to tweet a succinct message, a home video or an announcement of a tour, a residency or a new release. If, however, you at present don't find yourself with millions or even thousands of followers, use Twitter in this fashion - as a news reel. Follow artists, movements, music industry news that you have an affinity with, or interest in. Use Twitter as your custom news feed to educate yourself and keep up to date with current events, releases, drops, tours, etc. Then, when you see a post that motivates you, simply share it to your followers. Sharing reputable posts that resonate with you will gain credibility and put you on the radar of those who have authored the post you are now sharing.

INSTAGRAM

Instagram is a free photo and video sharing app available on iPhone and Android and also available on desktop. Unlike Facebook, which relies on both text and pictures, or Twitter, which essentially relies on text alone, Instagram's sole purpose is to enable users to share images or videos with their audience. It has quickly risen to be one of the most popular social media apps in the world due to its simplicity of visual storytelling. Major artists, bands and brands have gravitated to Instagram as most find it to be an effective social media platform for fan following, loyalty, and engagement.

TIK TOK

TikTok – formerly known as Musical.ly – was originally a popular short-form (15 seconds) video streaming and sharing app, with over 1 billion downloads. This short-form, (now long form) video-sharing app allows users to create and share videos on almost any topic. The app is popular with content creators as a platform to create compelling, viral content. Adapters to this platform have quickly learned to create short content that provides humor, amazement, and live music performances all having a poignant value. Musicians who have amassed major followings on the platform, have often been able to translate the following into a heavy increase of Spotify plays, monthly listeners, and followers. With celebrity endorsements and influencer marketing, TikTok has quickly risen to be "the '' desired platform for young adults.

YOUTUBE

You must have a video. Today there is little or no excuse to not have a music video. If you have the luxury of a storyboard, a budget to hire professional cinematographers . . . wonderful. But with a level playing field, you can engage the assistance of friends, videographers, fashion students, lighting designers; there exist more resources than you can image. Network and tap into your resources at your college, or put the word out through your network of friends, family, etc. Collaborate. In the end it's a win / win situation for all parties.

TWITCH

Perhaps here today, gone tomorrow, but . . . Twitch gained popularity among artists for their live streaming capabilities. The live streaming service encompasses content spanning: gaming, entertainment, sports, and music.

While we are on the subject of livestreaming, some things to consider for your marketing plan: Create an interesting livestream session with your fans
1. Quarantunes - Lukas Nelson used this in 2020 to appeal to his fanbase who were stuck at home during the pandemic.
2. Thematic – Perform 2-3 songs live every Friday night at 6:00 PM to your Instagram Live audience and create graphics to promote this weekly event to build a steady ongoing audience.
3. Acoustic concert – An acoustic solo, due, trio or group mini concert for your fans once a month.

4. Full Band show from the studio – Show them your rehearsal space, dress it up, give it some personality and mood lighting and go live as if you were at a club or live music venue or coffeehouse.
5. Q&A / AMA – Ask me anything. Discuss the background, the inspiration, the writing and recording of your new single, a book you've read, a new wine you've discovered, ask me about my rig, a recipe, practicing, or my workout routine, et al.

LIKE A VIRGIN

OK – now that we have covered the basic platforms of social media, let's get down to business in determining how best to strategize the use of each of your platforms of choice for your emerging/developing brand. Don't forget, just like SEO for your website, consistent content marketing for social media is vital. It's all about Content Marketing; continually creating and distributing interesting content equals selling. By consistently (daily,) engaging in content marketing on your social media platform(s), you will create increased search in Google SEO. Benefits derived from content marketing include; attracting leads, promoting products & services, and marketing your business. Don't forget to embed links throughout all the media/ websites/platforms you're engaged with to help increase crawling.

IMAGING

Capture images to enhance your photo and video collection – capturing video footage of you, your instruments, your gear, your recording studio, shows you play *and* attend (tag all the artists involved), utilize your local areas as landscapes and backdrops. Get a pal and do a miniature photoshoot with various landscapes and several wardrobe changes if that's something you feel would complement your strategy. Perhaps find a cool store, restaurant, etc. that you like and looks cool. Take a picture and tag them. Perhaps they'll reshare for their own media. It could potentially even lead to a future partnership. Consider content with subjects such as webisode themes, location themes, acoustic vs. studio vs. live footage, live streams, and tutorials. Create and establish your views, your persona, and your voice.

Video in today's world is a necessity for garnering traction and engagement. Will you or your band have acoustic videos or studio photos or a behind the scenes montage of photos from the forthcoming music video for pre-release. Are you on a tour and are you sharing life on the road and reposting fan stories who attended? Would you be receptive to recording a personalized video explaining the meaning of a song and debuting it in the form of an acoustic version from your living room? Where to release a new video is then the big question. Will you tease a portion of the track on TikTok, Instagram Reel, or on YouTube?

If, due to financial constraints the reality is that you will be releasing a single absent of an accompanying music video, then think of alternative new release options. In lieu of a video, host a livestream or record release party at a record store, a pub, or a live music venue in support of your new single.

STYLING

Think about selecting the primary colors for you, your band or brand or logo usage/placement. Determine how you'll create content. What style is representational of your brand and how do you keep it authentic. Practice doesn't make perfect, but it does create authenticity. Being transparent, honest and real on social media creates your uniqueness, signature, and brand image for your content.

ARTWORK

Build out your website, and your social media channel with the artwork from your most recent release. Ensure there is total integration of your newest artwork across all social media channels as well as your website. Make sure all platforms convey the same imaging – that of your most recent release. Consider how often you will change out your banners and profile photos and Spotify photos. If you change one, change them all to keep your image and brand consistent.

CONTENT DEFINITION

Deciding what and when to post is a determination you will ultimately have to make. Now's the time. Decide; once a day, twice, 3 times daily, – ultimately, you'll will have to make a decision, stick with it, and see if it's working. Do research on what the best posting times are for your respective platforms, see if they are effective for you as well. Many social media sites have insight tools, to help you track the activity of your followers, as well as the success of each of your posts. If you notice a certain day works better, designate that day for your more important posts. Keep a log of all of this (as well as overall engagement rates, any follower spikes that you notice, etc.), so that you have analytics that you can quickly reference while determining your future strategies. Based on shares and engagement you may come to realize less is more – posting once daily on your two preferred platforms may be ideal. Build a content strategy plan based on your resources and your comfortability with creating and editing content. Then determine when and how you'll release this new content incorporating hashtag usage with platforms like Twitter and Instagram. Recognize social media is a global story-telling platform. It's likely you'll have fans in Eastern Europe, Asia or anywhere in the world for that matter. Polo G. had early plays with fans of hip-hop in Eastern Europe. Be aware of who you are, and what traits you may possess or communities you may be a part of. Lock-in with them! They'll engage because they'll relate. Self-effacing humor typically resonates well with audiences. A comedic touch – if that's something in your DNA will likely be received positively. We've all made dumb mistakes, and if you were to be honest and show, just like everybody else, that you're not perfect and expose your vulnerable side (after-all, we all have one), will be perceived as ingratiating to your followers'. Superficiality seems to be something frequently associated with social media in pop-culture, yet this doesn't have to be the case for your digital-media brand to be successful. In fact, some of the most successful influencers/digital-media brands are the ones that are most truthful. People want to see themselves in your brand. To be something too perfect, too exclusive, and too unobtainable could deter potential new followers. As cheesy as it sounds, just be yourself. You'll garner fans that want *you*, instead of a persona you've created for your social media (unless of course, a character is the whole point of your brand).

RE-POSTS VS. REAL TIME POSTING

Evergreen content is timeless content, worth resharing; a momentous photo, show, event, or celebration are deemed social media re-posts. Postings that are not time sensitive and can be reposted to highlight a previous event. Real Time Posting, as the word implies is live or in the moment. Posting live photos / video from Lollapalooza is great. A throwback using another photo from Lollapalooza the previous year connotates evergreen content and will develop credibility amongst your fans. Depending on your strategy you may want to employ both methods and be more lenient in re-posting if you have a busy schedule. Part of your strategy may be creating content and writing social media posts for the entire week on the weekend while you work on your craft during the week or while juggling a part-time day job, creating social media content and strategy at night.

STRATEGY

Your social media strategy should be all about views, conversions, shares, and engagements. Set a strategy – post on Instagram 3-4 times per day, or once – it's up to you. There are no rules. See what's working, what's not, and what's getting engagements. If you're posts aren't working, change them / modify them. If your posts aren't getting reactions, shares, and likes, change your strategy. Recognize what's working and not working. Rethink it. Pivot – let your fans see another side of your persona – what do you do for fun, do you cook, skateboard, etc. Offer a window into your world outside of music. And then connect with those communities. Don't feel limited to collaborate and reach out to solely music-related brands. Connect with any brand/community that you're a part of, relate to, or are similar to (same demographics, style, etc.). The more brands/communities you can connect and collaborate with, the more your brand will grow. Be authentic and true in providing an inside glimpse of your everyday life. For some, social media is second nature, while others may find this difficult to master. The reason you have a team around you is to provide opinions and provide perspective and direction. Be open to tapping into mentors, friends, or family members who may be able to provide feedback or input in helping you design (or redesign) your plan. They may see something that you've forgotten about or help you see it from a different perspective.

Will you use memes? Will you utilize Reels and TikTok and if so, how do you plan to do so? Will you create tutorial videos on YouTube? Will you place a carousel ad or an advertisement through the Meta Dashboard? Another idea, create a personalized video or vlog once a month? These are all various content strategies to consider. Quality over quantity and less is more is the social media etiquette.

FREQUENCY

In developing the social media marketing plan and timeline, it's advisable to keep yourself accountable. Again, determine how much time you can allocate per day, however, bear in mind, that the more time you designate to social media marketing, may quite possibly be a better use of your time than practicing scales or writing a tune. Make a commitment to what you can implement on a daily basis. Monday AM is the best time to post. Think about posting 6 days a week, taking one day off. Take the same day off per week. Many new artists proclaim they'd prefer to forego this part of the business and dive right into social media without a plan or any form of structure. For some, this may work. However, for the vast majority you should think this through and be honest with oneself about frequency and consistency. How many posts per week will you commit to posting on social media to support that frequency? Frequency is a vital component to your strategy.

Be mindful of social media burnout syndrome. It's a real thing and a problem that is often swept under the rug. Post a nominal yet not obtrusive number of posts per day on Instagram. Beware of spamming on social media – there's no need to document your every action or movement. Excessive activity will result in your fans unsubscribing or unfollowing. The frequency with which to post is a variable answer based on the individual and amount of content, time, and interest dedicated to continuing to grow your audience.

REACH & ENGAGEMENT

The various platforms you choose to utilizing will all provide insightful analytics. This data (numbers) is then captured and presented to you in an understandable and comprehendible fashion. Collectively these analytics will help you understand the value of your relationships with your readers / fans or customers. Referred to as reach and engagement. Reach is the number of people who are exposed to your marketing message. Engagement is the number of interactions, comments, forwards, shares, etc. of your marketing message. One of the most important activities you must take on is audience engagement. Ask them questions, seek opinions on publicity photos for example. Always respond to comments and questions on your social media feed. Keep the conversation with them going – this is a monetary tool that will increase loyalty and develop new casual fans into superfan status. How will you choose to engage with your audience? Are you open to developing a DM (direct message) relationship with your fans if they reach out? Will you create a CTA (call to action) asking people to vote on the artwork for your forthcoming single or provide topical suggestions for the lyrical content of a new song? Utilize the social media tools provided to enhance your community. Engagement is simple: It's an online mono / mono conversation with your committed fans.

ADVERTISING

However modest ($2-3 dollars per day) you should incorporate a social media advertising budget into your marketing plan. Now, consider how you will be spending it and where. Set a daily, weekly, or monthly budget to invest in your release. To supplement your modest social media advertising budget, consider your investment in time as money. Content marketing comes into play here. Content creation, by definition, has no direct cost associated with it. You may need to put more time into the campaign creating content targeted towards fans you feel would find your music appealing. Does your music sound and resonate to fans who like Sam Hunt or Drake Future, Jack Harlow, Taylor Swift, Ed Sheeran, AC/DC or Bebe Rexha? Make Google your friend by finding identifiable targets that are in line with your perceived audience – for both your personality and for your music. Many artists forego advertising altogether and create content that is so utterly unique that their content is shared over and over again where "word of mouth" (or EWOM – electronic word of mouth) takes precedent and substitutes for advertising. Consider hashtags and tagging when appropriate as another social media monetary tool. Collaborating with a brand/artist with a bigger following than your own, may also help substitute for advertising.

We've stated this before but, a common trap many artists fall into is spending their entire budget in the recording studio and believing their music is so utterly awesome that people will naturally flock to it. Are you kidding me? If you are one of those folks, we implore you to read every single word of this book, and the myriad of online tutorials for artists. Social media parleys your skills in creating and performing music – both can always be improved and refined: practice, practice, practice.

THE SOCIAL MEDIA TIMELINE

Create a social media timeline to coincided with an event, a new release, or a video debut. Delineate (lay out for 30 days) a plan of what you want to achieve. What are your KPIs (key performance indicators)? Allocate a modest investment - as little as 2-3 bucks a day to boost or advertise your posts. At the very minimum, allocate a dollar a day in social media marketing. Monitor the ROI. It may be the case that if done correctly, (remember the age-old additive the more money you spend the more money you make) may be applicable here. Spend $200 dollars a month and see if the additional investment provided you with a corresponding or correlating number of new fans. What was the ROI? If you were to spend ten bucks and then gained 35 new followers, your CPA (cost per acquisition) at .35 cents would be minimal and worth the spend. Think of a financial spend in social media as a marketing investment. Consider as well, if you'll focus your financial investment on one of your two choice social medias or will allocate it between the two. If investing in one, seems to work better than the other, double down. Set your goals and action points and a budget for how you'll execute your plan and monitor how this strategy is working in terms of new Followers, Listens, Likes, etc. Create a realistic plan of what you feel would be a representation of your personality, your voice, your image and how that would all tie in together.

- Will you use Instagram Reels differently than TikTok or YouTube shorts?
- How will you uniformly brand your channels?
- How comfortable are you behind or in front of the camera?
- Can you capture an acoustic performance video from anywhere to share?
- Tour photos, rehearsal and recording session pics

Set up a social media marketing calendar to monitor and stay accountable to your goals. Be open minded and flexible to change it on the fly. There are apps available that help schedule posts as well. If you want to make a post at 11 AM, but are working your day job, schedule it the night before, so that the post can come out on time, without you having to actively post it in real time.

By now your *Bandzoogle* or *WordPress* website should be established and looking good. When creating/ registering your social media sites, try to find a URL / name that will be easy for branding and easy for fans to remember. Incorporate that into your flyers, your website, and your entire online presence whenever you have the opportunity to do so. Create a Linktree on your website. Use content marketing to increase SEO, attract new followers and fans, promote your merch and music to organically market your music and personality simultaneously from your social media presence. Effective social media marketing takes into account each platform's unique audience, demographic and offering, features and functions, and then builds a campaign around them. Promoting the release of a single or a show is a micro marketing opportunity that deserves a modest 7-day plan, at minimum. You wouldn't rent an apartment without first seeing the floor plan, this is no different. Create a blueprint for your release.

THE DASHBOARD

The dashboard for all the social medial portals can offer and provide you with valuable analytics about your fans. You can ascertain the 'reach' of each post – what content / posts are resonating with your audience. There's no reason to guess on your fan's demographics (or in some cases even their daily activity). Analytics will provide this. Analytics such as age, gender, and top markets (cities) can aid you in booking a tour, performing in markets where you already have a built-in (large or small) audience is far more prudent than going into a market as a completely unknown entity. Through Ad Manager and Reporting, you can see organic spread vs. advertised. Additionally, events and commerce managers are provided as well as traffic analysis, audience insights, A/B testing, integrated apps and more. The point being – the dashboard of your social media platform(s) can provide you with tremendous strategic advantages and insight on your audience, your posts and, in essence, can assist you in refining your strategy to grow and reach a larger audience.

CONCLUSION

Without a doubt, the end game of social media is to create awareness of your brand, events, and releases, and to ultimately drive traffic to your website. There is no cookie cutter approach to social media. Every artist is unique and different which makes marketing all that more defined and pinpointed for you as the artist, band, or brand. Are you an ardent supporter of LGBTQ+ rights, Black Lives Matter, Stand with Ukraine? Building trust, and establishing effective messaging is the objective. It's about portraying and magnifying a passion, your music, your personality, a cause, etc. Ultimately, your social media voice and brand should act as an 'amplifier' for you as the ambassador of your brand. Being authentic is the answer. Learn best practices of social media as part of artist development.

RESOURCES

Social Media Revolution 3 (4:15 version via Erik Qualman)

The Social Media Content Calendar Template Every Marketer Needs [Free Template] courtesy: HubSpot

How To Promote Your Music On Social | WHAT To Post And WHY – Adam Ivy

10 Best MUSIC Social Media Strategies in 2022 | Learn How MAJOR Artists Use Socials | Ditto Music

16

TAXES FOR SELF-EMPLOYED ARTISTS, MUSICIANS & CREATIVES

As the famous quote from Benjamin Franklin says, "...in this world nothing can be said to be certain, except death and taxes." Recognize the minute you begin earning money from music you are a business. By default, you may be a sole proprietorship. Or you may have entered a partnership (in writing), or you may have formally organized your business as an LLC. Regardless, you are a business. Consider for example a professional bassist in Chicago. The best of them are in demand for recording sessions, live performances on stages in jazz clubs, rock venues, or in large society orchestras. All are hired with the assumption that each is an *independent contractor*. Technically, this means you are self-employed and completing work or providing a service to an organization or individual. You are not employed by them in this circumstance. In any of these scenarios, when one's performance is compensated in the form or cash or check, it should be declared as taxable income. Assuming the bassist is a member of the AFM and plays for 14 consecutive nights in a pit orchestra on *Broadway In Chicago,* that individual will be hired by the 'contractor,' who will in turn engage the musicians' services (in a Work for Hire Agreement) as an independent contractor. As a freelancing / working musician, you will in all likelihood be considered an independent contractor in most of the work you engage in. This "work for hire" situation is true not just for musicians but anyone doing work for others and has not been hired as an employee of the organization you are completing this work for. With that come two primary responsibilities:

1. Keeping track of all income (cash, checks, royalties, advances, loans, etc.) and
2. Keeping records of all receipts – so that you might take advantage of the tax breaks and benefits the government allows to independent contractors.

> Sidebar: I distinctly recall being introduced to the legendary jazz record producer, Bob Thiele (John Coltrane, Louis Armstrong, Duke Ellington, et al). Upon simple introductions, Bob said to me "kid, the best piece of advice I can give you is to keep all of your receipts." Bob and I became fast friends after that. – Kent Anderson

We fully recognize that talking about taxes is about as exciting as talking about golf, yet if you take the time to understand and implement best practices as they pertain to your tax liabilities, this may quite possibly prove to be the single most valuable chapter in the book.

What if you were to learn that by taking advantage of the legal deductions you are allowed, it lessens your taxable income which in turns lessens your tax liability. And while no one has ever been able to successful argue *the only two things certain in life are death and taxes*, recognize you're not exempt: this includes you. And although this chapter falls outside of the scope of marketing, it does provide you with recommendations which can most certainly impact your bank account. Think of it this way, should you choose not to implement the suggestions and ideas set forth in this chapter, once again, you will be leaving money on the table, but this time in reverse fashion – paying more money out than is necessary.

Like it or not, you're running a business. That's why it's called the music business.

As outlined in chapter 4: the advantages of creating an LLC are substantial and include;
a. The ability to obtain a tax ID and then have the ability to;
b. Open a separate / business checking account.

In many instances, you may have not done any of the above. This is easily understood, as most great, dedicated, and gifted musicians', artists, background singers, etc. are by default - self-employed independent contractors. If you were to be offered and hired for a wedding band, you would agree on a performance fee for compensation. For our example let's assume the fee is $200. Typically, at the end of the gig you would be paid in either the form of cash or a check. This would be a common example in which you would be considered a self-employed, independent contractor. In all likelihood, you did not have the option nor opportunity to have taxes withheld. So, if we explore this example further, understand the entire 200 bucks is not yours to keep. The rule of thumb of the percentage one must set-aside of your taxable freelance income is 25% to 30%. Thus, netting our $200 down to equal $150-$170. It would be highly recommended that you open a savings account, and after every gig, transfer 25-30% of the cash or check to this savings account. It will accrue interest and at the end of the year, you will have the cash on hand to pay the taxes you owe to the Internal Revenue Service (IRS). Understand the IRS does not accept IOUs. You will be required by law to submit payment when filing both your state and federal taxes. Failure to pay taxes you owe and on time will result in you owing even more money as interest will accrue. For musicians who gig regularly throughout the year, the amount you may owe on taxes may be largely based on your ability to be organized with you receipts and documents you may utilize as legal deductions. If you or your artist accepts cash as agreed upon compensation for a gig you would not be declaring any taxes on the money at that time. However, as illustrated, you would be doing the right thing by putting a percentage of this money aside.

Conversely - when you are paid as an employee working for a company, taxes are taken out of your paycheck each pay-period and may include benefits such as medical and 401k plans. There are far fewer eligible taxable deductions an individual can take as an employee.

Being self-employed - keep all your receipts, find a qualified accountant, and develop a relationship with them. That's the best advice we can give you. Tax laws and provisions change yearly both on a state and federal level. A qualified accountant will be well versed on the year's changes and modifications. In turn, your business will benefit from taking advantage of new tax laws as they are passed into legislation. The challenge is to not only be aware of them but keeping records of both income and expenses (allowable deductions). Lastly, it is ill advised to inflate them. The last thing you need in developing your career is an audit from the IRS.

It's understandable that you have given little thought into taxes, tax preparations and deductions. To clarify; the authors of this book are not CPAs or accountants, yet there are a few simple tax deductions that you, as a self-employed individual, legal deduction you should be aware of, prepare for, and take advantage of. Tax deductions are legal expenses you have incurred to create or enact your business which had tangible costs. By declaring these costs, it reduces your gross income, making your taxable income less.

TAXABLE INCOME

Recognize that monies earned from numerous categories large or small, substantial, or not, collectively aggregate to a specific year-end gross earnings amount. This amount is taxable.

Taxable income may include, yet may not be limited to the following;
- Earned money from your distributor (streaming income)
- Live Performances
- Music Publishing
- Merch Sales
- Advances & Royalties
- Endorsements & Sponsorships
- Licensing
- Profits from Investments, it's all income.

ALLOWABLE DEDUCTIONS

Many independent creators invest more than their time. Necessary tools of the trade such as guitars, keyboards, amps, and studio hardware equipment are acquired. Additionally, you might outlay cash for a rehearsal space or a recording session. With few exceptions, these are obvious cash-outlay investments in your career and therefor equate in whole or in part to the taxable deductions you are entitled. If you sell a t-shirt for 30 bucks, you didn't make 30 bucks, after printing and shipping you may have netted half of that 50%. That equals $15 dollars of taxable income not $30. Now extrapolate the numbers, and you may begin to understand that tax deductions, and transparent accounting, are important and will most notably, be in your best interest.

As a jobbing musician, most often it is up to you, at your expense to get to a show, an airport for an out-of-town gig, drive to an audition or a rehearsal. Whatever mode of transpiration you choose, your own automobile, Uber or Lift, mass transit, you should be able to deduct all, or a portion of the cost associated with your getting from point A to point B and back. As a result, one of the most common and significant deductions a jobbing music can take is the automobile mileage deduction. Here's how it can be implemented; suppose you live in the suburb and have a gig in the city 16 miles away representing a 32-mile round trip. You cannot deduct your automobile payment, or fuel, or car insurance, you can however deduct your mileage. The current government reimbursement for an automobile is .56 per mile. So, in our scenario that would equate to $17.92. + parking. Choose a tool for tracking and calculating this expense. You may wish to download an app, utilize an appointment book, or your calendar.

Possible tax deductions you may be eligible for may include the following;
- Taxis, subways, buses, ride-shares
- Automobile mileage
- Costs associate with registering for a business license
- Agency / Management fees
- Legal fees (Including the previous year's tax preparation)
- Membership fees to the likes of A2IM, the Recording Academy, the AFM, etc.
- Costs associated with the manufacturing and shipping of merch
- Hourly rates and fees for recording, mixing, and mastering
- Music video production (including wardrobe, hair, and make-up, etc.)
- When attending an industry event or convention all costs associated with the registration, ground transportation, airfare, hotel, and meals
- Marketing and promotion (including social media advertising)
- Domain registration and website hosting
- Health and instrument insurance
- Manufacturing of physical product (L.P.s, CDs, etc.)
- Business meals
- Business gifts
- Concert tickets (+ parking) and
- Streaming subscriptions in the name of research

The most basic recommended way of setting up your business (regardless of legal entity) may be to establish a 2nd savings and checking / debit and credit card accounts. Here you can transfer money to set aside for taxes. The bank statements will then provide details of transactions for tax purposes.

Changes in the tax laws of recent years have provided some significant benefits for creators. Previously, costs associated with recording, mixing, and mastering a recording were amortized over a seven-year period. Today, you may amortize these costs over a three-year period. To be eligible you must declare your purchase of tangible property (a sound recording, mix console, Pro-Tools, etc.) be declared as safe harbor. You may then take advantage of the write-off with a 50% deduction in year 1 and 25% deductions in years 2 & 3.

Again, save ALL receipts, your accountant will assist in ascertaining what are allowable deductions. Mileage is a big one, subscription services, concert tickets, and parking may be submitted as research. AdWords, social media advertising, and marketing costs in general are considered acceptable deductions.

EMPLOYEE VS. INDEPENDENT CONTRACTOR

Under common-law rules, anyone who performs services for you is your employee *if you can control what will be done and how it will be done*. This is so even when you give the employee freedom of action. What matters is that you have the right to control the details of how the services are performed.

People such as doctors, dentists, veterinarians, lawyers, accountants, contractors, subcontractors, public stenographers, or auctioneers who are in an independent trade, business, or profession in which they offer their services to the general public are generally independent contractors. However, whether these people are independent contractors or employees depends on the facts in each case. The general rule is that an individual is an independent contractor if the payer has the right to control or direct only the result of the work and not what will be done and how it will be done.

If you are an independent contractor, then you are self-employed. The earnings of a person who is working as an independent contractor are subject to self-employment tax. To find out what your tax obligations are, visit the Self-Employed Individuals Tax Center. [Reference: irs.gov]

A major rock and roll band such as the *Rolling Stones* have established their entity as a corporation. A business entity such as a corporation provides salaries for its workers including business managers, office staff, and touring personnel. They are all considered employees. For example, a full-time member of the Chicago Symphony Orchestra is compensated in the form of an annual salary with benefits including; health, dental, life and disability insurance; a retirement plan; transit and parking programs; and complimentary tickets, designating them as an employee.

The Manager of a recording studio, the reception staff, a music instructor at a public school or university, and certainly an employee of one of the major record labels working in music or publishing would all be examples of salaried employees. In its simplest of definitions', if an individual is guaranteed an annual salary, is provided with certain benefits, (health, 401k, bonus plans, paid vacations, etc.) are all indicative of designation as an employee.

INDEPENDENT CONTRACTOR

A legal category of worker that is distinct and different from an employee. The key to the definition is that, unlike employees, independent contractors retain control over how they do their work. Employers are not required to withhold and pay federal, state, and Social Security (FICA) taxes on behalf of independent contractors, as they must do for employees. [Cornell Law School]

As artists / creators and entrepreneurs, it is probable that you will declare you tax status as an independent contractor. In instances where you have multiple revenue streams, some part-time ongoing work with multiple employers, or financial compensation for a specified period of time, (such as a tour) and where you select the work you are offered and accept, would all be typical characteristics of an independent contractor.

Although there is great potential upside in being an independent contractor (a hired gun essentially) recognize the downside. With your freedom comes a new responsibility, in addition to saving for taxes, you must provide for your own healthcare, retirement saving plan (in absence of a 401k), pension, or other typical corporate benefits.

Many creators, by choice, declare themselves as freelancers or independent contractors.

WORK FOR HIRE AGREEMENT

As a side artist working in a recording studio or out on a tour it would be customary for the production assistant to provide you with and ask you to sign a *Work For Hire Agreement*. This is a legally binding agreement with language which would presumably include the following:

I represent to COMPANY that I, _____, am a party to a fully executed and binding agreement with Artist, for which there is adequate consideration (the "Sideartist Agreement") with respect to have agreed to render my services as a background musician ("sideartist") on the following recordings (the "Recordings"):

Each of the Recordings [made under the Sideartist Agreement] (including "out takes"), together with the results and proceeds of my services embodied therein, is intended to be, and shall be deemed a "work made for hire" (as that term is defined and used in the United States Copyright Act) for COMPANY. COMPANY shall have the sole and exclusive right to copyright the Recordings in its name as the owner and author thereof throughout the world for the full term of copyright, including any renewals and extensions thereof. If any Recording shall not constitute a "work made for hire" for any reason, I hereby irrevocably assign to COMPANY all rights in and to such Recording, including but not limited to the sound recording copyrights therein.

Without limiting the foregoing, COMPANY and its designees shall have the sole unlimited and perpetual rights to distribute, manufacture and promote sound recordings and video recordings derived from the Recording Session and to exploit the same throughout the world and to use my name and likeness in connection therewith.

Essentially, the provisions in a Work for Hire Agreement stipulate the following:
- artist name, track title or name of tour or show for which you are performing the work
- the name and publishers of the tracks if it's a recording session
- the date(s) of the session or tour
- the ability to use your name and likeness in promotion and marketing
- that here are no royalties or additional payments due you beyond a one-time fee.
- That you will have no copyright ownership of the composition or master sound recording (unless of course, you are a songwriter on the track).

Don't be taken aback if someone asks you to sign a Work for Hire Agreement. Think of it this way, the leader / organizer of the session, or tour has their business acumen together. This is all quit standard and customary, in a professional setting. If presented to you, read it and be sure you understand it. However, assuming it stays within the scope outlined above, you should feel comfortable in signing the document without seeking legal advice. In other words, its standard and customary at major recording sessions, for tours and events. If you are unsure about what you are being asked to sign, seek the advice of an industry attorney.

W-2 — GETTING PAID AS AN EMPLOYEE

Should you be hired as an employee, you will be required to complete a W-4 form, this document indicates to your employer how much taxes you would like withheld from the gross amount in each pay period.

In this instance where the employer is responsible for the withholding and payment of income tax, social security, and Medicare on your behalf, would designate you as an employee.

A W-2 form should be sent to you sometime in the three months prior to the tax filing deadline in April. This form will report your annual wages earned from that employer and the amount of taxes withheld.

W9 — GETTING PAID AS A FREELANCER OR INDEPENDENT CONTRACTOR

With a part-time or full-time gig (as a barista, bassist, waitress, or band member), you may be required to fill out a W9 form from your employer. Should they anticipate your earnings with them to exceed $600 for the year, you will be asked to complete a W9 form. If you do freelance work, the person / business paying you may ask you to fill out a W9. Understand this is customary and required by law. It is important to note:

- Businesses are required to keep track of and report who they pay for services and how much they pay them.
- The form would include your name, address, number of deductions you are claiming, and your tax identification or social security number.
- As a freelancer, filling out this form typically means you'll receive a Form 1099 from the business if they paid you at least $600 over the course of the year.
- The Form 1099 should be sent to you sometime in the three months prior to the tax earned for performances, publishing, advances, royalties, etc. As a freelancer, it's quite conceivable that you may receive multiple 1099 forms in the mail. Keep track of them, as they will be required to be incorporated in your tax preparation and filing.

FILING TAXES

In all likelihood, as a freelancer or independent contractor, you will utilize the 1040 form in filing your taxes. This will be the primary form used in determining how much you earned and how much you owe. Note that as a freelancer, typically there are no withholdings from your payments from gigs for example. Therefore, like all other Americans, it will be necessary for you to pay into Social Security and Medicare, plus state and federal taxes. Essentially, you can declare your tax status as self-employed.

However, if you have progressed to establishing your business as an LLC (or Corporation) the current applicable form for you to complete and submit to the IRS would be a 1065

> Form 1065: U.S. Return of Partnership Income is a tax document issued by the Internal Revenue Service (IRS) used to declare the profits, losses, deductions, and credits of a business partnership. 1 In addition to Form 1065, partnerships must also submit Schedule K-1, a document prepared for each partner. [Investopedia]

Should you be a member of a Partnership, an LLC, or a Corporation, it would be prudent for you to seek the advice of a tax advisor or an attorney. One piece of advice, ask for recommendations for accountants, CPAs, and tax advisors from your peers in the music business. Although not contributing on a daily basis, ideally, this person (Business Manager) will be a long-term member of the team.

Any entity, individual, LLC, essentially all of us, file two tax returns – the Federal Tax filing with the IRS and the second with the state (where one resides). As mentioned, you can establish a savings account whereby you might put aside 25% - 30% of gross revenue (earned money) to save for quarterly or yearly tax filings. It may be wise to seek the advice of a CPA or accountant to assist in setting this up and to file taxes on your behalf.

For musicians, artists and creators that receive 1099 forms, in lieu of filing an itemized return, there is a new standard 20% deduction you can take. This applies to pass through entities such sole proprietorships and partnerships. Consult your tax advisor to see if this is a viable and advantages option.

CONCLUSION

Once again, it's not all about the music, but the business - including the business of building a brand around your band, or brand as well as business management and making sure your financial affairs are in order. Attaining financial success / stability is an art in and of itself. To paraphrase, you would be well advised to set up your business as an LLC and register your logo or brand with the US Trademark & Patent Office. Once this is done, keep all your receipts, your mileage, and network to find the most appropriate CPA or tax advisor for assisting in filing your annual tax returns. The objective is to report your earnings while providing legal deductions thus minimizing your tax obligations. Should you care to approach the benefits of taking legal advantages of the tax codes, guess what – there are even apps for that.

DISCLAIMER

What is presented in this chapter is gives you a basic understanding of the tax provisions. The content of this chapter is for informational purposes only. Please consult a CPA, tax advisor or accountant for specific federal and state permitted deductions, depreciation schedules, allowances, etc.

17

MUSIC INDUSTRY DATA ANALYTICS

~ Robert DiFazio

MS in Management Information Systems
Clinical Assistant Professor and Coordinator of Music Business –
University of Illinois at Chicago
Research Scientist – Songsleuth.io

ACKNOWLEDGEMENT

A special thank you to my friend Na'el Shehade of the duo DRAMA, for generously donating his time to be interviewed for the chapter, and for providing analytic examples used throughout.

DRAMA is a duo from Chicago consisting of producer Na'el Shehade and vocalist Via Rosa. Their sound is often described as a blend of R&B and dance. The band is known for their DIY approach to creating and releasing their music and have attracted a global fanbase as independent artists. Before forming DRAMA, Shehade worked on projects with Chance The Rapper, Kanye West, Chief Keef, and Vic Mensa among others.[1] I recently sat down with Na'el to talk about the growth of DRAMA and the role analytics have played in that growth. For more information visit thedramaduo.com

"The majority of the people are like me, and I feel like what DRAMA is doing and what I've done can be replicated. People can take what I've learned, and I've done, and use it and apply it to what they do, and they will see the success." – Na'el Shehade

INTRO

The analytic dashboards of today's music platforms display a plethora of numbers, lists and charts describing listening trends, audience characteristics and more. These charts, and the data on which they are based, have become an area of significant interest in the music industry. They are read like treasure maps by artists and executives alike, however, these dashboards are only the tip of the iceberg of analytic insights used in the modern music industry. Techniques employed by labels and tech companies involve very advanced statistical analysis and machine-learning to describe complex relationships and make predictions. The rabbit-hole of data analytics is seemingly bottomless, but a basic understanding of how to work with data is all that is needed to begin harnessing the power of analytics. In many cases, simple analytic insights can be the most valuable of all.

The fascination with music industry data and trends is nothing new. Music popularity charts have held a prominent place in the mainstream media since the 1940's when Billboard Mag-

---

1. Julious, Britt (15 December 2016). "Drama ensures that dance has a mood". Chicago Tribune. Retrieved 27 September 2020.

azine published the first weekly listings of top singles and albums in the United States. Across the world, the phrase 'the charts' is used in reference to the top singles and albums in each country. All major music markets cover music charts in print, radio, television and online. Entire playlists of popular national radio broadcasts like the BBC's U.K. Official Chart program are dictated by the charts, keeping listeners in a state of suspense about what new records will debut on the charts and who will be #1. The use of charts, however, no longer applies to just top artists. Now everyone can dig-into volumes of detailed music industry data as much as they please. In the world of streaming and social media, data are everywhere, and their uses are seemingly endless. Today's artists are using data in almost everything they do.

Everything, Everything is a vivid example of a charting band with a considerable interest in data analytics. In June of 2022, the band's sixth studio album *Raw Data Feel* debuted at number four on the U.K. Top 40 Album Chart, the band's highest-charting project to date. As the album's name implies, the band took a data-driven approach to the project from the start.

The songwriting and much of the promotional process for *Raw Data Feel* involved the use of data-mining techniques and machine learning algorithms trained on information from four sources: LinkedIn's terms and conditions, the epic poem Beowulf, 400,000 posts from the message board 4chan, and the sayings of Confucius.[2] Ultimately, data models contributed roughly 5% of the album's lyrics, a song title, and the imagery for both the album artwork and the promotional campaign.[3] While this level of analytics is not-typical, the general use of data analysis is expanding in both creative and commercial ways, as is the volume of data available to analyze

Every day, millions of listeners generate overwhelming volumes of data that pour from streaming platforms, social media networks and the press, revealing ever more detailed trends in music consumption. The task of managing these data streams creates both a challenge and an opportunity. The now famous term 'big data' describes these large, hard-to-manage volumes of data that inundate businesses on a day-to-day basis.[4] Both because of the challenges involved in producing analytic insights as well as the payoffs. Those who can harness the power of data are in high demand.

---

2. Ackroyd, Stephen (7 February 2022). "Everything Everything on their AI-powered new album 'Raw Data Feel': "I didn't want to sing about the same shit anymore | Dork". readdork.com.
3. "'It feels like a fresh start': why Everything Everything turned to AI to write their new album". the Guardian. 18 February 2022.
4. "Big Data: What It Is and Why It Matters." Big Data: What It Is and Why It Matters | SAS, www.sas.com, https://www.sas.com/en_us/insights/big-data/what-is-big-data.html. Accessed 8 June 2022.

The music industry has long feted its star executives for their gut instinct and intuition. But for the past few years, the world's biggest record company has started evaluating employees by a less sexy measure: their interest in big data. – The Wall Street Journal[5]

But before we talk about using analytics to grow your career, let's say what analytics aren't.

Analytics are not a deliverer of guaranteed success. As has been mentioned in this text on several occasions, your music needs to find an audience for your career as an artist to grow. *"People have to understand, it's all about having a good product. Product is the most important. You cannot have any of the other stuff without a good product."* - Na'el Shehade

Analytics are also not a perfect substitute for a gut feeling. There are times when a decision should be made entirely based on instincts and creativity. Artistic aspects of your career such as songwriting, record production, and your overall style should generally not be over-analyzed. Producing great art is typically not about analysis, but business decisions do lend themselves to data analysis quite well. However, even in a business context, analytics are not the answer to every problem and being entirely analytical is not the point. The point is to recognize when an analytic approach is preferable and to use sound thinking in making business decisions.

Lastly, it is important to be skeptical of data. Ideally, data are facts, but they are sometimes faked, omitted, or erroneous. It is often said that data do not lie, but consumers are not always told the full story of how those data materialized. Even in today's digital world, all data cannot be taken at face value, however, far more data can be obtained and analyzed than ever before.

HISTORICAL BACKGROUND OF MUSIC INDUSTRY ANALYTICS

The origin of the famous cliché *"What gets measured gets done."* may go back as far as the sixteenth century, initially meaning something closer to, *"If you can measure it, you can man-*

5. Karp, Hannah. "Music Business Plays to Big Data's Beat - WSJ." WSJ, www.wsj.com, https://www.wsj.com/articles/music-business-plays-to-big-datas-beat-1418603548. Accessed 8 June 2022.

age it."[6]. At least since the 1940's with the emergence of LP's and mainstream radio, music managers have measured the performance of their products as well as the composition and tastes of the market to get a sense of the facts. However, until the mid-1990's, the lack of accurate and comprehensive data meant that most decisions were made without the support of data analysis.

Charts of the 1940's tracked physical sales, radio spins, sheet music sales and jukebox performances. Some early billboard charts counted these data with equal weight when creating the rankings.[7] Until the 1990's chart data were compiled from store managers' oral reports.[8] Given the financial effect of chart position, many labels went to great lengths to influence these data. Some store managers could be influenced by industry stakeholders to doctor record sales. Paying off store employees with free albums, concert tickets and alike was a standard method manipulating record sales figures throughout the era of physical recordings.[9]

Early examples of Billboard Charts listed records in descending order of popularity and used basic data segmentation. ***Segmentation*** is the process of grouping examples into categories or segments based on characteristic that they share. Early charts segmented national sales data into two groups, East, and West.

Retailers still report physical sales data to distributors who then present the data to labels. Reports for the sale of cassettes, vinyl and CDs include data such as the name of the retailer, the location of the store, the retail price of the product, the date of sale, etc. By analyzing data about the sale of their own products, companies in the pre-digital era could learn about the results of their marketing efforts and reconcile shipments and return data for accounting purposes.

Sales reporting evolved with technology, moving from hand-written ledger to computer software applications as the method of recording data, but the manual nature of the work remained constant through the 1980's. Unlike automated methods, manual reports were not always submitted by retailers on-time, some reports were late or not completed at all.

---

6. Ellevate. "What Gets Measured Gets Done. Or Does It?" Forbes, www.forbes.com, 8 June 2015, https://www.forbes.com/sites/ellevate/2015/06/08/what-gets-measured-gets-done-or-does-it/?sh=400ab70713c8.
7. Trust, Gary (July 27, 2021). "Happy Birthday, Billboard Charts! On July 27, 1940, the First Song Sales Survey Debuted". Billboard. Retrieved December 26, 2021.
8. Are Pop Charts Manipulated? (Published 1996)." Are Pop Charts Manipulated? (Published 1996), www.nytimes.com, 25 Jan. 1996, https://www.nytimes.com/1996/01/25/arts/are-pop-charts-manipulated.html.
9. iBid

In 1991, Billboard implemented a product offered by the Nielson company called **_SoundScan_** to track sales data digitally and automatically. As the name implies, data were obtained at reporting retailers whenever a music product was scanned at checkout. There was some initial resistance to automatic reporting technology. Observers say that was because record labels had learned how to "work" the old system, influencing which acts were reported to Billboard to get additional radio airplay and attention.[10] But, as the technology became widely adopted, managers began to rely more heavily on these data.

But even in the world of automation, businesses would often need to estimate sales in the case of missing or incomplete data. For example, only a small fraction of independent stores reported to Soundscan. One record sold at an independent store would be weighted by Soundscan as three records sold in order to estimate total sales.[11] Sales data were also prone to error and even corruption. "There's no question that our old system was subject to manipulation and that people abused it."- Timothy White, editor-in-chief of Billboard.[12]

Figure 002 is an example of a Soundscan report for a fictive album circa 2003. The segmentation shows that chain stores and mass merchants are the major retail outlets for the sale of the album and that suburban stores sell more units than those in cities or rural areas. Just from these basic insights, a manager can learn which type of retailers are the primary movers and which are below expectations. Insights like these could be compared to trends in the industry at large to inform decisions related to distributing, marketing, and promoting new records.

Today's charts combine data from many types of transactions to estimate total sales. Streaming, downloading, and physical sales are all used to create album chart data, but in the case of each there are nuances. The **_Track Equivalent Album_** (TEA) system emerged in the era of downloading to equate downloads, a new medium at the time, with physical album sales for the purposes of tallying the charts. In the TEA system, ten song downloads from the same album are equivalent to one album unit.[13] Currently, most charts use the **_Streaming Equivalent_**

---

10. "POP MUSIC; Technology Gives the Charts a Fresh Spin (Published 1992)." POP MUSIC; Technology Gives the Charts a Fresh Spin (Published 1992), www.nytimes.com, 26 Jan. 1992, https://www.nytimes.com/1992/01/26/arts/pop-music-technology-gives-the-charts-a-fresh-spin.html.
11. Are Pop Charts Manipulated? (Published 1996)." Are Pop Charts Manipulated? (Published 1996), www.nytimes.com, 25 Jan. 1996, https://www.nytimes.com/1996/01/25/arts/are-pop-charts-manipulated.html.
12. "POP MUSIC; Technology Gives the Charts a Fresh Spin (Published 1992)." POP MUSIC; Technology Gives the Charts a Fresh Spin (Published 1992), www.nytimes.com, 26 Jan. 1992, https://www.nytimes.com/1992/01/26/arts/pop-music-technology-gives-the-charts-a-fresh-spin.html.
13. "Frequently Asked Questions (FAQ)." *CHART DATA*, chartdata.org, 1 Sept. 2017, https://chartdata.org/faq/#:~:text=SEA%20means%20streaming%20equivalent%20albums,equivalent%20to%201%20album%20unit.

FIGURE 002 – Soundscan National Sales Report

Title Report: National Sales

Title:	ExampleSong	Label:	XYZ
Artist:	ExampleArtist	Config:	ALBUM
Report Type:	All	Format:	ALL
Catalog:	19287	Release Date:	6/15/99
Week Ending:	2/23/03	Report Date:	2/27/03
Weeks TOP 200:	0		

1991 to Date

LP	0
CA	924943
CD	10283756
DvD	0
MD	0
Total	11208743
2003 YTD	0

1991 to Date

LP	0
CA	924943
CD	10283756
DvD	0
MD	0
Total	11208743
2003 YTD	0

	This Week	Last Week	2 Wks Ago	3 Wks Ago	TD Total
Total	3453	4677	3973	4291	11208743
Store Strata					
Chain	1889	2456	2071	2190	6153196
Independent	303	312	299	356	1045849
Mass Merchant	1192	1804	1477	1634	3914790
Non Traditional	69	105	126	111	94908
Geographic Region					
Northeast	179	265	195	234	696687
Middle Atlantic	336	509	440	513	1602326
East North Central	452	646	530	591	1652981
West North Central	218	284	252	260	602670
South Atlantic	598	816	662	725	1903533
South Central	560	764	650	666	1445056
Mountain	316	448	390	426	895347
Pacific	792	944	852	873	2410106
Geographic Place					
City	668	782	777	835	2310482
Suburb	1623	2202	1773	1871	5340687
Rural	1160	1692	1423	1585	3557582

Albums (SEA) metric to calculate total streams by equating 1,250 premium streams or 3,750 free streams from the same album to one album unit. Some artists have used these equivalences to their advantage. The 2017 release Heartbreak on a Full Moon by Grammy award winning artist Chris Brown contained 45 tracks and clocked in at 2 hours 40minutes.[14] Assuming a listener streams the entire album, each listen of Brown's album will carry four times the weight of a ten-song album in terms of chart data. Upon its release, Brown gave specific instructions to his fans about how to listen to the album. He urged his fans, *"DO NOT listen to the album on iTunes, it does NOTHING for Chris' album sales/streams"*. He went on to encourage all fans to create free streaming accounts on multiple platforms and leave the album playing on repeat for the following three days until the charts data are reported. Unlike other means of manipulating chart data, this strategy is totally legitimate and transparent, but nonetheless shows that in some cases there may be more to the story than the raw data suggest.

In 1991, Billboard adopted another Neilson product called ***Broadcast Data Systems*** (BDS) to track the performance of music on terrestrial radio, a transaction known as a ***spin***. BDS implemented early forms of audio recognition technology that allowed for automatic reporting of

---

14. Andrews, Travis M. "Chris Brown's New Album Has 45 Tracks. That's How You Climb the Charts in the Streaming Era. - The Washington Post." Washington Post, www.washingtonpost.com, 1 Nov. 2017, https://www.washingtonpost.com/news/morning-mix/wp/2017/11/01/chris-browns-new-album-has-45-tracks-thats-how-you-climb-the-charts-in-the-streaming-era/.

radio spins, replacing manual reporting. Access to more comprehensive datasets with greater accuracy gave labels and publishers the ability to see the results of their radio promotion efforts more precisely. If a radio promoter claimed to have achieved 100 spins in a given week, and the BDS report showed a very different number, then a label could make decisions about their future strategy based on the data and not a personal relationship with the promoter or a best guess.

Automatic reporting technology for tracking radio spins is not immune from issues of accuracy and authenticity. In the famous 2005 investigation into music industry payola by the State of New York, Sony BMG was found to have bribed radio D.J.'s, paying them outright for spins.[15] Emails discovered in the process included blatant evidence of faking spins data. One Sony employee said in an email, "Please be advised that in this week's Good Charlotte Top 40 Spin Increase of 61 we bought approximately 250 spins at a cost of $17k... which means in reality we were down almost 200 spins for the week..."[16] The BDS system was also manipulated by more technical means. The system's automatic recognition technology used short clips of recordings as fingerprints, as opposed to full-length recordings. By obtaining the timing of the short clips used by BDS for individual recordings, labels were able to gain credit for full spins by running 30-second commercials using fragments of the full recording.[17]

Pollstar Magazine has supplied concert industry data to promoters, agents, and the public since 1981. They provided one of the earliest sources of subscription-based syndicated data about the concert business called **_tour histories_**. Tour histories include data for each performance by a given artist over the course of their career, such as venue name, date, ticket price, gross revenue, and the number of tickets sold. Insights into these data gave promoters and agents the ability to make more informed decisions about routing tours, selecting venues, and choosing ticket prices based on historical facts. The magazine, which is the premier trade publication for the concert business, features charts of top grossing tours in much the same way as the Billboard Magazine.

It was not until the 1980's that detailed data about listeners came to inform music marketing decisions in a major way. By and large, audience data are facts used to describe characteristics, behaviors, and even the inner desires of music consumers. Audience insights are numerous, but can be segmented into types including demographic, psychographic, behavioral, and technographic.

---

15. Ulaby, Neda. "Payola: The Beat Goes On : NPR." NPR.Org, www.npr.org, 9 Aug. 2005, https://www.npr.org/2005/08/09/4785403/payola-the-beat-goes-on.
16. https://ag.ny.gov/sites/default/files/press-releases/archived/payola.pdf
17. iBid

**Demographics** describe knowable facts about audience members such as age, gender, location, income, etc. Before the 24hour-a-day demographic survey known as social media, managers typically gained insights by attending performances and observing the audiences. This is a common data-gathering tactic used by labels to this day. Executed by local college marketing representatives whose responsibilities include posting flyers, staffing merch booths, and taking copious measurements describing audiences in detail. While these observations have always influenced marketing decisions, detailed and accurate insights into demographic characteristics did not emerge until the 1980's.

Demographic insights have a major role in music related advertising and publicity. Advertisers often place ads in vehicles whose audiences have similar characteristics to the artist's audience. To help advertisers find a good match, vehicles such as glossy magazines and radio stations publish media kits which display key data about the readership or listenership of the vehicle. Figure 003 is an example of insights typically available in a media kit. This example describes demographic characteristics of Rolling Stone Magazine's readership circa 2014.

It is helpful to connect demographic traits of your audience with other media, however listening habits do not track perfectly with demographics because music is a hedonic product. Its consumption is driven by emotion and people of all demographic backgrounds listen to a wide variety of music. Therefore, it is helpful to understand what audience members feel inside to make more informed marketing decisions. **Psychographics** are distinct from demographics and describe audience member's lifestyle and desires. Prior to streaming and social media, companies produced their own psychographic insights through custom surveys, interviews and focus groups.

Figure 003 – Media Kit Data		
	Audience	% Comp
Adults	12430000	
Men	7784000	62.6%
Women	4646000	37.4%
Age 18 to 24	3326000	26.8%
Age 25 to 34	2892000	23.3%
Age 35 to 44	2466000	19.8%
Age 45 to 54	2125000	17.1%
Age 55+	1621000	13.0%
Age 18 to 34	6218000	50.0%
Age 18 to 49	9752000	78.5%
Age 25 to 49	6426000	51.7%
Age 25 to 54	7483000	60.2%
Age 21+	10729000	86.3%
Median Age	35	
White	8929000	71.8%
Black	2071000	16.7%
Asian	317000	2.6%
Other	1351000	10.9%
Hispanic Origin	1926000	15.5%
Metro	10179000	81.9%
Rural	2251000	18.1%
Employed	8979000	72.2%
Any College	7679000	61.8%
Grad College +	3243000	26.1%
Attending College	1893000	15.2%
Single	6207000	49.9%
Married	4382000	35.3%

The earliest example of psychological consumer segmentation is the Values and Lifestyles (VALS) research methodology developed in 1978 by sociologist Arnold Mitchell at SRI International.[18] The VALS system used a survey of specific questions to allow researchers to segment consumers into groups based on lifestyle. The first VALs survey in 1980 segmented 1635 consumers into the following segments: survivors (4%), sustainers (7%), belongers (35%), emulators (9%), achievers (22%), I-am-me (5%), experiential (7%), societally conscious (9%), and integrated (2%). With these insights, businesses could make marketing decisions based on how certain groups see themselves and how they have been shown to respond to certain products.

"The idea was to create a rigorous tool for measuring a whole range of desires, wishes, values, that prior to that time had been kind of overlooked... We were basically telling manufactures that if you're really going to satisfy not just the basic needs but individuated wants, whims, and desires of more highly developed human beings, you're going to have to segment." [19] - Jay Ogilvy, Director of Psychological Values Research, SRI 1979-88

This type of psychological connection with the audience is a strong area of interest in all media including television. MTV, the leading music television station of the early twenty-first century, learned that a strong connection with their audience was key to turning their business around in the wake of low ratings in the early 2000's. But they would need the data to do it. By conducting focus groups at in-home interviews with fans carefully chosen for their specific traits, MTV accumulated increasing amounts of data and insights into the minds of their fans.

"MTV felt like we needed to get a closer connection to the audience. We said, "If we know more about them - know more about their lives, know more about who they are, what they want, what they don't want - we can make a better MTV that has a better connection with the audience if we talk to them and listen to them a lot more."[20]- Dave Sirulnick, MTV Exec VP of Programming and News

We immersed ourselves in research about the fall of '97... and now our rankings, when it comes to creative or original or funky or anything you would care about musically relevant, have went

---

18. Yankelovich, Daniel; David Meer (February 6, 2006). "Rediscovering Market Segmentation" (PDF). Harvard Business Review: 1–11. Retrieved 7 June 2011.
19. executive producer, Stephen Lambert ; written and produced by Adam Curtis ; RDF Television ; BBC. The Century of the Self. Wyandotte, MI :BigD Productions, 2009.
20. "Transcript | Merchants Of Cool | FRONTLINE | PBS." Transcript | Merchants Of Cool | FRONTLINE | PBS, www.pbs.org, 18 Nov. 2015, https://www.pbs.org/wgbh/pages/frontline/shows/cool/etc/script.html.

way, way up, and our ratings are their highest in their history."[21]- Brian Graden, MTV President of Programming

Other types of insights that inform music managers are **behavioral insights,** which describe patterns in the activities of an audience such as how often fans exercise or whether they drink coffee and **technographic insights**, which relate to the technology audience members use and how they use it. Behavioral insights are used in much the same way as psychographics, segmenting consumers into groups based on similar patterns in their activities. Technographic insights such as what type of a phone fans use or how often they comment on social media are very useful in today's technological world but did not play a major role in the pre-digital era as most consumers used comparable technology.

Over the course of the 2010's, as more and more data were generated through streaming, platforms began to offer data to the public via Application Programming Interfaces (APIs), which are tools for transmitting data between a platform and applications written by independent developers. Companies like Google have a strong interest in providing data to developers via API's in order to expand the reach of its products in other applications. *Google's mission is to organize the world's information and make it universally accessible and useful. Through products and platforms like Search, Maps, Gmail, Android, Google Play, Chrome and YouTube, Google plays a meaningful role in the daily lives of billions of people.*

The emergence of API's made it possible for companies large and small to get their hands on Big Data reliably and at scale. Countless music industry start-ups emerged in the ladder half of the 2000's to track and make-sense of these data. Major streaming platforms acquired many tech start-ups in the 2010's, folding the new technology into their business. Famous acquisitions of data analytics firms include the acquisition of NextBigSound by Pandora and The Echo Nest by Spotify.

It is now typical for music companies to employ in-house business software developers and a host of third-party tech companies to obtain and analyze data. But no matter whether you're a label, researcher or just a hobbyist, anyone can interface with APIs and conduct an analysis of music industry data.

Today's charts are powered by Big Data from numerous API's and exquisitely designed using the latest data visualizations. Companies like Chartmetric.com offer subscription access to

---

21. iBid

data and displays that incorporate almost every online service available for almost every artist. A growing list of data providers now offer insights into artists, radio stations, playlists and more. Now any artist can not only track and analyze their own data, but the data of all artists around the globe.

Even modern music technologies are not infallible. Online streams and views can be bought for pennies and delivered in bulk, inflating popularity data.[22] Payola of this kind is forbidden by all major streaming platforms, but while some offending data are removed, there is evidence that many fraudulent data remain.[23]

UNDERSTANDING DATA AND OPERATIONS

Data has become the single most valuable commodity in today's business world. Perhaps one of the most important considerations in understanding the value of data is that it may not always directly translate into cash, but this doesn't make it any less valuable.[24]

The analytic process is the process of turning data into information. Information can be used to gain knowledge and ultimately make a smart decision. But what are data and how are they turned into information?

Data are facts or measurements about the world that are obtained for record-keeping or analysis. ***Data analysis*** is the process of systematically applying statistical and/or logical techniques to describe, illustrate and evaluate data.[25] Analytic information can be something as simple as a word, a number, a list, or a chart, but regardless of their complexity all analytics are based on data. Analytic techniques can be mathematical or statistical and they may be complicated, but they only need to be logical and thoughtful to be effective in most music industry cases.

22. Keller, Michael H. "The Flourishing Business of Fake YouTube Views (Published 2018)." The Flourishing Business of Fake YouTube Views (Published 2018), www.nytimes.com, 11 Aug. 2018, https://www.nytimes.com/interactive/2018/08/11/technology/youtube-fake-view-sellers.html.
23. iBid
24. Cherukuri, Vijay. "Data: The Most Valuable Commodity for Businesses - KDnuggets." KDnuggets, www.kdnuggets.com, https://www.kdnuggets.com/2022/03/data-valuable-commodity-businesses.html. Accessed 9 June 2022.
25. "Data Analysis." Data Analysis, ori.hhs.gov, https://ori.hhs.gov/education/products/n_illinois_u/datamanagement/datopic.html. Accessed 9 June 2022.

In the simplest terms, ***analytics*** are pieces of information that are based on facts and are useful in the context of business decision-making. Numeric analytic insights are often referred to as ***metrics***, which implies an observation or measurement of some kind. An ***analytic dashboard*** is a collection of analytics displayed to users, either as a document or via a webpage.

The organization of data is usually in reference to a subject about which you are collecting data, which is known as an ***object***, ***instance,*** or ***example***. If collecting data about people, then each person is one instance in your dataset, whereas collecting data regarding a concert tour, each performance in the tour would be an example.

Data collected for each example are known as ***variables***. The words ***attribute*** and ***feature*** are sometimes used interchangeably with variable. For instance, you might measure the number of streams you have accumulated on various platforms, in which case, the examples would be different platforms and the single variable would be the number of streams. Figure 004 describes an example where the number of streams on each platform varies. These data are organized as a ***table*** of data, which is a tabular method of organizing data where columns represent variables, and each row represents a single example. The purpose of a table is to allow a user to identify the relationship between and given example and variable.

FIGURE 004 – Streams per Platform	
nameOfPlatform	**numberOfStreams**
Spotify	24397096
Apple Music	42401261
Amazon Music	13824507
Pandora	14510023
Deezer	26643938

Before conduction analysis or producing visualizations, it is important to consider the level of information of the data collected. Psychologist Stanley Smith Stevens published a four-tier data classification system in a 1946 Science article titled "On the Theory of Scales of Measurement"[26]. Figure 005 shows his typology in which data are classified into four levels: nominal, ordinal, interval, and ratio. Nominal and ordinal data are ***qualitative***, meaning these data cannot be operated on using mathematical operations such as addition, subtraction, multipli-

---

26. https://symbiosiscollege.edu.in/assets/pdf/e-learning/tyba/Economics/Scales-of-Measurement-6.pdf

cation, and division. Interval and ratio data are **_quantitative_**, meaning they measure quantities and can be operated on, thus providing the potential for higher-level analysis.

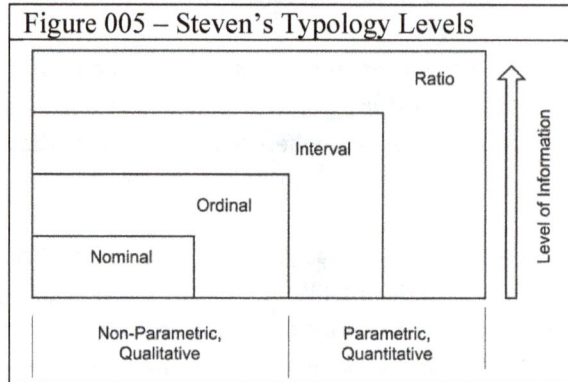

Figure 005 – Steven's Typology Levels

Nominal data are those that use a simple naming system as a label for each example. Nominal data are typically **_categorical_**, meaning that different values can be used to categorize examples into groups. The term nominal comes from the Latin "nomen", meaning "name", and implies that all examples with the same name have that fact in common. Location, gender, and many other data commonly depicted in analytic dashboard are often nominal.

While location data can be expressed numerically using longitude and latitude measurements, location data used in the music industry are typically nominal. Nominal location data are labels that identify the location of each example by the name of the territory. Location can be captured at any level such as country, state, county, city, zip code, etc. In Figure 006 each fan is labeled with the name of a city. Gender is a categorical measurement that is not quantifiable and is therefore always recorded at the nominal level. Figure 007 is an example of gender data.

FIGURE 006	
Name	**City**
Fan 1	Chicago
Fan 2	Detroit
Fan 3	Miami
Fan 4	Chicago
Fan 5	Los Angeles
...	

FIGURE 007	
Name	**Gender**
Fan 1	Female
Fan 2	Male
Fan 3	Non-Binary
Fan 4	Female
Fan 5	Other
...	

Although nominal data cannot be operated on directly does not necessarily mean they are not enumerated. Some numbers serve only as a label, not a measurement. Examples of enumerated nominal values include the jersey numbers worn by athletes and zip codes; both are recorded as numbers but are not intended to be used in mathematical operations, neither can be added or subtracted to produce meaningful information.

While nominal data are non-numeric, counting-up the number of examples for each name forms a large part of most analytic dashboards. Counting the number of examples in each segment allows for sorting segments by size, allowing a user to easily identify the largest and smallest segments.

Ordinal data are categorical, qualitative data where labels are organized in a set order such as the values low, medium, and high or freshman, sophomore, junior, senior. The ordering of values does not imply that the categories are equally spaced, although they may be. In the case of ordinal data, the order of values cannot be altered, else the values are incorrect or misleading. As an example, January always comes before February; those months must come one after the other. Ordinal data are usually categorical, meaning an example can only be a member of one group.

The interval scale is not very common in business analysis but is conceptually important. Like ordinal data, *interval data* are data ordered in a set sequence with values that are equally spaced, however these data are quantitative measurements. The defining factor of interval data is that the interval scale has no true zero value. Depending on what you are measuring, it may be the case that the value cannot be zero. Data expressed in the interval scale would include temperature (theoretically there is no such thing as zero degrees) and an intelligence scale like the IQ scale on which a score of zero is not possible. Because the values are equidistant, the values can be added and subtracted, but since there is no true zero these data cannot be multiplied or divided. For instance, the sum of 40 degrees and 6 degrees is 46 degrees. However, ten degrees multiplied by four is not 40 degrees.

Ratio data are numeric data where all values are equally spaced and there is a real zero. These data can be summed, subtracted, multiplied, and divided and used in a variety of advanced statistical models. Most numeric measurements used in the music industry are ratio data. Numeric data about the price of a product, the age of a fan, the population of a city are all examples of ratio data.

In addition to simple mathematical operations, managers often want to know the central tendency of their data. The **_central tendency_** of data describes the middle point of the data and is commonly associated with the term 'averaging', although the average is not always the best measure of the center of a variable.

Three common measurements of central tendency are mean, median and the mode. Mean commonly describes the arithmetic average, or the sum of all values divided by the total number of examples. The ratio data shown in Figure 009 describes the age of a given set of fans and the expression to find the average age of this set.

FIGURE 009	
Name	**Age(yrs)**
Fan 1	18
Fan 2	75
Fan 3	22
Fan 4	24
Fan 5	18
$(18+75+22+24+19) / 5 = 31$ mean age	
$18 \mid 18 \mid \mathbf{22} \mid 24 \mid 75 , 22 =$ median age	
$\mathbf{18} \mid \mathbf{18} \mid 22 \mid 24 \mid 75 , 18 =$ mode of age	

Although the average is the most common example of central tendency, it is not always the most appropriate. Data usually values that is far outside of the normal range of a variable called **_outliers_**. Outlier has a strict statistical meaning, but in a non-scientific sense the value of 75 seems like an outlier in this case as far from all other examples. In the case of data with high or low outliers, what is known as skewed data, the average may be misleading. The high outlier in this case pulls the average up, farther away from the median than would be found in more normal data and so in this case the median is preferable to the mean.

The mode of data is a measure of the label or number with the most occurrences. In the case of nominal data, the only operation that can be applied to the data itself is counting and therefore the mode of nominal data is central tendency.

However, from counts of nominal data, more analytic information can be produced. For instance, counting the number of fans in Chicago shown in FIGURE 006 and dividing by the total number of fans describes the percentage of fans in Chicago as shown in FIGURE 010.

FIGURE 010 – Percentage of Fans in Chicago
2 fans in Chicago / 5 total fans = 2/5 = 40% of fans are in Chicago

The world of statistics is vast, and many statistical measurements and models exist to describe data in very precise terms. However, basic operations and measurements such as counting and averaging account for most of the information displayed in modern music industry dashboards.

ANALYTIC DASHBOARDS

"One hit today has ten-billion micro-transactions... creators can pull-up their smartphone and see in real-time what is going on in the world, and all the data".[27] - Willard Ahdritz, Chief Executive Officer, Kobalt Publishing

Platforms have commercial interests in providing quality analytics to their users. Data and insights are in demand, and so offering superior analytic products help platforms stay competitive. Advertising platforms like Google and Metaverse have an interest in providing access to quality audience data in the hopes of attracting and retaining new clients. Platforms know that helping advertisers analyze past campaigns and improve on future campaigns will attract large accounts. Many digital distributors earn a percentage of their user's revenue, and therefore have an interest in providing their clients with data and insights to help them grow; each new dollar earned is shared by both the distributor and the client. User generated content platforms like YouTube are specifically interested in sharing data with their content creators. As new video views are earned, channels create revenue for YouTube. By helping their clients learn to grow their businesses, platforms help themselves.

---

27. "How Kobalt Is Transforming the Music Industry." YouTube, www.youtube.com, 9 May 2018, https://www.youtube.com/watch?v=aOVmmiA0l-k&t=63s.

Users never see all the data because platforms also have strong interests in withholding data. Platforms maintain detailed data describing the who, what, where, when why and how of all action users take, revealing patterns that may have real value. Data and insights that would be useful to competitors are typically not shared via dashboards or APIs. Many data collected are private details, protected by federal law, and are never available to users.

Some platforms may share data for philanthropic or charitable purposes. Sites like Music-Brainz.org are ***open-source*** platforms where all data and source code are made freely available. MusicBrainz.org is a music database with the stated aim of providing a reliable and unambig-uous form of music identification, enabling both people and machines to have meaningful conversations about music.[28] It is an example of a non-commercial ***wiki***, or a website whose content is created and modified by its userbase.

All platforms offer some level of analytic insight to users by providing access to raw data, met-rics, and charts that follow a relatively consistent set of conventions. The raw data is never bad to have, but they can often be overwhelming. It is more common to consume information by reading a metric or a visualization, and so much of analytic dashboards consist of data visual-izations.

Visualizations help get the point of an analysis across in a way that can be interpreted as information much easier than the data itself. Imagine trying to gain information from looking at thousands of rows of numeric data. On their own the data are too numerous to use as actionable information. In the era of big data, the data themselves are not particularly helpful without some analytics that present the data in a concise way. As the famous cliché goes, "a picture is worth a thousand words".

Figures 011 and 012 depict streaming data from Figure 004. Figure 011 displays these data as a ***pie chart***, while FIGURE 012 uses a ***column chart***. Both charts are designed to visualize the number of streams on each platform, however the primary purpose of the column chart is to show a comparison while the primary purpose of the pie chart is to show composition. Com-position refers to the shares of each example as a fraction of 100. Both charts offer a concise view of the data, but there are trade-offs between the ***visual cues*** used in each chart.

------

28. https://musicbrainz.org/

IT'S ALL ABOUT THE MUSIC MARKETING STUPID

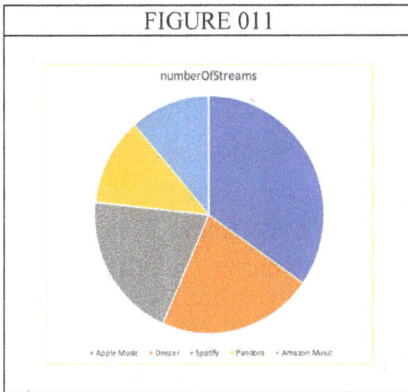

FIGURE 011

numberOfStreams

• Apple Music • Deezer • Spotify • Pandora • Amazon Music

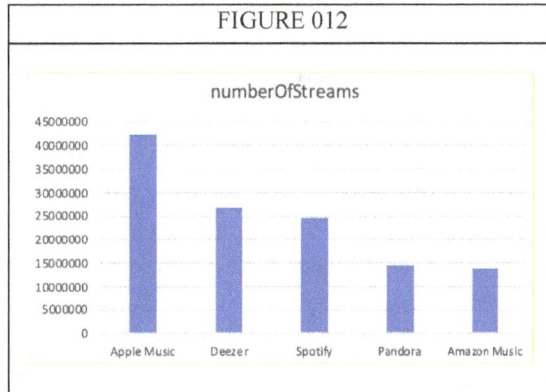

FIGURE 012

numberOfStreams

Visual cues are common components of a chart such as distance, size, shape, color that are interpreted by the human eye-brain system. Whenever we look at a chart, we are performing the elementary task of comparing values based on visual cues. In some cases, one cue may be more precisely interpreted by the human eye-brain system than another. In 1984, William S. Cleveland and Robert McGill published the first peer-reviewed research showing that certain visual cues are more accurately understood by the human eye-brain system than others.[29] FIGURE 013 describes the cues evaluated in their study; the top left cue being the most accurate with other cues listed right to left in descending order of accuracy.

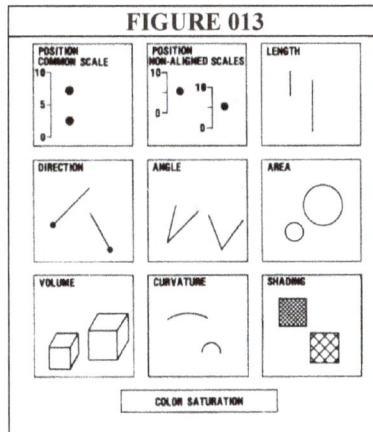

FIGURE 013

POSITION COMMON SCALE | POSITION NON-ALIGNED SCALES | LENGTH
DIRECTION | ANGLE | AREA
VOLUME | CURVATURE | SHADING
COLOR SATURATION

---

29. Source: Journal of the American Statistical Association , Sep., 1984, Vol. 79, No. 387 (Sep., 1984), pp. 531-554

The essential task of interpreting these cues is to infer comparison and composition based on some aspect of the image, such as determining how much longer one line is than another, or how much more curved one surface is than another.

Choosing the right cues is an important aspect of visualizing data. The column chart in Figure 012 displays values using the height of columns. The height of columns can be compared using their positions on the number line along the y-axis. Cleveland and McGill showed that position along a common scale as the most accurately interpreted by the human eye-brain system and therefore a column chart is a staple of analytic dashboards. The pie chart shown in Figure 011 uses the angles of a circle as the primary visual cue, which is less accurately interpreted by the human eye-brain system than position on a common scale. This pie chart also uses color as a cue to differentiate examples. This cue works in this case, but color shading and color saturation are relatively inaccurate cues when there are many examples and data are distributed across a large range. Such a case requires many different colors, and as more colors are added it becomes difficult to distinguish between closely related colors. As one of my professor's once told the class, "Do not let your charts end up looking like a rainbow lollipop".

It can be helpful to think about the goal behind a visualization when choosing a chart, as some goals can lend themselves well to the use of charts. Figure 014 describes numerous possible goals of a visualization and relates them to specific charts that can best display data for that purpose. For example, a line chart is appropriate for displaying sales data over time whereas a pie chart is a good choice for showing the composition of streams as parts of a whole.

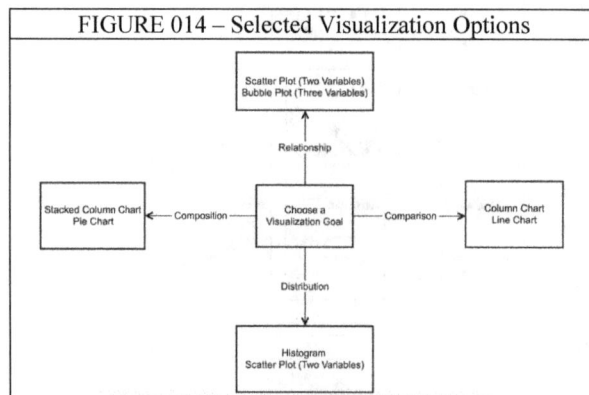

FIGURE 014 – Selected Visualization Options

Commonly used visualizations in music industry analytic dashboards include the column and pie charts as well as maps, line charts, and histograms.

In my experience, managers seem to be particularly interested in maps; they want to 'see the whole picture'. In many cases a map can be very insightful, but in some cases a simple list will do. In the case where you have sparse data, a map is unnecessary as most of the map will be blank. As an example, it would not be necessary to use a map of the world to visualize top countries if you only have fans in three countries. Conversely, if you have very detailed data and you wish to use a map you may run into problems. Maps can either display color cues to show the data or simply display the measurements themselves on the map. Color, however, does not do a good job of accurately describing detailed numeric data. Figure 015, a map of search traffic from Google Trends for an unnamed band, is an example of a map where color is used as a cue. From the color saturation of each state, it is clear that Tennessee, Iowa and Kentucky are top states. But what about California, Nevada, and Oregon? They appear nearly identical because the data in this example is too detailed to be accurately shown as individual shades of blue. The other option, displaying numbers on the map, is not ideal in this case because there is not enough space to display numbers on smaller states. Maps are a good option to display the big picture but not the fine details.

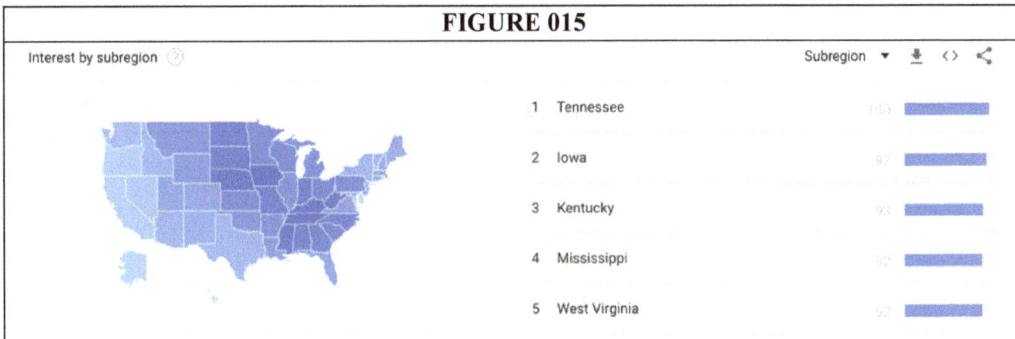

FIGURE 015

The use of multiple maps can often provide the detail a manager might need while still using the convention of a map. As is the case with most platforms, Google Trends allows users to zero-in on territories such as states, counties and even cities, showing macro and micro trends in geographic data. Figure 016 is an example of city-level data showing a band's top cities in Tennessee.

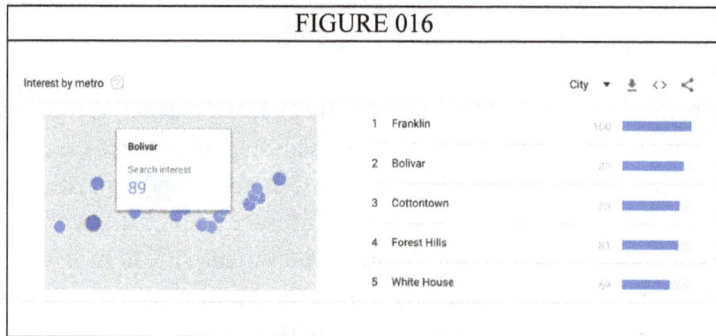

FIGURE 016

Interest by metro

	City	
1	Franklin	100
2	Bolivar	89
3	Cottontown	83
4	Forest Hills	81
5	White House	69

Bolivar
Search interest
89

Visualizing the changing value of a variable over time is typically accomplished with the use of a **_line chart_**, also known as a **_time series chart_**, which connects points plotted on a timeline to show the trend in the changing variable over time. Two variables are plotted in a line chart, time on the x-axis and the value of any variable you wish to track on the y-axis. Observable trends and peaks in the data may be useful in learning the response of fans to various events in an artist's career. Figure 017 displays a count of daily Spotify listeners of DRAMA's music over time. Here we see peak daily listenership in January and February of 2021, coinciding with the release of the single _"You've Done Enough"_ with British electronic duo Gorgon City featuring DRAMA.

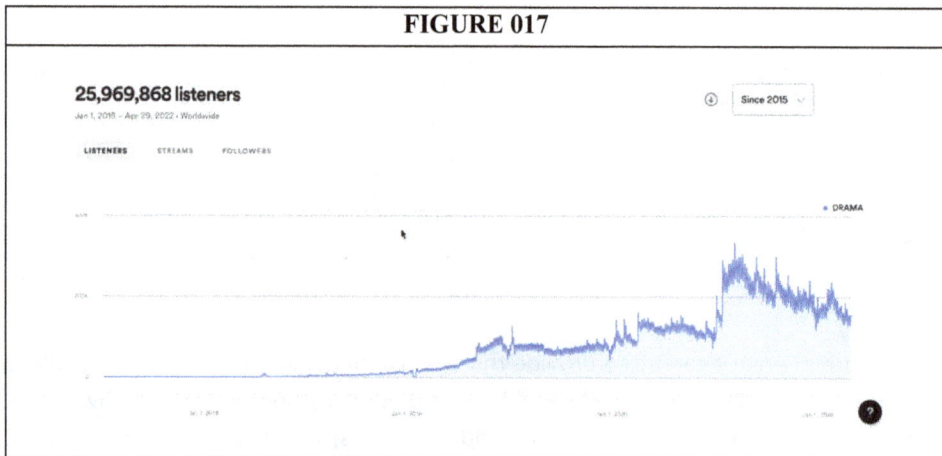

FIGURE 017

25,969,868 listeners
Jan 1, 2018 - Apr 29, 2022 · Worldwide

LISTENERS   STREAMS   FOLLOWERS

• DRAMA

The public's taste in music changes over time. Data about search engine queries can be a good indication of interest in a subject and are also quite getable. Google Trends is a premier source of this type of insight. Google searches of a term indicate interest in that term, therefore, tracking search volume for a term over time can reveal interesting trends. Figure 018 displays weekly Google Trend data for three duos over the last 12 months.

Figure 018			
Week	Gorgon City	Big Gigantic	Krewella
6/6/21	27	35	47
6/13/21	26	27	37
6/20/21	33	34	49
6/27/21	40	20	48
7/4/21	37	14	48
7/11/21	34	24	64
7/18/21	19	22	47
7/25/21	22	14	56
8/1/21	18	7	49
8/8/21	14	7	47
...	...	...	...

Google trend values represent search interest relative to the highest point on the chart for the given region and time. Here the values are not literal; they do not reflect a count of searches. For instance, a value of 100 does not mean 100 searches. A value of 100 refers to the peak popularity for the term in a given timeframe. A value of 50 means that the term is half as popular as compared to 100. A score of 0 means there was not enough data for this term.[30] Therefore, if the term has enough interest to be tracked by Google Trends, the data will have one peak of 100 and all other points will be below that point.

Google Trends presents the data in Figure 018 as a time-series chart as shown in Figure 019, which displays weekly data over the past 12 months. From this visualization we can see that Gorgon City and Krewella seem comparable in terms of popularity, with the highest peak of search volume for Gorgon City in November 2021. However, this chart only displays data from the last year. By increasing the time range as shown in Figure 020 we can see trends going back to 2004, revealing more information.

---

30. https://trends.google.com/

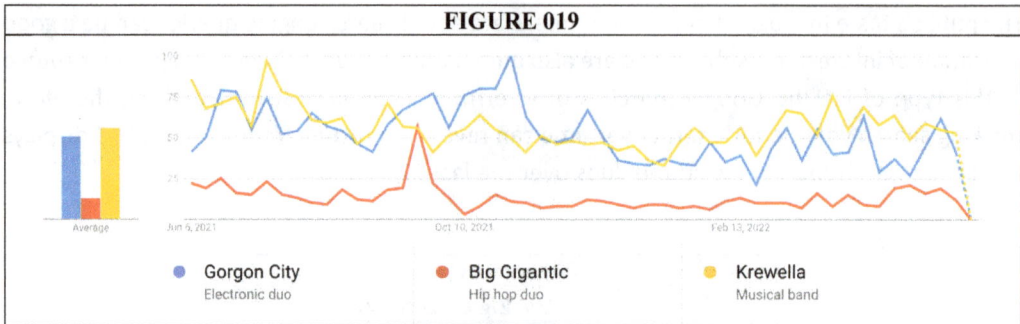

FIGURE 019

Gorgon City	Big Gigantic	Krewella
Electronic duo	Hip hop duo	Musical band

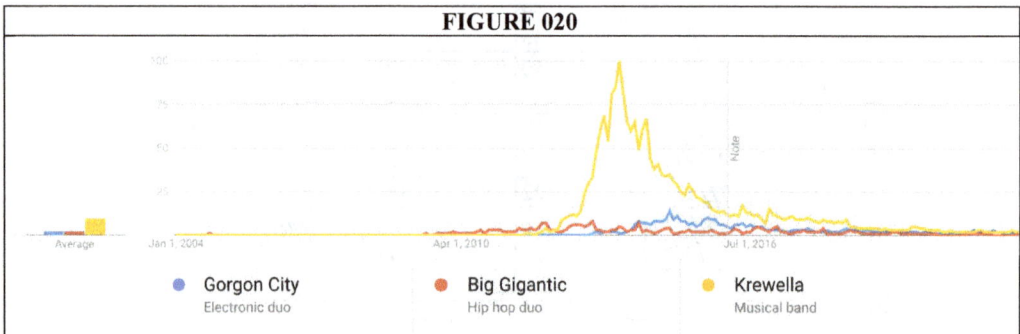

FIGURE 020

Gorgon City	Big Gigantic	Krewella
Electronic duo	Hip hop duo	Musical band

The distribution of data can have many meanings, however in common music industry analytics *__distribution__* refers to the spread of numeric data for a single variable. A common example is the distribution of the age of listeners. A *__histogram__* presents values using column height as a cue for the count or percentage of examples that fall into specified ranges known as bins along the x-axis. Any number of bins can be used, but analyst typically do not use more than ten bins in a histogram. The range of each bin can be altered to show varied levels of detail, but the range is usually uniform across all bins.

The histogram in Figure 021 displays the distribution of gender by age for the Facebook audience of Gorgon City as a histogram with six bins. Along the x-axis the six bins are shown in order. The bins have a range of nine years except for the outer bins. The lowest bin has a range of six years, and the highest bin is unbounded as there is no maximum age. The choice of the nine-year bin range is a choice made by the developers of the Facebook Ad Manager. In making your own histogram you may choose the overall number of bins and bin range based on how you want to segment the data.

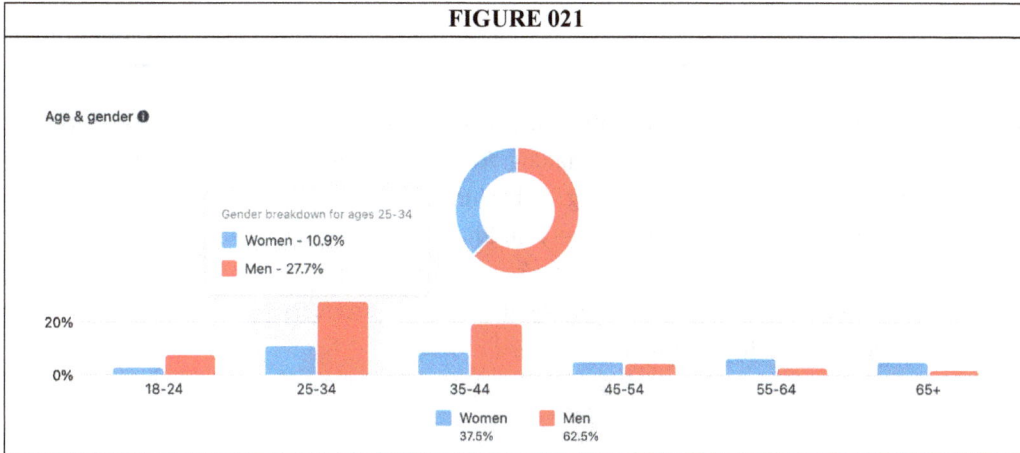

FIGURE 021

Age & gender ⓘ

Gender breakdown for ages 25-34
- Women - 10.9%
- Men - 27.7%

Women
37.5%   Men
62.5%

Interpreting these simple charts can give artists a handle on basic facts about their audience. The histogram in FIGURE 022 depicts the distribution of age and gender for Spotify listeners of DRAMA's music. In this example the Spotify developers elected to make each bin range unique, presumably to segment music listeners into meaningful categories. In this case we can say that the audience is equally split between male and female and more than half of the total audience is between 23 and 34 years old.

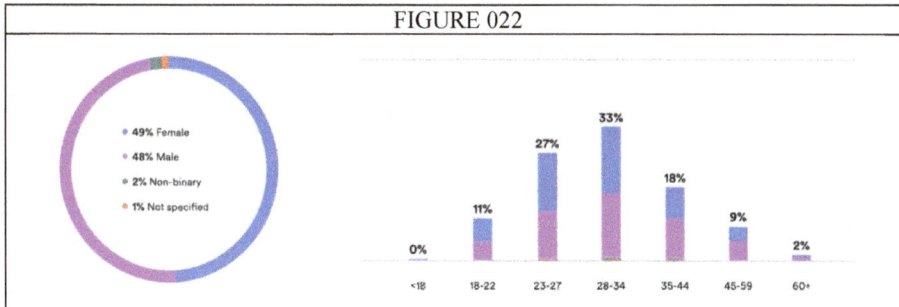

FIGURE 022

- 49% Female
- 48% Male
- 2% Non-binary
- 1% Not specified

CONCLUSION

Over the past decade, data and analytic information have become powerful tools in almost every area of music business decision making. The analytic mindset has become a central tenet of company culture in the recording, publishing, and concert promotion industries. But this power is not limited to the few or the well-financed. Today, all artists can see their data and know the facts of their business. *"There's no excuse anymore not to put it in the world. Everything is there for you. It's just a matter of putting good products out there, applying it and seeing what happens".*- Na'el Shehade

`

18

NETWORKING

Developing relationships and maintaining them will be essential to building a career in the music industry. You should prepare a self-assessment of your strengths and weaknesses and consider how you will/are perceived by those around you and those who you need to connect with. Ask yourself these important questions:

- What does your ideal professional network look like in order to reach your goals?
- Who do you need to connect with and why?
- Can you leverage your existing network of people and in what way?
- In what ways are you going to create opportunities to make connections and build relationships?
- Are you located in a place or in proximity to where you need to be to reach your goals?
- How can you share information about yourself in a professional manner and manage the contact details of the people you hope to work with?

Building a network takes time and dedication. Be ambitious and do not be afraid to engage with people. Learn something about them and share your background and interests with them. We're in the business of being discovered. Think about it – whether you're an aspiring artist, photographer, producer, beat maker, you want to be discovered so people need to learn about you. If you find people that you're comfortable with or folks who might be interested in working with you, think of ways to make it happen. What can you do for them? Relationships should be reciprocal. Be sure to stay connected even if you don't find some common ground to work with right away. You never know when the stars might align, and you have an opportunity to work together. Be careful not to burn any bridges. Also, look for some common ground and relationships that are mutual. Do you have some common friends, or do you know some of the same people? This might be the way to get the ball rolling. Promote yourself. Be visible, both online (in zoom meeting and on social media) and off, in person. Make yourself known, interact and put yourself in places and positions to engage with people.

Although we have proclaimed that the music marketing element is of vital importance, there are three other qualifications which we should discuss in closing:
- Be a nice person. It never hurts to put your best foot forward and get a leg up on everyone else by being friendly and approachable. Know something about the people you hope to deal with and do your best to make sure they know who you are and what you're about.
- Be reliable, prepared, and on time. Nothing speaks louder than actions and you want people to want to work with you and be able to count on you.
- Continuously honing your craft of making / creating art. If being an artist is your goal, then this should be an easy one. Creating art should be something you can't live without doing.

The Founder/CEO of a successful indie label was delineating that he's done chasing social metrics as the majors can always find them first and/or out bid him. He explained there were three (3) traits he looks for in signing an artist to his roster;
1. They are able to connect with a live audience
2. They are good people that have it together, and;
3. They are full time 'artists'

If you're an aspiring artist or manager, or anyone wanting to get into the business, make sure you or the people in your orbit address and meet these three criteria.

If you were offered and accepted a "proper position" (a day gig) with a salary and benefits, one of the first things you might be provided with would be an office/workspace. OK so if you're self-employed then build an "office" in your apartment, or spare room, or at your kitchen table. And the most effective and cheapest form of marketing is the other marketing tool you would be provided with at any straight job, a business card. Though they're not as convenient or as practical in the post-pandemic world, physical business cards can still come in handy. Make them online and have them printed, with a nice quality stock. Of course, we can easily digitally transfer contacts, however, also do it old school and surprise people. Not everyone is comfortable going the digital route. Also, if they/you are in a hurry, and if you want to impress, slip them a business card. Remember the age-old adage: There's' nothing like making a first impression.

You don't have to necessarily be an artist to be in this business. Don't forget there are multiple jobs and positions in all facets of music marketing, recording, touring, et al. Being a friendly person, responsible, and reliable are three of the vital components of this business. Time waits for no one here. Lobby calls, load-ins, sound checks are all part of having a career in the business. In addition to your talent one of the most important qualities is your ability to be on time, reliable, rehearsed, and a good hang. One thing for certain about the music business is that positive word of mouth is critical. Essentially, it's a small industry and word gets around. Be exceptional at your gig / job, be cool, and humble. Having a good sense of humor is a bonus.

Dress the part. Look appropriate for your 'gig'. Be on time. Set multiple alerts. Practice. Attend any opportunities to write, record, or jam. Sit-in where you can.

Always be humble. Here's a true story. The roster for a label had to be cut down. There were two artists', both having sold 40,000 copies each and having identical recording budgets. It was kind of like comparing *apples to apples*. However, the difference being, one had a very experienced, professional, and polite manger. The other guy had several and was for the most part, self-managed and was himself high maintenance. Guess who got dropped?

The point being, look the part, be outgoing, meet others in your field, be prepared, do the work, and be nice. You'll have a very good chance of finding a gig in the music business.

MD's (Music Directors) for tours don't always hire the absolute most badass bass player, drummer, vocalist, or anyone for that matter on a tour. Of course, they must be more than competent, maybe even exceptional on their axe or at the gig. But the overriding qualification may be one's personality. After all you may find yourself traveling in a small or large tour. Then the challenge that may ultimately determine the trajectory for your career, equally as your knowledge and expertise, may be your ability to get along with others. Your likability or simply the ability to be someone everyone wants to hang with could be important. Networking will be key in making it in the entertainment business.

RESOURCES

If you've not yet been in the industry, find / get an internship. Set up a Google alert for once a day for 'jobs in music' in your city or market. Have your bio and resume looking good and ready to go. Be prompt and on time. Even better – arrive early. And always be polite, respectful, and humble.

8 Effective Networking strategies for Professionals - indeed
Jobs in the Music Industry – DIGITAL MUSIC NEWS
Music Industry Jobs – MUSIC BUSINESS WORLDWIDE